Foreword

As more and more countries compete to attract foreign direct investment (FDI) – through, for example, the liberalization of FDI policies, privatization and promotion programmes including the granting of incentives – their regulatory frameworks for FDI are becoming similar. As a result, the appeal of any particular host country to potential investors is increasingly determined by factors other than FDI regimes. These include the nature of its macroeconomic environment, the size and growth of its market, the quality of its physical infrastructure and the skill composition of its human resources. The importance of these factors in any particular location varies according to the global investment strategy of each transnational corporation (TNC). Governments need to understand these corporate strategies – and the broader determinants of FDI decisions in today's world economy – if they are to interact with TNCs and compete successfully for scarce investments.

This study was prepared at the request of the Government of Brazil to support its objective of increasing the inflow of FDI as part of a wider policy of accelerating the growth of the country's economy. The research was started in 1995 when many TNC executives were cautious about prospects for profitable operations in Brazil and sceptical about the effectiveness of the reforms aimed at stabilizing the economy. Though both the economy and TNCs' attitudes have changed considerably since 1995, the study is still useful for Brazil as the introduction points out. Equally important, it contains many valuable lessons and insights for all countries wishing to improve the effects of their dealings with TNCs.

The study shows clearly the range of considerations that lead international investors to choose one location over another. Shifting competitive and technological structures have acted to alter investors' weightings of traditional considerations and to add new ones. Most importantly, a survey of senior executives' opinions reveals starkly that investors' perceptions can be more important than "reality" in influencing an investment decision. Those perceptions can be shaped by experience and access to data: asymmetries in information are important determinants. Perceptions can also be shaped by beliefs about longer-term prospects for an economy and the "climate" for doing business.

There is often a lag between changes in policy that affect a country's relative locational attractiveness and investors' reactions. This lag – or "hysteresis effect" – can work in both directions: greater attractiveness does not immediately yield greater FDI inflows; and diminished attractiveness can be disguised by continuing inflows. Policy makers need to be aware of such dynamic effects as they compete for scarce wealth-creating investments.

These dynamics and asymmetries in information and interpretation of data show up markedly in the differences in attitude and behaviour of investors already experienced in a host country compared to the attitudes held by those remaining outside. In Brazil's case in the mid-1990s, investors with negative or no experience of the country tended to emphasise the disincentives to investment. By contrast, those with good experience emphasised the positives. Though this difference is to be expected, it is often overlooked. Part of the reason, no doubt, is the tension that exists between the investors' desire for stability and consistency in policy and governments' needs to adjust policy to changing circumstances and development priorities.

iii

Strengthening the success of the incumbents – assisted, perhaps, by an appropriate public-private sector dialogue in the framework of a business advisory council and reinforced by an investment promotion agency – and publicizing that success are important aspects of the Government's role in fostering a welcoming investment climate. After all, there are no better "ambassadors" for a country's investment climate and attractiveness than foreign affiliates that perform well, are fully integrated in a country's economic fabric and contribute to its growth and development.

What matters, therefore, is not only the quantity of the FDI that a host country receives, but also its quality in terms of a country's needs and priorities. While this issue (including the consequent effects of FDI on the balance of payments) are beyond the scope of this study, it must be kept in mind that, ultimately, it is the contribution of FDI to development that matters most and that will determine the choice of policy. Indeed, there is no doubt that policy matters, not only to attract FDI but also to realize its benefits for development. To this end, Brazil needs to pay special attention to policies that strengthen the role of FDI in facilitating technical change and technological learning, and in promoting exports. Backward and forward linkages are particularly important in this respect as they also help to integrate foreign affiliates more tightly in the domestic economy and, in this manner, contribute to the creation of a vibrant domestic enterprise sector.

The message of the study is that, in today's world economy, Governments that seek to attract FDI and that seek to benefit from the investment that they have attracted need to be pro-active in their policy stance. The increasingly specialized forms of international investments being made by TNCs as they search for distinctive strategies suggest that any Government, if it wishes to harness the wealth-creating assets controlled by TNCs, needs to define its role as that of a partner in progress. From the perspective of firms, the need for partnership is increasingly being stated in terms of such considerations as the ability to provide resources that enhance efficiency and productivity in a global framework. From the perspective of Governments, of course, the need for partnership revolves around the imperative of furthering national economic growth and development.

Geneva, January 2000

Rubens Ricupero
Secretary-General of UNCTAD

Acknowledgements

This study was made possible through the financial support of the United Nations Development Programme (UNDP). It was sponsored by Grupo de Analise e Pesquisa, an advisory group to the Presidency of the Republic of Brazil. Luciano Martins provided – in his capacity as Special Adviser to the President of the Republic of Brazil and the Brazilian counterpart for this project – the overall framework for the study.

John M. Stopford prepared the study, with the assistance of a team comprised of Jamuna Prasad Agarwal, Chong Ju Choi, Yoko Ishikura, Peter Nunnenkamp and Peter Smith. The project was directed by Karl P. Sauvant and coordinated by Zbigniew Zimny, project officer. They, together with Mark Knell and Kumi Endo, finalized the study for publication. Chiraz Baly, and Lizanne Martinez provided statistical assistance and Florence Hudry and Jenifer Tacardon provided production assistance. Teresita Sabico desktop-published the study. The study benefitted from comments from Constantine Vaitsos. Comments were also received from Fernando Mello Barreto, Ana Galvao, Neil Hood, Sanjaya Lall and Ludger Odenthal.

Contents

Page

Boxes

Figures

Tables

Page

INTRODUCTION

Foreign direct investment (FDI) worldwide has been growing much more rapidly than world trade and world gross domestic product (GDP) since the mid-1980s. For an increasing number of countries, it is becoming a key link to the world economy. Virtually every country – developed and developing, large and small alike – have sought FDI to facilitate their development. Brazil was the single largest host country to FDI among developing countries until the late 1970s, but began losing its appeal to investors in the 1980s and early 1990s (its FDI inflows in the early 1990s were below the level of the late 1970s). Only recently has it regained some of its former importance, moving up the ranking in terms of FDI stock from fifth place among developing host countries in 1994 to second place by 1998.

The relative decline of Brazil among host countries was due both to internal factors (such as indebtedness, slow growth, macroeconomic instability and restrictive FDI policies) and external factors (such as good economic performance and increasing openness to FDI elsewhere, and intense competition for FDI among host countries). During the early 1990s, Brazil introduced a stabilization programme that successfully restored macroeconomic stability and economic growth. To support both its short-term stabilization programme and long-term economic objectives, Brazil also liberalized its FDI policy. While this has contributed to increased FDI inflows, the amounts initially involved were not adequate to satisfy the needs of the country nor did they reflect its economic potential. FDI inflows began to grow rapidly only from 1995 onwards, reaching almost $29 billion in 1998 and over $31 billion in 1999. Yet, as the report discusses, they are well below FDI flows into China in recent years. Moreover, on some FDI performance measures, such as the ratios of inward stocks and flows to GDP, they are only now catching up with averages for developing countries. In addition, a considerable proportion of the recent growth of FDI is attributed to the granting of public service concessions and to the privatization of State-owned enterprises in the services sector. It remains to be seen what the full impact will be for manufacturing. More generally, Brazil has not yet realized its full potential in terms of both the quantity and quality of FDI it attracts.

As Brazil is just beginning to take advantage of the increasing FDI inflows that are part and parcel of a liberalizing and globalizing world economy, this raises two important questions: First, can Brazil sustain the increased inflows and raise them even further, to a level reflecting its economic potential? Second, can it interact effectively with transnational corporations (TNCs) to maximize the potential developmental benefits from FDI? Both are challenges faced by many host countries. There is no doubt that policy matters for attracting FDI and for realizing the development benefits that FDI can yield. However, any policy aimed at achieving these objectives requires an understanding of the principal factors that determine investment decisions of TNCs in a liberalizing and globalizing world economy.

The objective of the study is therefore to analyse the factors that shape FDI decisions by TNCs. This is done at three levels:

- Analysis of the global patterns and characteristics of FDI, as these indicate the nature of the phenomenon and the opportunities it entails.

- Investigation of the strategies of TNCs and especially the key factors molding their strategic choices.

- Discussion of the implications of the patterns of FDI and TNC strategies for Brazil and other host countries, taking into account the views of corporate managers.

The primary aim of the original study was to assist the Government of Brazil in formulating its FDI policy. Recent changes in this policy reflect many of the suggestions contained in the original report. The subsequent growth of FDI indicates that these suggestions may also be useful for other host countries wanting to devise effective FDI policies.

The study sought to indicate those considerations that provided incentives to investment (for example, restoring political stability, improving the regulatory framework and devaluing the Real) and those that provided disincentives (for example, an inefficient infrastructure and restrictions on the freedom of managers to operate and to optimize their corporate systems across borders). Given a certain sense of continuing under-performance relative to other countries, there is more work to be done on both agendas if the growth of new inward FDI is to be sustained and complemented by rising levels of reinvestment in the country.

Part of the study draws on interviews, based on a questionnaire, with senior executives in the headquarters of 32 TNCs with affiliates in Brazil, selected by the Brazilian counterpart in the project (see annex 1). They were supplemented by telephone interviews with 25 important competing TNCs not yet prominently established in Brazil. The selection of TNCs narrows the scope of the study of TNC strategies and FDI determinants to manufacturing industries, although chapter I examines FDI trends and determinants in all three sectors.

The study is structured into four chapters:

- Chapter I provides an overview of the changing patterns of FDI in the 1990s and their implications for host countries, including Brazil. It shows that competition is not only important between firms, but also between countries. The increasing number of TNCs has been accompanied by a diversification of home countries, sectors and industries. This has provided greater opportunity for host countries to attract increased flows. These overall trends raise important issues for national Governments about the dynamics of FDI and the opportunities they create in the highly competitive world FDI market.

• The overall patterns also provide the context for managerial choice and the development of TNC strategies, which is the focus of chapter II. Here, the argument concentrates on several central issues, including the overwhelming need for investors to retain managerial control over their far-flung operations; to organize their international networks in a manner that increases internal efficiencies while simultaneously retaining an ability to adjust to changing circumstances; and to choose locations in which the costs of adaptation are minimized. In general terms, the chapter argues that TNCs seek to develop distinctive strategies that cannot be easily emulated by others, thus giving them a competitive edge. It therefore provides pointers on how host countries can interact with TNCs; in the case of large projects, in particular, Government interaction needs to be "custom made".

• In chapter III, the analysis of the questionnaire data is focused on the question: How do major manufacturing TNCs perceive the FDI environment in Brazil? The data show that perceptions are strongly influenced by the investor's experience of operating in the country; but even firms that are not significant investors have their own perceptions. For better or worse, these perceptions influence locational decisions. Partly as a result, the data show widely differing responses on such important issues as the significance of the MERCOSUR in stimulating new FDI, and of Brazil as a worldwide source point for specialized output. The strong differences in opinions and practice underscore the importance for host countries to undertake efforts to change perceptions and, in particular, to convince the international investment community that the reforms are indeed well on track and will lead to an even better investment climate.

• Chapter IV pulls together the broad range of TNC perspectives on the attractiveness of host countries and their commentary on a number of related public policy issues. The chapter first describes the conditions under which TNCs determine their individual strategies and the implications that these diverse strategies have for policy-makers. It then explores what executives consider to be important when choosing a particular location to invest. The chapter concludes with some suggestions about practical means to promote further inward investment.

*   *   *

The basic premise underlying this report is that, in a world of limited resources (and especially managerial resources) available to firms, managers have to make specific choices, and these are often done in ways that reinforce the unique characteristics and strengths of their enterprises. A consequence is that there may be many different strategies chosen within any one industry. The questionnaire data did not test this proposition directly, but provided strong implied support to a number of dimensions in these strategies. Supporting evidence shows that the turbulence in contemporary markets forces firms to move away from a belief in any single dominant strategy that represents best practice in a given industry.

The importance of this proposition lies in the implication that firms in the same industry will provide seemingly contradictory information about, for example, investment priorities. Furthermore, it challenges many of the standard assumptions in industrial organization economics and in FDI and trade theory, by showing that the structure of an industry is not necessarily the primary determinant of corporate performance. These observations complicate the interpretation of the results of the questionnaire data. To gain full value from the analysis, one needs to have a focus not just on firms, but also on their different strategies. This task is, in its fully articulated form, beyond the scope of this enquiry. As chapter IV notes, the implications go beyond this effort to include the nature of the intelligence that government agencies in host countries increasingly need to have if they are to interact effectively with foreign investors.

It is important to remember that the interview data contained in the study reflect opinions and perceptions, not necessarily facts. How those opinions and perceptions have been formed is a question that has not been pursued in this study. Still, they can be more important in determining behaviour than the underlying reality. In addition, it needs to be kept in mind that TNCs are not internally monolithic. Internal political behaviour, reflecting differing opinions and perceptions, contributes therefore to the outcomes of corporate strategy.

CHAPTER I

CHANGING PATTERNS OF FOREIGN DIRECT INVESTMENT AND IMPLICATIONS FOR BRAZIL

Until the end of the 1970s, Brazil was the largest host and home country for foreign direct investment (FDI) among developing countries. The debt crisis in the 1980s, together with the ensuing reduction in Brazil's creditworthiness and macroeconomic stability on the one hand, and the increased attractiveness of Asian developing countries for FDI on the other hand, considerably reduced the global importance of Brazil as importer and exporter of equity capital. Although a combination of notably improved domestic economic conditions and the global boom in FDI have spurred a fresh growth in inward FDI, this growth might well have been even greater if Brazil's size and growth potential had been better understood by key decision makers in transnational corporations (TNCs).

One of the conditions to attract even more FDI is for policy makers in any country to have a good grasp of the forces shaping FDI flows in today's hyper-competitive world, and of the characteristics of these flows. This chapter analyses these forces and characteristics as they relate to the changing pattern of global FDI. The single most important key feature of this pattern has been that, both outflows of FDI and the number of TNCs have grown at unprecedented rates during the past 15 years, as managers of TNCs have increasingly realized the importance of FDI as a means for accessing resources and markets for (final and intermediate) goods, skills and technology and for developing a portfolio of locational assets. The total number of TNCs in 14 leading developed countries more than quadrupled from the late 1960s to the mid-1990s, and continues to increase every year. In the second half of the 1990s, the total number of TNCs in the world economy was estimated at almost 60,000 parent corporations with over half a million foreign affiliates (UNCTAD, 1999, pp. 5-6).

The increasing number of TNCs has resulted in a diversification of FDI sources in terms of home countries, sectors and industries, as well as types of enterprises. These various new sources have their specifics as regards their impact on FDI and implications for host countries, including policy implications. They are discussed in separate sections: section A deals with home country diversification, while sections D, E and F discuss issues related to the sectoral and industrial diversification of FDI sources. Section G deals with the emergence of small- and medium-sized enterprises (SMEs) as a significant source of FDI. Other forces and characteristics examined in this chapter include the growing number and diversification of host countries (section B); the role of regional integration (section C); associated and sequential investment (section H); privatization programmes (section I); interlinkages with trade (section J); and the emergence of integrated production systems (section K). For each of these forces and characteristics, possible implications for Brazil are discussed, as an example of implications of the pattern of FDI for host countries.

A. The increasing number and diversification of home countries

1. Pattern

Until the early 1970s, the FDI scene was dominated by a few actors and was largely limited to a few areas. It consisted mostly of United States investment in European manufacturing, European countries' investment in North America and of FDI by a handful of firms from developed countries in the primary sector, especially in the petroleum industry, of a few developing countries. There was also some manufacturing investment in a selected number of developing countries. In the late 1960s, the United States alone accounted for almost 60 per cent of FDI outflows from developed countries. With the United Kingdom – the second largest home country – added, the two countries were responsible for almost 70 per cent of outflows (UNCTC, 1978, pp. 238-239). This began to change in the second half of the 1980s, when firms from Japan, countries of continental western Europe, Canada and Australia began to invest abroad on a much larger scale than before, challenging the domination of United States and United Kingdom firms, not only in third countries, but also on their own territories. Though, on average, United States outflows during 1986-1990 were five times higher than in 1967-1969, the United States share fell to only 15 per cent of outflows from developed countries. While this share had doubled by the mid-1990s, reaching 30 per cent in 1996, it declined to 22 per cent in 1998. Yet the average annual FDI outflow per developed country increased 40 times, from $0.6 billion in 1972 to $24 billion in 1998, or about 10 times in real terms.[1]

Today, FDI originates from almost all developed countries. The amounts invested every year by firms from these countries are at levels never reached before and they are growing rapidly. The number of firms undertaking FDI within these countries has also been growing rapidly. Increasingly they include SMEs, as will be seen in section G.

In addition to the quantitative changes in FDI – the increasing number of firms and countries – there have been also a number of qualitative changes:

- During the 1990s, TNCs originated from all sectors of economic activity, and increasingly from the services sector (section D). Within sectors, and especially within the manufacturing and services sectors, they originated in an increasing number of industries. As a result, FDI is also undertaken in a much wider range of industries of host countries. For example, until recently, FDI in the services sector was mainly in trading and financial services, but today it is expanding rapidly into virtually all service industries including telecommunications, air transportation, business services and tourism. The result is that the supply of resources that TNCs are ready to deploy in host countries – capital, technologies, skills, managerial and organizational practices and access to markets – has increased considerably, not only in quantity but also in their range and quality.

• The motives of TNCs for investing abroad have expanded, and include not only access to natural resources and protected national markets, but increasingly also cost and efficiency considerations, access to strategic assets, advantageous price/ quality ratios of inputs (including skill/cost ratios of labour) and access to large liberalized markets (box I.1).

Box I.1. A typology of outward FDI

According to the motivations of investors, FDI can be divided into the following four main types: natural resource-seeking, market-seeking, efficiency-seeking and strategic asset-seeking:

Natural resource-seeking FDI

Natural resource-seeking FDI is the oldest form of FDI. One of the prime motives of such early foreign investors as the East India Company, the Virginia Company and the Massachusetts Bay Company in the seventeenth century was to search for raw materials, besides extending trade and creating settlements (Colebrook, 1972, p. 9). Natural resources absorbed until recently (1984) one third of the United States and United Kingdom outward FDI stock. Since then, the share of this sector in the total stock of outward FDI of most of the major home countries has slumped (UNCTAD, 1999, annex tables A.I.20 and A.I.21).

The wave of nationalizations in the 1960s and early 1970s spoiled the climate for new foreign equity investments in the primary sector. But now many developing countries are reopening this sector to foreign investors. This gives firms from those developing economies, which are less endowed with natural resources, but more advanced in terms of technological development (such as from the Republic of Korea and Taiwan Province of China), greater chances of investing in this sector to strengthen their resource-based competitiveness.

Market-seeking FDI

Market-seeking FDI is attracted by the size and growth prospects of host country markets, advantages linked to a direct presence in customers' vicinity, avoidance of import barriers, discriminatory Government-procurement policies and high transport costs in supplying markets through exports. Market size and growth have proved to be the most prominent determinants of FDI in most empirical studies (Agarwal, 1980; UNCTC, 1992; UNCTAD, 1999). Market-seeking FDI can also be a result of oligopolistic competition, as TNCs try to get a foothold in each other's market. Much of intra-industry FDI is associated with oligopolistic competition.

Market-seeking FDI became the predominant motive for investing in the manufacturing sector of developing countries in the 1960s and 1970s during the heyday of import-substitution industrialization. This motivation also was paramount in the wave of United States manufacturing investments in Europe in the early postwar period and in Japanese investment in the United States since the early 1980s. Recently, the formation or strengthening of regional groupings has given rise to significant investments in order to serve the enlarged markets of the integration schemes (as will be discussed in section I.C).

Until recently, all FDI in services could be regarded as market seeking, because services were largely not tradable internationally. The services sector accounts for more than half of all outward FDI flows and stocks from major developed countries (table I.10). The picture is similar for major home developing economies: of the total outward FDI stock of the Republic of Korea, Taiwan Province of China and Thailand, 35 per cent, 43 per cent, and 69 per cent, respectively, were in this sector (UNCTAD, 1996, p.10). The technological revolution in communication and data transmission has now made it possible to produce some services in one country and consume them in another one (e.g. software). However, the share of such services in total FDI is still small (Agarwal, 1996), and most of FDI in services remains market seeking.

/...

(Box I.1, concluded)

Given that services dominate FDI flows and stocks and that much manufacturing FDI is market seeking, market-seeking FDI is still the most important. But the trend is towards an increasing relative importance of the two other types of FDI discussed below.

Efficiency-seeking FDI

Efficiency-seeking FDI is attracted generally by lower costs of labour or environmental resources in host than in home countries. The oldest such investments have been labour-seeking ones. As wages rose in home countries, TNCs sought to obtain access to low-cost labour in developing countries through locating labour-intensive industries or segments of their production processes in them. This has been a characteristic of Japanese investment in the textile industry in Asia; United States investment in *maquiladoras* in Mexico, Central America and Asia; and European investment in Central and Eastern Europe. More recently, as real wages have risen over time in some of the Asian countries – first to industrialize with an outward-oriented strategy – labour-seeking investment has moved on to other, lower-wage Asian countries, such as China (UNCTAD, 1997b, p. 10).

Other, more complex, forms of efficiency-seeking investments are closely related to the emergence of integrated international production (see section I.K. and II.B.2). One increasingly important form for developing countries is component outsourcing which requires greater skills and higher productivity than is typical of labour-seeking FDI, and is therefore concentrated in the relatively industrialized developing countries (UNCTAD, 1995a, chapter IV). It has also been extensively used by United States TNCs in such industries as automobiles, electronics and personal computers. The extreme form of component outsourcing is original equipment manufacturing, wherein a firm in a developing country undertakes to supply a TNC with a fully made manufacturing product that will bear the brand name of the TNC. Several firms from the Republic of Korea began their penetration of markets of developed countries through the production of original-equipment manufacturing products, which they later replaced with their own brand names.

Still another form of efficiency-seeking FDI is horizontal FDI in differentiated products; this is less common in developing countries and tends to be associated largely with investment flows (for example, in automobiles, computers, chemicals and consumer goods) among developed countries. It occurs because of the need to adapt products to the tastes or quality requirements of a particular market. These investments require a relatively large market, as they are related to the demand for different brands of a similar product in industries that are characterized by significant economies of scale. As the markets of developing countries are enlarged through regional trading arrangements, such investments are likely to become more common in those countries as well.

Strategic asset-seeking FDI

Strategic asset-seeking FDI usually takes place at an advanced stage of the globalization of a firm's activities. Firms, including a few from developing countries, may invest abroad in order acquire research and development (R&D) capabilities (e.g. Japanese or Korean investment in microelectronics in the United States), as noted in section I. K and chapter II. Integrated international production involves the location of *any* component in the value-added chain where it contributes most to a TNC's competitiveness, and ultimately to its profitability. Thus, it may be efficient for a firm to relocate design, R&D (or other high value-added activities) from its home base to an overseas affiliate. Some developing countries are, or can make themselves, able to attract this kind of FDI through investment in human resources and infrastructure; for example, the availability of skilled personnel and the requisite telecommunications infrastructure have contributed to the location of R&D centres and headquarters' services by TNCs in Singapore; software development in India; and service centres for airline reservations in the Caribbean (UNCTAD, 1997b, p.12).

Source: UNCTAD.

- Partly as a result of the diversification of FDI sources, TNCs' strategies have also diversified. To a certain extent this is obvious, as TNCs in non-tradable services can not have the same FDI strategies as TNCs in tradable goods. Most importantly, however, the strategies of TNCs originating in the same industry and frequently in the same country have diversified too, as will be discussed in chapter II. There is no such thing as an industry recipe for success. In fact, increasingly TNCs see distinctiveness as a source of acquiring a competitive edge.

A remarkable feature of the diversification of source countries has been the extension of home countries to include more and more developing countries. Until the early 1980s, 99 per cent of the world's FDI originated in developed countries. Until then, only firms from Brazil, Kuwait, Singapore, Colombia and the Republic of Korea were noticeable (above $10 million of annual outflows at the country level) investors abroad (table I.1). Since then, the number of developing economies that are sources of FDI has increased considerably. With many joining the ranks of significant (above $50 million)[2] direct investors abroad in the 1990s, they are now the headquarters for a growing number of billion-dollar TNCs. At the same time, the size of annual outflows from the ten largest investor countries – mostly developed countries – increased from $ 676 million to $ 47 billion between 1977-1980 and 1995-1998. Nevertheless, the share of developing economies in world outflows rose from 1 per cent in 1975-1979 to 12 per cent in 1995-1998 (table I.1). The significance of this increase is, however, mediated by the fact that much of it originates in a few economies in Asia,[3] and that outflows from developing countries are largely directed to other countries in the same region.

The trend towards outward FDI from some high-performing developing countries is likely to be reinforced in the future (despite weakening during the financial crisis), as there remains great potential for firms based in developing countries to increase their FDI outflows. In 1995, their share of outward FDI was well below their shares of global exports (25 per cent) and world GDP (18 per cent).[4] Because trade flows, and especially manufacturing exports, are similarly concentrated in relatively few countries, the implication is that the same forces that have been acting to link the trade and investment flows in developed economies are now spreading in their impact on developing countries. To the extent that growth in outward FDI is associated with trade-related investments, it increases the linkage between the trade and investment agendas of countries (see section J).

Latin American and Caribbean countries contributed, on average, 2.5 per cent of global outflows of FDI from 1995 to 1998. Their share almost tripled during the first half of the 1990s compared with the second half of the 1980s, indicating a strong recovery from the consequences of the Latin American debt crisis and its effect on the investment capacity of domestic firms (see box I.2). In comparison to the late 1970s, however, Latin American countries have not kept pace with Asian developing countries, which accounted for almost 70 per cent of FDI outflows from all developing countries in 1998 (table I.1). In the late 1970s, Brazil was the largest outward direct investor from developing countries. Since then, its share in global FDI outflows declined from 0.5 per cent (1980-1984) to 0.1 per cent (1990-1994). This trend was reversed in the second half of the 1990s, raising Brazil's share of FDI outflows to 0.4 per cent in 1998.

Outward investment from developing countries is largely intraregional. It goes primarily to neighbouring developing countries and is influenced by close cultural links and regionally integrated markets (table I.2). Excluding Mexico (because of its significant FDI in the United States due to membership in NAFTA), 57 per cent of outward FDI from Latin American countries in 1992 was directed towards other countries of the same region.[5] Chile has been one of the

Table I.1. FDI outflows from regions and selected economies[a], 1975-1998

(Millions of dollars and per cent)

| Region/economy | Annual average | | | | | | | | | | | | 1998 | |
| | 1975-1979 | | 1980-1984 | | 1985-1989 | | 1990-1994 | | 1995-1998 | | 1990-1998 | | | |
	Millions of dollars	Share (per cent)	Millions of dollars	Share (per cent)	Millions of dollars	Share (per cent)	Millions of dollars	Share (per cent)	Millions of dollars	Share (per cent)	Millions of dollars	Share (per cent)	Millions of dollars	Share (per cent)
World	**37 454**	**100.0**	**49 918**	**100.0**	**140 099**	**100.0**	**234 827**	**100.0**	**465 622**	**100.0**	**337 403**	**100.0**	**648 920**	**100.0**
Developed countries	**37 052**	**98.9**	**47 378**	**94.9**	**130 896**	**93.4**	**208 576**	**88.8**	**406 803**	**87.4**	**296 677**	**87.9**	**594 699**	**91.6**
European Union	16 342	43.6	24 308	48.7	69 892	49.9	113 602	48.4	236 704	50.8	168 314	49.9	386 161	59.5
United States	16 062	42.9	13 113	26.3	20 480	14.6	49 540	21.1	102 423	22.0	73 043	21.6	132 829	20.5
Japan	2 134	5.7	4 280	8.6	24 591	17.6	26 372	11.2	24 051	5.2	25 341	7.5	24 152	3.7
Central and Eastern Europe	**12**	..	**8**	..	**14**	..	**146**	**0.1**	**1 723**	**0.4**	**847**	**0.3**	**1 903**	**0.3**
Czech Republic	..	..	..	..	..	..	46	..	67	..	56	..	55	..
Hungary	..	..	..	..	..	..	17	..	238	0.1	115	..	481	0.1
Russian Federation	..	..	..	..	..	..	49	..	1 190	0.3	556	0.2	1 027	0.2
Developing countries	**391**	**1.0**	**2 532**	**5.1**	**9 188**	**6.6**	**26 105**	**11.1**	**57 096**	**12.3**	**39 879**	**11.8**	**52 318**	**8.1**
Africa	**70**	**0.2**	**923**	**1.8**	**1 031**	**0.7**	**842**	**0.4**	**589**	**0.1**	**730**	**0.2**	**511**	**0.1**
Liberia	..	..	23	..	48	..	111	..	167	..	136	..	167	..
Nigeria	1	..	819	1.6	839	0.6	511	0.2	195	..	371	0.1	114	..
Latin America and the Caribbean	**175**	**0.5**	**470**	**0.9**	**776**	**0.6**	**4 012**	**1.7**	**11 441**	**2.5**	**7 314**	**2.2**	**15 455**	**2.4**
Argentina	- 17	- 0.0	- 40	- 0.1	13	..	565	0.2	2 057	0.4	1 228	0.4	1 957	0.3
Bermuda	..	..	65	0.1	23	..	151	0.1	1 246	0.3	637	0.2	2 365	0.4
Brazil	152	0.4	236	0.5	212	0.2	344	0.1	1 488	0.3	852	0.3	2 609	0.4
Cayman Islands	..	..	98	0.2	72	0.1	128	0.1	1 388	0.3	688	0.2	2 900	0.4
Chile	4	..	2	..	6	..	375	0.2	1 667	0.4	949	0.3	2 799	0.4
Colombia	20	0.1	60	0.1	28	..	96	..	481	0.1	267	0.1	529	0.1
Mexico	..	..	30	0.1	142	0.1	397	0.2	562	0.1	470	0.1	1 363	0.2
Panama	6	..	34	0.1	110	0.1	230	0.1	738	0.2	456	0.1	1 362	0.2
Venezuela	..	..	5	..	151	..	456	0.2	356	0.1	412	0.1	140	..
Virgin Islands	..	..	..	..	..	..	1 252	0.5	1 674	0.4	1 440	0.4	- 830	- 0.1
Asia	**145**	**0.4**	**1 135**	**2.3**	**7 365**	**5.3**	**21 228**	**9.0**	**44 916**	**9.6**	**31 756**	**9.4**	**36 182**	**5.6**
Bahrain	..	..	..	..	13	..	68	..	95	..	80	..	90	..
China	..	..	0	..	671	0.5	2 429	1.0	2 069	0.4	2 269	0.7	1 600	0.2
Cyprus	..	..	54	0.1	1	..	10	..	100	..	50	..	2	..
Hong Kong, China	..	..	361	0.7	1 985	1.4	10 535	4.5	23 675	5.1	16 375	4.9	18 762	2.9
India	..	..	3	..	6	..	20	..	122	..	66	..	19	..
Indonesia	..	..	4	..	15	..	204	0.1	356	0.1	272	0.1	44	..
Korea, Republic of	16	..	81	0.2	715	0.5	1 501	0.6	4 357	0.9	2 770	0.8	4 756	0.7
Kuwait	32	0.1	140	0.3	513	0.4	81	..	890	0.2	440	0.1	1 873	0.3
Malaysia	..	..	245	0.5	231	0.2	1 111	0.5	3 142	0.7	2 014	0.6	1 921	0.3
Philippines	..	..	10	..	4	..	130	0.1	219	..	170	0.1	160	..
Singapore	90	0.2	106	0.2	325	0.2	2 121	0.9	5 096	1.1	3 443	1.0	3 108	0.5
Taiwan Province of China	4	..	45	0.1	2 384	1.7	2 903	1.2	3 961	0.9	3 373	1.0	3 794	0.6
Thailand	2	..	2	..	49	..	242	0.1	597	0.1	399	0.1	122	..
Turkey	..	..	..	..	2	..	28	..	195	..	102	..	307	..

Source : UNCTAD, FDI/TNC database.

a   Countries/economies with $50 million or more of annual average outflows in 1990-1998.

Box I.2. A new wave of FDI from developing countries: Latin American TNCs in the 1990s

Several Latin American countries (Argentina, Brazil, Colombia, Mexico and Venezuela) were involved in the "first wave" of FDI from developing countries which took place in the 1960s and 1970s. It consisted mainly of market-seeking FDI, motivated by the existence of trade barriers in host countries (Lall, 1983). Latin American countries lost ground in the 1980s during the "second wave" of outward FDI from developing countries, which was led by Asian firms (Dunning, Van Hoesel and Narula, 1998).

The "third wave" of FDI from developing countries, which began during the 1990s, has been led by Latin American firms, mainly from Argentina, Chile and Mexico and, to a lesser extent, Brazil. Assets abroad by firms headquartered in these countries can be estimated at between $40 and $50 billion. Only a few of these firms started their foreign investments in the first wave, though many have been operating for a long time in their home economies.

The current wave of Latin American FDI cannot be separated from the adoption of more outward-oriented economic strategies and of structural reform programmes – including trade liberalization, privatization and deregulation – in most Latin American countries in the 1990s. These programmes have significantly increased competitive pressures on domestic firms, and have induced processes of restructuring in the economies of the region. In this sense, it is not surprising that Chile and Mexico were the first countries to enter the third wave of outward FDI from developing countries in the early 1990s, followed by Argentina a few years later, while Brazil is still lagging in this respect. FDI outflows from Chile increased from an annual average of only $6 million during 1985-1989 to $375 million during 1990-1994 and to $2.8 billion in 1998. In Mexico, official figures – which do not fully capture the magnitude of this phenomenon – indicate that from an annual average of $142 million during 1985-1989, FDI outflows reached nearly $400 million in 1990-1994 and, after the financial crisis, amounted to almost $1.4 billion in 1998. In Argentina, the outward FDI "boom" began in 1994. FDI outflows increased from an annual average of $13 million during 1985-1989 to $565 million during 1990-1994 and to over $2 billion during 1995-1998 (table I.1). In this sense, the sequence in the countries' FDI process is to some extent a mirror of the sequence of the structural reform processes in their home economies.

Chile is the country in which outward FDI stock in relation to GDP is the highest among non-offshore financial centres, while in Brazil it is among the lowest. Mexico and Argentina are in-between cases. Among the factors that foster outward FDI in these countries are the relative size of their home economies, the sequence and timing of structural reforms, the insufficient availability of raw materials in the home country and the fact that many firms have already acquired dominant positions in their domestic markets.

The majority of FDI from the region has been made by domestic economic conglomerates, though some Brazilian medium-sized enterprises made significant investments as well. Some of these large firms are trying to gain world leadership in specific market segments. Cemex (Mexico) for instance, is the second largest world producer of cement, with plants in the United States, Europe and Asia; and Techint (Argentina) accounts for 30 per cent of the world market in seamless pipes for the oil industry and operates a global network with a productive presence in Argentina, Mexico and Italy. As a rule, ownership advantages of Latin American TNCs are based more on management capabilities, knowledge of well-diffused technologies, efficient quality and production management, sound marketing experience and access to financial resources, rather than on technological assets. In some cases, ownership advantages are also strongly based on the capability to work in similar cultural environments and on knowledge of tastes and specific conditions in certain markets, due to geographical, cultural, linguistic or other forms of proximity.

/...

(Box I.2, concluded)

Even those few Latin American firms operating in advanced technology industries so far do not seem to have embarked upon a path of technological accumulation (Cantwell and Tolentino, 1990) to become genuine innovators. As a result, contrary to what happened with Asian TNCs that tend to operate in skill-intensive industries, Latin American firms invest very little in developed countries' economies. In addition, their outward FDI takes place more specifically in services, mature industries or resource-based activities, though some cases of FDI in more skill-intensive and more technology-oriented activities can be found: in pharmaceuticals, custom-made capital goods, telecommunications and information services in Argentina; in autoparts and transport equipment in Brazil; and in biotechnology, television, telecommunications and transport equipment in Mexico, for instance.

Two opposite forces are at work, which have an impact on the maintenance (or development) of this third wave of outward FDI by Latin American companies. On the one hand, for a growing number of firms, an FDI strategy is becoming indispensable for their own survival and expansion in the new context of globalization. Hence, it is plausible to assume that a growing number of Latin American firms will embark upon a global FDI path and acquire a portfolio of locational assets, to maintain or strengthen their competitive position in a global environment; by investing abroad, domestic firms can better exploit their tangible and intangible assets and achieve economies of scale. This situation can be summarized in the dilemma faced by many domestic firms "to buy or to be bought", in a scenario in which foreign TNCs have shown a growing propensity to invest in Latin America.

On the other hand, the relatively small size of Latin American firms, compared with TNCs from developed and even developing Asian countries, may be a constraint for a sustainable FDI path. The costs of obtaining financial, technology and human resources are greater than those faced by their competitors based in developed and Asian countries. In addition, not only are Asian firms generally more transnationalized than Latin American enterprises, a number of them have also made more inroads in technology and skill-intensive activities.

The significant financial, technological and human resources constraints faced by Latin American enterprises are, to some extent, a consequence of the many weak points that characterize their home economies including, in some cases, relatively small domestic capital markets mostly geared towards short-term finance, educational systems not generally producing the kind of human power and management required for competing in open economies, and an inappropriate level of infrastructure. Overcoming these structural problems needs time, as well as systematic efforts and well designed and implemented public policies.

Source: Chudnovsky, Kosacoff and López, 1999.

---

most active regional investors, especially in the energy and financial services sectors of Argentina, Peru and Brazil. It was also the largest Latin American investor in Argentina in 1994 (besides Brazil), and the fourth largest holder of FDI stock in Peru in 1995 (IADB-IRELA, 1996, p. 60-61). And about half of all Chilean outward FDI goes to countries in the "Mercado Común del Sur" (MERCOSUR) or the Southern Common Market.

Brazilian outward FDI stocks in Latin American countries increased from 39 per cent of total outward FDI in 1986 to over 60 per cent in 1991 (table I.2). Prospects for a more integrated MERCOSUR market have since then bolstered the intraregional FDI of Brazil, especially in the automobile industry. Investment flows from Brazil to Argentina amounted to $500-800 million in 1994, and more than 300 Brazilian firms had started investment projects there by that year (Ibid., p. 61). At the same time, Argentine firms have been investing primarily in distribution networks in Brazil rather than in local production.

The regional orientation of FDI in the developing countries of Asia is also strong. Yet its degree has varied significantly from country to country, with a low level in China (18 per cent in 1997), and a very high level in Hong Kong, China (99 per cent). The group of Asian countries as a whole accounted for 87 per cent of the outward FDI from the region (table I.2). Hong Kong's (China) high ratio of intraregional FDI is explained by its special economic relations with mainland China (Chie, 1995, table 7), as many foreign affiliates with FDI in China are located in Hong Kong (China) (Low, Ramstetter and Young, 1996) and it is often used to recycle investment funds from China. However, some Asian countries, while retaining the regional orientation of their FDI in developing countries have significant extraregional FDI involvement in developed countries. Such investments by TNCs from this region, for example, Daewoo and Samsung from the Republic of Korea, appear to be the result of their progressing maturity and growing confidence that they can succeed in gaining market access in other regions (UNCTAD, 1996a).

An international comparison of FDI outflows based on absolute amounts may be a misleading indicator of outward investment intensity because it ignores the size of national economies. To avoid a large country bias, internationalization ratios (FDI outflows as percentages of gross domestic fixed capital formation) of Latin American economies are compared with those of other regions and the world as a whole (table I.3). These data show that the internationalization of Latin American countries as a whole is weak by international standards. Their internationalization ratios have been lower than those of Asia and sometimes even Africa, which, in turn, have far lower ratios than developed countries. Chile is, however, a major exception as its ratio of FDI outflows to gross domestic fixed capital formation jumped from 0.2 per cent (1986-1990) to over 10.0 per cent (1997).

2. Implications

The increasing number of home countries and TNCs is part of a broader trends towards vastly increased size and diversification of FDI outflows. This phenomenon is driven by the need of firms to undertake outward FDI, because, in addition to traditional motivations related to the expansion of markets, FDI is increasingly important to maintain or increase their competitiveness. A portfolio of locational assets (non-proprietary assets that cannot be moved freely across countries, such as land, climate, skilled and unskilled labour and infrastructure) increasingly complements the traditional sources of firm efficiency. These include a portfolio of firm-specific assets, natural or created (e.g. control acquired over natural resource deposits and/or patents) and their managerial expertise (in organizing production, product design, marketing etc.) (UNCTAD, 1995a, p.125).

In general, these changes in the supply of FDI have positive implications for host countries. As more firms from more countries and industries seek investment opportunities abroad, the range of choices for host countries as regards FDI increases. In a number of cases, host countries do not have to accept a single investment proposal as there are usually other TNCs that provide an alternative. There can also be competition among TNCs for specific attractive investment projects in host countries. This can be seen most clearly in the privatization programmes in Latin America and Central and Eastern Europe, where TNCs compete with each other to acquire enterprises to be privatized, especially in the natural resources and services sectors. Such competition can put host countries in a better position to benefit from FDI, provided that they have the negotiating skills permitting them to take advantage of their bargaining position.

Table I.2. Regional distribution of outward FDI stocks of selected Latin American (1986 and 1992) and Asian (1987 and 1997) economies
(Millions of dollars and per cent)

Home economy	Total[a] (Millions of dollars)		Geographical distribution (per cent)											
			Developing economies								Developed countries		Central and Eastern Europe	
			Africa		Latin America and the Caribbean[b]		South, East and South-East Asia		Others					
Latin America	1986	1992	1986	1992	1986	1992	1986	1992	1986	1992	1986	1992	1986	1992
Argentina	394	1 207	-	-	25.8	40.2	1.1	-	-	-	74.2	59.8	-	-
Brazil	1 497	4 123	1.1	0.4	39.0	60.4	-	0.4	0.9	0.3	57.9	38.5	-	-
Chile	30	713	-	2.4	53.5	90.8	-	0.4	-	-	46.5	6.2	-	0.1
Colombia	316	496	-	-	81.8	63.7	-	-	2.9	1.2	15.3	35.1	-	-
Mexico	891	1 365	-	-	4.9	4.8	-	-	-	-	95.1	95.2	-	-
Peru	39	63	-	-	57.7	74.0	-	-	9.9	6.0	32.5	20.0	-	-
Venezuela	590	599	-	-	19.3	20.7	-	-	-	-	80.7	79.3	-	-
Total	**3 755**	**8 566**	**0.4**	**0.4**	**30.3**	**48.8**	**0.4**	**0.2**	**0.7**	**0.3**	**68.1**	**50.3**	**0.0**	**0.0**
Asia	1987	1997	1987	1997	1987	1997	1987	1997	1987	1997	1987	1997	1987	1997
China	1 029	1 859	4.8	5.6	5.6	4.9	17.4	18.4	2.2	2.9	67.0	62.5	2.7	5.5
Hong Kong, China	16 887	279 754	-	-	-	-	91.1	98.8	-	-	8.9	1.2	-	-
Malaysia	1 812	12 737	1.2	1.1	-	1.4	58.4	48.8	-	0.7	37.0	41.8	-	-
Rep. of Korea	939	16 750	-	2.2	1.7	4.8	24.5	44.5	28.6	3.5	44.0	45.0	-	-
Singapore	7 808	39 800	1.0	0.6	-	-	51.1	57.3	-	-	27.4	25.3	-	-
Taiwan Prov. of China	375	15 314	-	-	4.7	34.1	27.9	35.2	1.2	0.2	65.2	29.3	-	-
Thailand	189	1 951	-	-	-	3.6	73.3	56.6	-	-	26.0	28.1	-	-
Total	**29 039**	**368 164**	**0.2**	**0.2**	**0.3**	**1.7**	**72.6**	**86.8**	**1.0**	**0.2**	**19.7**	**8.8**	**0.1**	**0.0**

Source : UNCTAD, 1999, annex tables A.I.13 and A.I.15.

Note : Data refer to the years other than those specified for the individual countries as follows : Brazil (1991 instead of 1992), Peru (1990 instead of 1992), China (1990 instead of 1987 and 1995 instead of 1997), Hong Kong (China) (1996 instead of 1997) and Singapore.

a Includes amounts which cannot be allocated by region.

b According to available data from national sources, the tax haven economies in this region (Bermuda, Cayman Islands, the Netherlands Antilles and Panama) received a significant part of total outward FDI stocks from the following Latin American countries: Brazil 17.4 per cent (1986) and 51.8 per cent (1991), Chile 25.6 per cent (1992), Colombia 49.8 per cent (1986) and 40.6 per cent (1992) and Peru 39.5 per cent (1986) and 24.3 per cent (1990).

This competitive pressure among TNCs applies also to large projects not involving privatization. A case in point is the automobile industry, where all major firms from developed countries have become TNCs. This was not the case some 20 years ago, when only United States producers were significant foreign investors. The result is that host countries with locational advantages in this industry (such as a large, dynamic market) have today a much greater choice of TNCs from home countries ranging from the United States through several European countries and Japan to the Republic of Korea. It is also important, as chapter II shows, that TNCs from different backgrounds and with different ownership-specific advantages may have different perceptions of the attractiveness of the same host country. Thus, if there is a lack of interest in a given host country on the part of one TNC or a set of TNCs (which some time ago could have meant that such a country would not receive FDI in a given industry), there may be TNCs from other countries interested in undertaking FDI in that country.

Table I.3. Internationalization ratio[a] of domestic investment, 1980-1997
(Per cent)

Region/country	Annual average				1997
	1980-1984	1985-1989	1990-1994	1995-1997	
Latin America	0.2	0.5	1.0	1.8	2.5
Argentina	-0.1	0.1	1.2	3.7	5.0
Brazil	0.5	0.3	0.4	0.7	1.1
Chile	0.5	0.1	3.6	7.2	10.1
Colombia	1.0	0.4	1.0	3.1	5.4
Mexico	0.1	0.5	0.6	0.3	1.4
Peru	..	..	0.1	0.2	0.5
Venezuela	0.1	1.4	4.5	3.5	3.2
Memorandum :					
World	2.4	4.3	4.9	6.8	8.0
Developed countries	2.9	5.0	5.7	8.0	9.7
European Union	4.2	7.7	8.1	12.0	14.8
United States	2.5	2.7	5.9	8.5	9.4
Japan	1.3	3.3	2.5	1.8	2.2
Developing countries	0.5	1.5	2.4	3.8	3.9
Africa	1.8	1.9	1.9	1.0	2.1
Asia	0.5	1.9	2.9	4.6	4.5
South, East and South-East Asia	0.4	1.9	3.5	5.2	4.9
Central and Eastern Europe	0.1	0.1	0.2	1.0	2.0

Source : UNCTAD, FDI/TNC database.

[a] Defined as a percentage share of outward FDI flows to gross fixed capital formation.

Thus, the greater number of actors providing outward FDI increases, on average, the number of candidates for individual FDI projects in host countries. Especially in the case of negotiated projects – e.g. as related to privatization – this can give a host country greater choice, enhance its bargaining power and lead to a bidding-up of the value of privatized assets or to better terms for the host country, thus potentially upgrading the quality of the FDI it receives.

New investment opportunities resulted in a rapid rise in outward international investment in the 1990s. Contrary to the common view some years ago that countries trying to attract FDI will divert scarce investment resources from other countries (especially developing countries), firms responded to emerging investment opportunities by increasing the supply of FDI capital rather than shifting given amounts of capital from one group of countries to another. There is no indication that FDI capital is scarce and that, because of a shortage, TNCs face hard choices among host countries. The amounts invested by TNCs abroad constitute a small share of the world's total investment: in 1995, outward FDI flows accounted for only 8 per cent of the world's gross fixed capital formation (UNCTAD, 1999, p. 501). Most likely, this share could increase easily in response to new opportunities.

Increased competition among firms for a portfolio of locational assets is balanced, however, by the fact that, as will be seen in the next section, all countries in the world now seek to attract FDI. This vastly increases the demand for FDI, providing TNCs with an increased range of choices as regards country locations. Moreover, as will be seen in chapter II, changes in the strategic investment behaviour of TNCs make them also more selective in their choice of investments, partly because of greater choice of host country locations and partly because of changing priorities and forms of investment (as later sections of this chapter will illustrate). Furthermore, while TNCs have been able to increase the supply of some types of investment resources in response to the increasing demand for FDI (especially the supply of outward FDI capital and certain intangible resources related to their expansion abroad through non-equity forms of investment), most of them, as will be shown in chapter II, face serious internal resource constraints, and especially managerial constraints, which put limits on the scope – or at least tempo – of their expansion abroad; this, in turn, makes them selective as regards the number of host countries in which they can operate.

The selectiveness of TNCs as regards FDI locations leads to considerable variations in the direction of the outward FDI flows among major home countries. For example, firms from Germany have invested proportionally much more in Brazil than have French and British TNCs. These differences may be due as much to industry effects and the perception of "economic distance" affecting the cost of home-host transactions as to firm-specific differences in the calculation of competitive advantage. The impact of "economic distance" upon actual investment decisions is highly variable. Though some Japanese firms blamed "economic distance" for the lack of any investment in Brazil (see chapter III), others disagreed: the share of Japanese FDI located in Latin America generally, and in Brazil in particular, has been close to the average world "weightings" for many years. The very fact of those differences suggests that (in this case) Brazil may have an opportunity to increase inward flows from those home countries that are currently under-represented in such terms.

A related consideration concerns the need for all Governments to balance a number of competing priorities in the pursuit of their development policies. How they do so sends signals that investors may interpret differently – partly explaining the differential patterns in flows. Given the strong examples of such high-growth economies as the Republic of Korea, and earlier Japan, where growth and wealth-creation has not been associated with inward FDI, it is not axiomatic that greater numbers of TNCs considering investment will increase the real development options for a given country. It is possible, however, that policies developed at the sectoral level can be refined to call for specific contributions that only some types of investors will be willing to provide. There is some evidence (Prahalad and Doz, 1987) of how smaller newcomers may be motivated by competitive forces to pay costs of entry that are higher than those offered by industry leaders and incumbent investors considering re-investment.

Another implication for host countries is that they have a further source of opportunity for increasing their inflows by actively taking into account non-traditional (i.e. developing country) home economies such as Argentina, Chile and Mexico in Latin America; and China, Hong Kong (China), the Republic of Korea, Singapore and Taiwan Province of China in Asia. Firms from these economies have built up sufficient ownership-specific assets and managerial expertise to be able to compete internationally. Moreover, they are striving for greater market shares through trade as well as investment and could be responsive to the economic priorities of particular host countries. How these firms might be persuaded of the merits of investing in a particular economy has much to do with thinking at the firm level.

A related issue that goes beyond the scope of this study, concerns whether firms from developing countries should be encouraged to invest abroad to increase their international competitiveness (box I.3).

Box I.3. Should firms from developing countries be encouraged to invest abroad?

There is a strong presumption that a country's economic performance mirrors the competitiveness of its firms. Therefore, measures that handicap firms in their efforts to increase competitiveness by acquiring a portfolio of foreign locational assets should be avoided. Governments of developing countries, especially in Asia, have recognized this, and are in the process of removing regulatory obstacles to outward FDI. Some are now actively promoting outward FDI, but there are strong differences among them in this regard. Developing countries with a successful export-oriented strategy have been more liberal in allowing firms to invest abroad. The primary motive is to facilitate market access of firms: allowing them to establish local production facilities in host countries is often necessary to expand market penetration and to avoid actual or anticipated trade barriers. More recently, access to technology has become an important additional motivation for developing countries to permit their firms to invest in developed economies (UNCTAD, 1995a, p. 322). Samsung's acquisition of Rollei Fototechnic GmbH in Germany in 1995, and its negotiations to acquire the bankrupt Dutch aircraft manufacturer, Fokker, are cases in point. A number of Asian developing countries (e.g. India, the Republic of Korea, Malaysia, Singapore and Thailand) have gone from permissive to promotional policies towards outward FDI. Hong Kong (China), the Republic of Korea and Taiwan Province of China became net exporters of equity capital by the end of the 1980s (UNCTAD, 1996a, annex tables 1 and 2).

The question of whether developing countries should pursue policies of domestic efficiency first and outward investment second is a question that goes beyond the scope of this study. Nonetheless, the example of Asian developing countries, which moved early to export-oriented development, indicates the long-term strengthening that has resulted from a combination of efficiency- and export-oriented policies that have led to outward FDI perhaps earlier than would have happened without specific policy intervention. As mentioned above, outward FDI can reinforce such strategies by providing access to new technologies, cheap labour and natural resources, thus helping to restructure the economy (see UNCTAD, 1995a, p. 322).

Promotional policies that enhance the ability of firms to invest abroad include (ibid., pp. 331-339):

- Information and technical assistance to one's business community, especially to small enterprises, as regards outward FDI opportunities. Lessons can be drawn from the experience of the Republic of Korea, Singapore and Thailand which actively support their domestic TNCs to invest abroad.

- Direct financial support and/or fiscal incentives to outward FDI are provided by a number of developing economies (the Republic of Korea, India, Singapore, Thailand, Malaysia and Taiwan Province of China). Such measures are often adapted from programmes used to promote domestic industrial development or inward FDI. They may evolve also from export-promotion programmes. However, it must be noted that capital exports that are excessively subsidized can lead to a misallocation of resources and a weakening of the firms involved.

- Investment insurance against non-commercial risks to domestic firms investing abroad. Where national insurance mechanisms does not exist, private investors can insure against such risks through the Multilateral Investment Guarantee Agency (MIGA) (ibid., p. 22).

Source: UNCTAD

B. The growing number and diversification of host countries

1. Pattern

The changes in the *supply* of FDI discussed in the preceding section have been accompanied, as already signaled, by significant changes on the *demand* side. While many countries were hostile or, at best selective, towards FDI some 10 to 15 years ago, nowadays virtually all countries – rich and poor, large and small, industrialized and industrializing – actively pursue policies aimed at attracting FDI. The liberalization of FDI regimes and effective promotion policies play a particular role in this respect.

Many economies have liberalized their FDI regimes and have undertaken internal economic reforms and legislative adjustments to increase their attractiveness to foreign investors (UNCTAD, 1999, tables IV.1 and IV.2). These efforts are taking place at the national, regional and international levels. This represents a powerful trend, one result of which has been that the demand side for FDI has become very crowded; both countries and regions within the countries are actively pursuing increasingly similar practices in their attempts to attract FDI. In addition, countries have put in place various promotional efforts by establishing agencies whose purpose is to target investors abroad, attract them and help them settle in host countries. The number of such agencies has increased substantially – as of 1 October 1998, 105 of them have joined together to form the World Association of Investment Promotion Agencies (WAIPA), supported by UNCTAD, UNIDO and MIGA. The resulting competition among countries is fierce. Furthermore, in many places this competition has led to the increased use of incentives (UNCTAD, 1996a). Malaysia, for example, calculates its incentive packages relative to those offered by neighbouring countries in an effort to stay ahead (Stopford and Strange, 1991). However, this example indicates that the impact of this policy competition on FDI inflows is not as straightforward as might be expected, and depends on the type of FDI (box I.4).

Box I.4. Competition for FDI in Asia

China's "open-door" policy and attractiveness to foreign investors has intensified competition for FDI in Asia, with possible implications for FDI flows to other host countries in the region. In the aggregate, FDI flows into the developing economies of South, East and South-East Asia, excluding China, grew fairly substantially during the early 1990s as compared with the late 1980s. However, the levels of FDI flows to China and their growth rate during 1992-1993 were substantially higher than those flowing to any other country in the region, while a number of them even experienced a decline in inflows. Liberalization measures implemented or introduced in 1993 and 1994 in countries such as Indonesia and Thailand may have been partly a response to the fear that they were losing out to some of the new investments going to other parts of Asia. However, the scope for investors to substitute actual or potential FDI in one host country by FDI in another country depends largely on the type of FDI as well as the sector or industry concerned (assuming, of course, that all countries permit such investment). The following factors need to be considered in this connection:

Market-seeking FDI. A significant portion of FDI in South, East and South-East Asia is of the market-seeking type that is unlikely to shift as long as there are profitable opportunities for production in a host country's market. The sheer size and income growth of many countries in South, East and South-East Asia have started to generate a consumption boom for goods and services. This points to a large market-oriented FDI potential that is not restricted to the newly industrializing economies (NIEs) alone. In India, for example, the potential for market-oriented FDI is enormous, especially as the effects of FDI liberalization are taking hold: FDI approvals

/...

(Box I.4, concluded)

rose dramatically from $165 million in 1990/1991 to $4 billion in 1993/1994, although actual inflows are still under $1 billion a year. Malaysia and Thailand have reached income levels at which it has become profitable to establish automobile manufacturing facilities for domestic (and foreign) markets.

If, however, a host country market is too small to exploit economies of scale, and an investment project has to be oriented to more than one country or to the region, then, of course, competition for such a project may arise. This may be costly and may distort investment and trade. Therefore countries that participate in regional integration schemes, which may attract such projects, sometimes agree on rules limiting such competition. If the integration scheme is sound and involves countries at similar levels of development, investors in complex projects (e.g. automobile industry) quite frequently locate production of different individual components in different countries.

Furthermore, the services sector is attracting more and more FDI flows, especially in the NIEs. Given the non-tradability of most services, markets can only be reached by FDI which, therefore, is difficult to divert. For example, in the Republic of Korea, the share of the services sector in total inward approved FDI stock was 37 per cent in 1994, compared with about one-quarter in 1981; in Taiwan Province of China, the share of services in FDI stock increased from 21 per cent in 1980 to 32 per cent in 1993. Recently, large-scale services-related FDI has been picking up in response to liberalization in such industries as power and telecommunications.

Natural resource-seeking FDI. Natural resource-seeking FDI, another important form of FDI in several countries of the region, is also largely location-specific. In addition to such inflows in established resource-abundant host countries such as Indonesia, Malaysia, Papua New Guinea and the Philippines, new entrants such as Viet Nam and Myanmar have begun to attract FDI in the primary sector, and this can be expected to grow.

Efficiency-seeking FDI. The situation differs, however, with respect to FDI in export-oriented manufacturing which is based on cost considerations. To the extent that locational advantages – especially regarding labour costs – differ or change, this can have an impact on such FDI, and can work to the advantage of China as well as other low-cost countries in the region. Indeed, it appears that TNC activities are gradually being restructured in Asia, with export-oriented labour-intensive manufacturing activity gradually shifting from the more advanced of the developing countries in the region to the less advanced ones. For example, in the Republic of Korea, average annual FDI inflows into the textile and clothing industries declined from $16 million during 1989-1992 to $5 million during 1993-1994 on an approval basis. Counterbalancing that, a number of Asian countries are increasingly attracting FDI in capital-intensive industries. For example, average annual flows to the chemical industry in the Republic of Korea increased from $24 million during the period 1982-1986 to $189 million during 1987-1991 and continued to maintain almost the same level during 1992-1994. Investment policies of countries in the region also reflect a recognition of this shift in locational advantages; countries such as Malaysia and Singapore are becoming more selective with respect to the kind of FDI they seek to attract, putting an increased focus on its technological content.

To sum up, several types of FDI do not lend themselves easily to shifting between locations, and this is one important reason for expecting continued growth of FDI in Asian and Pacific countries other than China. To the extent that FDI has shifted, this is likely to have been relatively limited and, in most cases, accompanied by industrial upgrading. In any event, the amount of FDI available to a region is not a fixed quantity. The pattern of flows to the region suggests, moreover, that a process of adaptation is under way in response to the changing locational advantages and capabilities of countries for hosting FDI in different industries and activities.

Source: UNCTAD, 1995a, pp. 54-64.

Thus, as countries' FDI policies become similar, the focus of their actions is shifting increasingly towards promotional efforts. However, many countries simply cannot afford incentives programmes that are too generous, especially if these programmes prove to have only a limited effect. Therefore, countries undertake other efforts to upgrade their various locational advantages, thus increasing the range of FDI opportunities available in the world.

Firms have been taking advantage of these new investment opportunities and all groups of countries have received increasing absolute amounts of FDI (table I.4). Between 1985 and 1998 (based on five-year and four-year annual averages to eliminate yearly fluctuations), FDI inflows increased uniformly, consistently and significantly into all three groups of countries. When, during the recession of 1991-1993, investment conditions in the developed countries deteriorated, the rate of increase of FDI inflows into this group was seriously reduced, while inflows into the other two groups continued to grow rapidly. When investment conditions in the developed countries recovered after 1993, annual FDI inflows more than doubled in every region in the period 1995-1998 compared with 1990-1994. In Central and Eastern Europe these flows quadrupled.

Table I.4. FDI inflows by host region, 1985-1998

(Billions of dollars)

Region	Annual average		
	1985-1989	1990-1994	1995-1998
World	129	202	409
Developed countries	107	136	288
Developing economies	22	63	145
Central and Eastern Europe	0.2	4	16

Source: UNCTAD, FDI/TNC database.

Judging from the rapid rise in FDI inflows, developing countries have now come fully within the purview of TNC executives, a situation quite different from that in the 1980s. The share of developing countries in world FDI inflows increased from about 20 per cent in 1990 to 38 per cent in 1996 and then fell to just under 26 per cent in 1998 (table I.5). Yet this development masks considerable differences among regions and countries within the group. In terms of shares in global FDI, Latin America and the Caribbean benefited somewhat less from the increased investment activities of TNCs than the developing countries in Asia. The latter increased their share between 1980 and 1998 by 3.7 percentage points, whereas Latin American countries increased their share by 0.8 percentage points. Still, FDI inflows per capita in Latin America and the Caribbean are almost 6 times higher than in Asia and have increased considerably faster than in Asia, doubling between 1995 and 1998 (UNCTAD, 1999, p. 21).

During the 1980s, the shares of the major Latin American countries in the global *stock* of inward FDI stagnated or even declined as a consequence of the debt crisis, economic stagnation or slow growth and macroeconomic instability. Policy reforms to restore stability and promote growth have helped in different ways to restore investors' confidence in the region (Funke, Nunnenkamp and Schweickert, 1992, p. 4). Some countries, such as Chile and Mexico, recovered their lost share relatively quickly. By contrast, Brazil's share of the Latin American stock of FDI declined by more than 5 percentage points through the early 1980s and 1990s. However, with the stabilization programme (Plan Real) and privatization, the trend reversed to give Brazil the same share in 1998 as it had in 1980. The almost fivefold increase in FDI inflows, from $5.5 billion in 1995 to almost $29 billion in 1998, accounts for the increase in Brazil's share.

2. Implications

Though international investors have been returning to Brazil in the late 1990s, the country is still below its potential to attract FDI. Continued FDI growth will depend, among other things, on whether investors regard Brazil's locational advantages as attractive enough – and perhaps even more attractive than those of other countries – to commit more funds and attention there.

Where does Brazil stand in this respect? As discussed in other sections of this chapter, it has considerable potential for inward FDI in all sectors of its economy.

- In the primary sector, Brazil possesses more natural resources than Argentina, Chile, Colombia, Mexico, Peru and Venezuela together (table I.6), and more than India and Indonesia (Hiemenz and Nunnenkamp, et al., 1991, p. 67). The vast majority of these resources are in mineral deposits. As of the late 1990s, Brazil has proven and estimated iron ore reserves of 48 billion tons, enough to supply global demand for the next 500 years. In addition, it has proven deposits of 208 million tons of

Table I.5. Inward FDI by region and selected host countries, 1980-1998

(Billions of dollars and per cent)

Region/country	Stocks						Inflows					
								Annual average				
	1980	1985	1990	1996	1997	1998	1980-1984	1985-1989	1990-1998	1996	1997	1998
						(Billions of dollars)						
World total	507	782	1 768	3 086	3 437	4 088	58	129	312	359	464	644
					Shares in the world total (per cent):							
Latin America and the Caribbean	9.4	9.8	6.5	9.5	10.1	10.2	12.2	6.1	11.4	12.9	14.7	11.1
Argentina	1.1	0.8	0.4	1.1	1.2	1.1	0.8	0.6	1.4	1.8	1.7	0.9
Brazil	3.5	3.3	2.1	3.5	3.7	3.8	3.6	1.1	2.5	2.9	4.0	4.5
Chile	0.2	0.3	0.6	0.7	0.7	0.7	0.4	0.6	0.9	1.3	1.2	0.7
Colombia	0.2	0.3	0.2	0.3	0.3	0.3	0.7	0.4	0.6	0.9	1.2	0.5
Mexico	1.6	2.4	1.3	1.5	1.5	1.5	3.7	2.0	2.8	2.6	2.8	1.6
Peru	0.2	0.1	0.1	0.2	0.2	0.2	0.1	-	0.5	0.9	0.4	0.3
Venezuela	0.3	0.2	0.2	0.3	0.4	0.4	0.2	0.1	0.6	0.6	1.1	0.6
Memorandum :												
Developed countries	73.8	69.7	78.9	69.2	67.3	68.1	68.3	82.7	65.3	58.8	58.9	71.5
European Union	36.6	30.2	41.7	36.8	35.8	36.4	26.5	33.8	35.3	30.4	27.2	35.7
United States	16.4	23.6	22.3	19.3	19.8	21.4	31.1	37.7	22.0	21.3	23.5	30.0
Japan	0.6	0.6	0.6	1.0	0.8	0.7	0.5	0.1	0.5	0.1	0.7	0.5
Central and Eastern Europe	-	-	0.2	1.7	2.0	2.0	-	0.1	3.0	3.5	4.0	2.7
Developing countries	26.2	30.3	21.0	29.2	30.7	29.8	31.7	17.2	31.8	37.7	37.2	25.8
Africa	2.7	3.0	2.1	1.9	2.0	1.8	2.0	2.3	1.5	1.6	1.6	1.2
Asia	13.8	17.3	12.1	17.5	18.4	17.5	17.1	8.6	18.7	22.9	20.6	13.2

Source : UNCTAD, FDI/TNC database.

manganese, 2 billion tons of bauxite and up to 400 million tons of nickel. It also has 90 per cent of the world market in gems. Nevertheless, FDI in this sector is minimal. If Brazil wishes to attract TNCs to exploit these natural resources, it will, to some extent, have to meet the policy challenges discussed below (section F).

- In the services sector – and despite the considerable increase in the share of services in Brazil's total inward stock of FDI – the relative size of the stock is still small, compared to most Latin American countries. A number of service industries appear to be significantly underrepresented in that FDI stock (section I.D).

- In the manufacturing sector, the FDI stock is sizeable with a considerable potential for sequential investment. Brazil's degree of industrialization holds potential for the participation of its firms in international mergers and acquisitions (on both the inward and outward FDI side), an important form of worldwide FDI, which accounted for a substantial share of annual flows in the 1990s.

The inward FDI potential in all sectors could be considerably enhanced by a full-fledged privatization programme (as discussed below) cutting across all sectors. The launching of the programme contributed to the surge of FDI inflows in the late 1990s despite the financial crisis.

Brazil stands out among developing countries and countries in transition in terms of market size. It is by far the largest country in the region with the largest population, area and gross domestic product (GDP) (table I.6). In 1998, its GDP ($748 billion) was not much lower than of China ($900 billion) and higher than that of the Russian Federation ($338 billion). In terms of population, Brazil ranks only behind China, India and Indonesia, but it has much greater purchasing power, measured by GDP per capita, ranking 72 out of 210 economies in 1998 (World Bank, 1999, table 1), and therefore a significantly larger market (in terms of GDP size) than India ($421 billion) and Indonesia ($139 billion).

Market size is generally seen to be one of the most important determinants of inward FDI. From the point of view of a company that considers substituting FDI for exports to a host country (a typical motivation for companies to undertake FDI), the size of a host country market in terms of being able to accommodate an efficient plant is of key importance. Consequently, countries with large markets can potentially accommodate more foreign investors in various branches of their economies than countries with small markets.

However, if a large market is stagnant or shrinking, or an economy or a country is unstable – or is considered to be unstable or risky – market size is not sufficient to attract considerable amounts of FDI (UNCTC, 1992). Brazil, from the 1980s until the early 1990s, is a case in point. By all standards, its market size at that time was no smaller when compared with other countries than it is today: in 1986, it was the seventh largest market in the world and, despite of its economic problems, it was the largest market among developing countries (UNCTAD, 1989, pp. 422-428). But until the mid-1990s, it failed to attract much FDI. One major reason was precisely that its market was stagnant – in 1981-1992, Brazil's real GDP per capita declined by 0.5 per cent per year. Another reason was that its economy was unstable with an annual average inflation rate during that period being very high (table I.6). Only when the economy began to grow again and returned to stable conditions, and other locational advantages improved, did Brazil begin to reappear as one of the largest host countries among developing countries.[6]

Table I.6. Selected indicators of locational competitiveness of Brazil vis-à-vis other selected economies

Economy	Population (Millions) 1998	Area 1000 (sq. km.)	Natural resources[a]	Energy reserves[b] 1995	GDP[c] Billions of dollars 1998	GDP[c] Annual average growth 1981-1992	1993-1994	1995-1998	1998	Per capita GDP[c] Dollars 1998	Per capita GDP[c] Annual average growth 1981-1992	1993-1994	1995-1998	1998	Inflation[d] 1981-1992	1993-1994	1995-1998	1998
Brazil	166	8 547	7 665	3 862	751	1.4	5.4	2.6	0.2	4 524	-0.5	3.9	1.3	-0.9	371.7	2114.5	22.4	0.0
Latin America	235	8 831	2 275	32 605	970	1.8	4.8	3.1	2.9	4 162	-0.2	3.0	1.4	1.2	114.1	17.0	19.4	11.2
of which:																		
Argentina	36	2 780	114	985	332	0.6	7.0	3.2	3.9	9 193	-0.8	5.6	1.9	2.6	341.3	4.3	0.7	-2.0
Chile	15	757	281	1 321	70	4.7	7.2	6.8	3.4	4 752	3.0	5.3	5.4	2.0	19.0	11.6	5.6	5.1
Colombia	41	1 139	211	5 198	86	3.3	5.7	3.0	0.6	2 095	1.2	3.7	1.0	-1.4	24.8	24.5	18.2	17.5
Mexico	96	1 958	1 107	9 873	337	1.8	3.3	2.6	4.8	3 521	-0.3	1.4	0.8	3.1	55.8	8.9	24.4	13.8
Peru	25	1 285	80	1 349	65	-0.4	9.3	4.4	0.7	2 639	-2.5	7.7	2.6	-0.9	280.8	32.1	8.9	5.4
Venezuela	23	912	482	13 879	80	2.0	-0.7	1.8	-0.7	3 465	-0.5	-3.0	-0.3	-2.5	22.1	46.4	53.2	21.2
Asia	2 637	16 034	643	232 312	1 871	7.5	9.8	7.1	4.2	978	5.6	8.2	5.6	2.8	..	..	..	..
of which:																		
China	1 239	9 597	-	119 846	900	9.5	13.1	9.2	7.8	727	7.9	11.8	8.1	6.9	5.9	17.2	4.6	-1.3
India	980	3 288	-	71 340	397	5.3	6.5	6.3	5.0	405	3.2	4.7	4.5	3.2	8.9	9.7	7.0	5.6
ASEAN-4	362	3 048	-	40 943	163	4.6	7.0	2.1	-7.9	1 476	2.8	5.1	0.3	-9.4	7.9	7.4	16.2	44.3
NIE-3	56	101	-	183	411	7.6	7.1	3.7	-4.8	10 378	6.5	6.0	2.4	-5.7	7.1	5.5	4.1	4.5

Source : United Nations and World Bank, UNCTAD's own calculations.

Notes: ASEAN-4 includes Indonesia, Malaysia, the Philippines, and Thailand. NIE-3 includes Hong Kong (China), the Republic of Korea, and Singapore. Regional data aggregate country totals except for GDP and per capita GDP growth rates and inflation which are a weighted average of the country total.

a   Mineral reserves, including oil and gas, valued at world prices of 1985-1988, in billions of dollars. Data are taken from Heimenz and Nunnenkamp (1991).

b   Recoverable reserves in millions of metric tons. They include coal, peat, crude oil, oil shale and natural gas (converted to oil equivalent). Data are taken from the United Nations, *Energy Statistics Yearbook 1996* (New York, United Nations).

c   Calculated as exponential growth using 1995 United States dollars.

d   Annual average growth of the GDP implicit deflator.

If Brazil maintains its dynamism and macroeconomic stability, the size of the Brazilian market will undoubtedly be a great asset in the country's efforts to attract FDI and in its dealings with TNCs, though, as suggested below, the relative importance of this asset is diminishing.

Whether, and to what extent, Brazil's substantial potential for inward FDI can be exploited, will depend on many factors, a number of which are examined throughout this study. These factors belong not only in the area of objective locational determinants, but also in the area of perceptions of those TNC executives who take FDI decisions concerning such matters as the credibility of reforms, prospects for market growth and degree of macroeconomic stability. As suggested in chapters II and III, it is one thing to implement reforms but quite another to convince investors that these reforms will hold.

There are also more specific policies that are relevant in this respect, including those concerning the investment regime, trade policies and various factors that determine transaction costs. The latter two can be particularly important in the context of attracting efficiency-seeking FDI and the possible inclusion of affiliates in Brazil in the international production networks of TNCs. Compared with its regional competitors and a group of Asian developing countries that have been successful in attracting FDI, executives view Brazil's policies as relatively more favourable to FDI. However, they also perceive Brazil as having average transaction cost-related barriers compared to those in Latin America, but below Chile, which scores higher on all but one of the individual items (tables I.7 and I.8). When compared with the 1995 rankings – by the World Economic Forum – when Brazil was below the Latin American average in both categories,[7] it had improved its ranking by 1999.

An important question that arises in this context is that among the various determinants of FDI and the possible actions Governments can take, which are the most important ones for attracting FDI? In this respect, a dynamic national market remains a powerful magnet for FDI, even though, in a liberalizing and globalizing world economy, markets are increasingly becoming regional or global in scope. Furthermore, given the worldwide competition for FDI, host-country stability has assumed greater importance in influencing TNC investment decisions. Thus, the continuation of Brazil's stabilization efforts are most likely to significantly affect future FDI

Table 1.7. Policies towards FDI in Latin America and selected Asian economies, 1999

	Brazil	Argentina	Chile	Colombia	Mexico	Venezuela	Latin America	China	India	ASEAN-4[a]	NIE-4[b]
1. Acquisition of control	8.6	9.3	9.2	7.7	7.3	8.1	8.3	4.4	5.8	5.8	7.4
2. Import restrictions	7.1	7.3	8.3	6.5	6.7	6.6	7.1	4.3	5.4	5.7	6.8
3. Equal treatment	7.7	8.1	9.1	7.0	7.3	7.5	7.8	3.9	5.3	5.5	7.1
4. Cross-border ventures	7.5	2.5	8.7	6.9	7.5	7.6	6.6	4.3	4.7	6.7	7.7
5. Employment of foreigners	6.4	8.5	6.9	5.9	5.3	5.8	6.5	5.9	5.5	5.4	5.8
6. Investment protection	6.3	6.3	7.4	5.1	6.3	4.7	6.0	8.1	5.7	6.6	6.9
7. Investment incentives	7.3	6.6	6.6	3.9	5.7	5.0	5.6	6.7	6.0	6.7	6.8
Total	7.3	6.9	8.0	6.2	6.6	6.5	6.8	5.4	5.5	6.1	6.9

Source: IMD, *The World Competitive Yearbook, 1999* (Lausanne, IMD).

Notes: Survey results are scaled from 0 (least favourable to FDI) to 10 (most favourable to FDI). The criteria are as follows: (1) foreign investors are free to acquire control in a domestic company; (2) national protectionism does not prevent foreign products and services from being imported; (3) foreign and domestic companies are treated equally; (4) cross-border ventures can be negotiated with foreign partners without government intervention; (5) immigration laws do not prevent your company from employing foreign labour; (6) investment protection schemes are available for most foreign partner countries; (7) investment incentives are attractive to foreign investors.
[a] Includes Indonesia, Malaysia, the Philippines and Thailand.
[b] Include Hong Kong (China), the Republic of Korea, Singapore and Taiwan Province of China.

Table 1.8. Transaction cost-related barriers to FDI in Latin America and selected Asian economies, 1999

		Brazil	Argentina	Chile	Colombia	Mexico	Venezuela	Latin America	China	India	ASEAN-4[a]	NIE-4[b]
1.	Legal framework	3.7	3.9	6.1	3.0	3.3	2.2	3.7	5.9	5.0	4.7	6.5
2.	Competition laws	5.1	3.0	6.4	3.3	5.4	5.0	4.6	4.2	4.7	4.1	5.7
3.	Transparency	5.2	5.4	6.4	5.2	4.6	3.4	5.0	6.4	3.8	4.9	5.8
4.	Bureaucracy	2.1	3.0	4.1	1.5	2.3	1.7	2.5	1.3	1.8	2.9	5.0
5.	Corporate taxes	4.2	3.1	7.6	5.4	4.0	5.7	5.2	4.8	6.4	6.4	7.1
6.	Corruption	2.7	1.4	6.1	1.4	2.0	1.4	2.4	2.0	1.8	2.2	5.7
7.	Culture	8.4	7.2	8.1	6.2	7.1	8.0	7.3	7.2	6.8	7.2	7.2
8.	Corporate governance	6.2	6.7	7.3	6.2	6.1	5.9	6.4	6.1	5.6	5.6	6.2
9.	Distribution system	3.2	4.2	4.7	1.9	4.5	3.4	3.7	5.5	2.3	4.8	7.0
10	Skilled labour	6.3	6.5	6.8	5.2	5.9	4.5	5.8	4.8	7.8	6.3	6.7
11.	Technological change	5.2	5.1	5.5	4.6	4.8	4.7	4.9	6.1	4.7	5.2	6.4
12.	Image abroad	3.9	6.0	7.4	1.7	4.8	3.3	4.6	7.8	3.4	4.7	6.9
	Total	4.7	4.6	6.4	3.8	4.6	4.1	4.7	5.2	4.5	4.9	6.3

Source: IMD, *The World Competitive Yearbook*, 1999 (Lausanne, IMD).

Notes: Survey results are scaled from 0 (least favourable to FDI) to 10 (most favourable to FDI). The criteria are as follows: (1) the legal framework is not detrimental to your country's competitiveness; (2) competition laws do not prevent unfair competition in your country; (3) the government communicates its policy intentions clearly; (4) bureaucracy does not hinder business development; (5) real corporate taxes (after deductions) encourage entrepreneurial activity; (6) bribing and corruption does not exist in the public sphere; (7) national culture is open to foreign influence; (8) rights and responsibilities of shareholders are well defined; (10) the distribution infrastructure of goods and services are generally efficient; (11) skilled labour (i.e. relevant to your economy) is available in your country's labour market; (12) the image of your company abroad supports the development of business.

[a] Includes Indonesia, Malaysia, the Philippines and Thailand.

[b] Includes Hong Kong (China), the Republic of Korea, Singapore and Taiwan Province of China.

inflows. Sustained macroeconomic stability is a major reason why Asian developing countries received the bulk of increasing FDI flows. But to the extent that this also happens in competing investment locations, an improvement in operating conditions for foreign affiliates becomes an important inducement to FDI, supplemented by carefully crafted promotion efforts.

C. Regional integration can stimulate and reorient FDI

1. Pattern

Regional integration groupings have proliferated in the world, encouraged by the success of the European Union. Economic integration increases market size and enhances economic growth. As market size and economic growth are in turn important determinants of FDI inflows, regional integration is often expected to stimulate FDI. Such FDI can come from member countries of the regional integration schemes, as TNCs reorient their strategies from national towards regional markets to realize economies of scale and face intensified competition resulting from the removal of national protection. For the same reason, higher FDI inflows can also be expected from third countries, especially if TNCs from these countries expect efficiency gains from producing in the integrated area.

The formation of the European Economic Community in the late 1950s led to increased FDI inflows during the 1960s (UNCTC, 1993). The same experience was repeated when the Community was enlarged successively. More recently, its deepening through the 1992 Single Market Programme brought about another increase in FDI inflows. A striking feature of this growth has been the surge in intra-European Union FDI (table 1.9), resulting from the efforts of European TNCs to rationalize their European Union (EU) production bases to achieve scale economies and efficiency. Between 1984 and 1990, the share of intra-regional FDI in the total stock of the EU's FDI increased from 20 per cent to 66 per cent. A significant proportion of this was in the form of mergers and acquisitions as firms raced to capture market positions (Centre for Business Strategy, 1990). The EU's share of FDI declined from 1990 to 59 per cent in 1993, partly because TNCs had largely completed their restructuring in the group's internal market even before the Single Market Programme itself had been completed.

The formation of NAFTA was also expected to induce higher FDI inflows. Yet Canadian and Mexican shares in the total outward stock of the United States declined from 19 to 13 per cent between 1990 and 1995 (table I.9). One explanation is that the removal of trade barriers may have stimulated United States firms to develop enhanced scale economies at home, rather than investing in Canada or Mexico. NAFTA did not promote Canadian FDI in the United States either. In 1994, the United States share in Canadian stock of outward FDI was 5 percentage points lower than in 1991 (OECD, 1996). Moreover, NAFTA as a whole lost considerable ground in worldwide FDI inflows: its share fell from 40 per cent in 1984-1989 to 24 per cent in 1990-1995 (UNCTAD, 1996a, annex table 1). The dominance of the United States as the regional hub for so many industries may be one reason for this fall; intra-regional trade creation, as in the EU, has been an important effect of trade liberalization.

Table I.9. Intraregional FDI, 1984, 1990 and 1995
(Percentage of total FDI stock)

Country or region	1984	1990	1995
European Union (12)[a]	19.5	65.8	58.5[b]
United States[c]	24.3	18.6	13.4
Japan[d]	25.1	15.3	16.4[e]

Sources: Eurostat (1995, pp. 158-159); OECD (1994); Lowe and Bargas (1996); UNCTAD (1996a, p. 82).

[a] Share of intra-EU outward FDI in total EU FDI stock.
[b] 1993.
[c] Share of Canada and Mexico in total outward FDI stock of the United States.
[d] Share of South and East Asia in total outward FDI stock of Japan.
[e] 1994.

Unlike the EU and the United States, Japan had no regional integration scheme with its neighbours until APEC was formed in 1989. But it had developed close economic relations with Asian developing countries since the early 1960s. Moreover, trade and investment flows among East and South-East Asian countries have increasingly intensified. Therefore, this region has often been regarded as experiencing market-driven regional integration (as distinct from the policy-led integration of the EU). In the early stages of this development, many Japanese TNCs invested in labour-intensive industries of neighbouring countries, to lower the costs of supply to world markets. Then they targeted domestic markets of Asian countries to take advantage of their rising income levels. After the appreciation of the yen, Japanese FDI moved to a third stage, in which Japanese firms relocated production to Asian countries with a view to re-export to Japan. The three types of linked trade and investment flows have been taking place within the framework of regional core networks of TNCs. Though these are becoming more complex and harder to manage, they continue to create value for the participants (Stopford, 1997a).

These contrasting indicators from the three regions suggest that the impact on FDI of regional integration depends both on the life-cycle and rationalization effects, as well as on the impact of a dominant country within the region. Japan's share of the stock of FDI in developing Asia fell from 25 per cent in the early 1980s to 21 per cent in 1993. The same relative fall was experienced by European and United States investors as an increasing part of the intra-regional growth dynamic was captured by investors from smaller countries in the region.

Similar factors may affect the medium-term impact of the MERCOSUR on FDI. Initial trade developments in the MERCOSUR have been in line with the European experience. Trade grew much more rapidly within the MERCOSUR, recording a growth of 250 per cent between 1990 and 1993, than it did outside the common market (29 per cent). TNCs accounted for 65 per cent of intra-MERCOSUR manufacturing exports (UNCTAD, 1995b, p. 83). As will be shown in greater detail in chapter III, most TNCs have responded positively to the common market, most notably those seeking regional scale advantages. The MERCOSUR was created by the Treaty of Asunción and signed by Argentina, Brazil, Paraguay and Uruguay on 26 March 1991. Chile and Bolivia became associate members in 1996 and 1997 respectively. Negotiations are currently underway with the Andean Community (Bolivia, Colombia, Ecuador, Peru and Venezuela) to create a joint free trade zone in 2000, which would have 334 million consumers spending more than $1.4 trillion, potentially fostering further trade and FDI expansion in the region (table I.10).

Table I.10. Market size and FDI inflows in an enlarged Latin American free trade zone

Country or grouping	Population (Millions) 1998	GDP per capita (Dollars) 1998	Total GDP (Billions of dollars) 1998	Share in world FDI inflows (per cent) Annual average		
				1990-1993	1994-1997	1998
MERCOSUR	211	5 123	1 078	2.3	4.4	5.4
of which:						
Brazil	166	4 524	751	0.7	2.7	4.5
Associate members of MERCOSUR	23	3 846	87	0.5	1.2	0.9
Andean Community	109	2 655	289	1.1	2.4	1.6
Latin American free trade zone	334	4 329	1 445	3.8	8.0	7.8

Source: World Bank and UNCTAD FDI/TNC database.

Notes: The MERCOSUR includes Argentina, Brazil, Paraguay and Uruguay.
Associate members of the MERCOSUR include Bolivia and Chile.
The Andean community comprises Bolivia, Colombia, Ecuador, Peru and Venezuela.
The Latin American Free trade zone includes the MERCOSUR, the Andean group and Chile.

2. Implications

Because many investors regard Brazil as the hub of the emerging regional economy, the country has every opportunity to reap considerable benefits from this boost to FDI. As the share of TNCs in intra-MERCOSUR trade indicates, they are seeking to exploit the advantages created by this integration effort. If Brazilian firms are to take equal advantage of the MERCOSUR, they too need to develop outward FDI and the associated managerial structures (Kotabe, 1996). Strengthening the framework both for tariff liberalization and firm-level support is likely to bring considerable gains to the Brazilian economy.

The importance of TNC actions in determining how Brazil might gain most from the MERCOSUR and a Latin American free trade zone will be addressed further in chapter III. The actions of TNC within any economic union need to be understood within the context of their global strategies. The spur for greater FDI depends critically upon the economics of the business, the nature of the desired linkages across internal and external borders, and thus the sensitivity to internal and external tariff policy and expectations of policy evolutions in the future.

D. The increasing share of services in FDI

1. Pattern

The share of service industries in global FDI inflows has risen significantly over the past two decades, increasing from 43 to 53 per cent in the developed countries, and from 25 to 41 per cent in the developing countries between 1988 and 1997 (UNCTAD, 1999, tables A.I.16 and A.I.17). Yet this increase is probably higher than that shown by FDI statistics, as many service providers have globalized by means of non-equity arrangements such as partnerships (e.g. in accounting), management contracts (e.g. in tourism) and franchising (e.g. in fast food and retail trade). Moreover, many manufacturing firms have also diversified into services, often investing abroad to obtain certain complementary undertakings to such as logistics and marketing services. These services are not always recorded separately.

For some major home countries, the services sector accounted for more than half (France and the United States) to nearly three quarters (Japan) of their total FDI outflows as early as the late 1980s (table I.11). This share has increased considerably over the past decade in Germany and the United Kingdom. Although the industry breakdown of FDI in services is incomplete, financial services (including banking and insurance) account for the highest share, followed by trade (which was especially important in France, Japan, the United Kingdom and the United States, and much less important in Germany).

Developed countries absorbed over 80 per cent of inward FDI in services throughout the 1980s (UNCTAD, 1993a, p. 62). The efficiency-enhancing aspects of these investments provide a link between the role of services in inward FDI and the services sector's contribution to GDP which, in turn, is positively correlated with an economy's per-capita income.[8] The deregulation and privatization of service industries, as well as their opening up to foreign competition provided further stimuli to inward FDI in service industries in developed countries. This trend was most pronounced at the regional level, especially within the European Union. At the same time, the liberalization of services entered the agenda of multilateral trade negotiations, signalling the importance now being attached to their role in fostering global development.

By the mid-1990s, the share of inward FDI flows into services going to the developed countries fell considerably. By contrast the share of inward FDI in services going to the developing countries increased from 14 per cent in 1988 to over 39 per cent in 1997 (UNCTAD, 1999, tables A.I.16 and A.I.17). Most of this growth went to relatively advanced developing countries, in which the services sector had reached a fairly high share of the GDP. For example, the share of services in inward FDI stocks of the Republic of Korea increased from 25-30 per cent in the early 1980s to about 35 per cent 10 years later (OECD, 1994; European Commission-UNCTAD, 1996, p. 34), parallel to the rise of the services sector's contribution to GDP from 45 to 50 per cent (World Bank, 1996). Likewise, in Taiwan Province of China, the share of services in inward FDI stock rose from 20-25 per cent in the early 1980s to nearly one third in 1993.

In Latin America as well, the share of services in inward FDI has increased since 1980 (table I.12), often as a result of the privatization of State-owned service firms.[9] In Peru, for example, FDI inflows of $2 billion related to the privatization of the telecommunications industry in 1994 represented about 60 per cent of total FDI inflows. To a lesser extent, FDI inflows induced by privatization were also significant in the service industries of Argentina, Mexico and Venezuela.

Table I.11. Share of services in FDI outflows of major home counties, 1987-1998[a]

(Per cent)

Home country	Total services	Finance and insurance	Trade	Transport, storage and communication	Construction	Other services
France						
1987-1990	51.1	30.5	3.9	0.9	1.7	14.1
1991-1994	58.6	22.6	6.2	1.4	2.2	26.2
1995-1998	69.6	10.9	12.9	2.8	1.8	41.2
Germany						
1987-1990	42.2	29.8	2.3	0.7	0.5	8.9
1991-1994	48.0	23.7	3.1	1.6	0.7	18.9
1995-1998	49.5	23.1	2.7	0.5	0.3	22.9
Japan [b]						
1987-1990	70.3	23.1	8.2	4.7	0.7	33.6
1991-1994	65.0	14.7	12.1	5.9	1.0	31.3
1995-1998	56.3	16.4	9.5	4.2	0.8	25.4
United Kingdom						
1987-1990	37.3	4.9	11.4	2.5	1.4	17.1
1991-1994	46.6	13.5	7.0	4.8	0.4	20.9
1995-1998	49.0	23.1	9.4	9.0	0.5	7.0
United States						
1987-1990	54.8	35.0	10.7	2.7	0.0	6.4
1991-1994	63.5	39.2	11.8	4.4	0.2	7.9
1995-1998	60.1	34.2	8.6	4.5	0.2	12.6
Memorandum:						
Share of services in FDI						
inflows of Brazil						
1987-1990	48.5	12.2	5.3	0.0	..	30.9
1991-1994	73.1	21.5	2.2	0.02	..	49.4
1995-1998	81.1	10.5	6.9	7.2	0.2	56.3

Source: UNCTAD FDI/TNC database.

[a]   Annual average. Non-specified other services including hotels and restaurants, as well as real estate, frequently account
     for a significant share of total FDI outflows in services.
[b]   Based on notification data.

Measured by the share of the services sector in total inward FDI stocks, Brazil appears to
fit perfectly into the trends portrayed above. During 1985-1997, the services sector's share
increased two and a half times (table I.12).   In 1997 the share of services in total inward FDI
stock in Brazil was well above the other Latin American countries except Peru, and was
considerably higher than that in the Republic of Korea and Taiwan Province of China. However,
some service industries, such as financial services and other business services still appear to be
significantly underrepresented in Brazil's inward FDI stock.   Several Latin American countries
emerged as significant hosts of FDI in finance and insurance. In Argentina, Chile and Venezuela,
per capita FDI stock in these industries soared by factors ranging from 5 to 8 since 1980. The
difference reflects, in part, different domestic policies towards services industries and differing
speeds of liberalization and privatization.

Table I.12. The role of services in the inward FDI stock of Latin American countries and FDI stock in services per capita, 1980-1997

(Percentage and dollars)

Host country		Percentage of total inward FDI stock				Stock in services (dollars per capita)			
		Total services	Trade	Transport and communication	Finance and insurance	Total services	Trade	Transport and communication	Finance and insurance
Argentina	1980	22.3	4.5	0.6	9.0	42.5	8.6	1.2	17.1
	1985	24.4	4.3	0.6	11.9	52.9	9.4	1.3	25.8
	1990	26.9	3.5	0.5	12.5	72.6	9.5	1.4	33.9
	1992	36.8	2.0	0.3	17.1	168.9	9.2	1.4	78.6
Bolivia	1980	18.0	2.1	0.1	8.1	14.1	1.7	0.1	6.3
	1985	14.3	1.8	0.1	6.6	14.4	1.8	0.1	6.6
	1990	15.4	1.4	0.1	5.4	18.9	1.7	0.1	6.6
	1994	13.3	0.0	0.0	0.0	23.4	0.0	0.0	0.0
Brazil	1980	21.9	3.7	0.2	3.8	31.4	5.3	0.3	5.4
	1985	21.5	3.9	0.2	4.1	40.7	7.3	0.4	7.9
	1990	27.8	4.1	0.2	6.3	69.8	10.4	0.4	15.9
	1993	39.5	3.3	0.1	4.6	118.8	9.9	0.4	13.7
	1997	56.6	6.8	0.1	6.0	227.3	27.2	12.5	24.1
Chile	1980	20.6	3.1	0.7	13.3	16.5	2.5	0.5	10.6
	1985	29.5	3.1	0.8	19.8	57.9	6.0	1.6	38.9
	1990	29.5	2.5	4.9	19.0	142.1	12.2	23.8	91.6
	1995	25.7	1.1	2.6	8.1	266.2	11.2	27.3	84.1
Colombia	1980	22.9	9.1	3.0	9.6	9.2	3.6	1.2	3.8
	1985	15.8	6.2	1.5	7.3	12.0	4.7	1.1	5.5
	1990	11.6	4.8	1.0	14.5	12.4	5.2	1.0	4.9
	1995	26.6	6.7	6.6	9.0	47.6	12.0	11.7	16.0
	1997	43.2	6.3	8.4	13.9	130.6	18.9	25.3	42.2
Ecuador	1980	31.3	13.5	1.1	8.8	28.3	12.2	1.0	7.9
	1985	28.2	11.8	1.4	8.6	30.4	12.7	1.5	9.3
	1990	28.1	11.8	1.4	8.6	37.6	15.8	1.9	11.5
	1994	17.6	7.0	1.0	4.3	42.7	17.0	2.4	10.5
Mexico	1980	17.4	8.9	..	..	21.8	11.2	..	..
	1985	20.3	7.7	..	..	39.3	14.9	..	..
	1990	35.8	6.8	..	..	130.3	24.7	..	..
	1995	44.9	9.0	3.2	5.0	268.6	53.8	18.9	30.1
Peru	1980	22.4	10.2	0.5	5.6	11.6	5.3	0.3	2.9
	1985	29.6	14.5	0.6	8.2	17.5	8.6	0.3	4.9
	1990	28.3	15.7	0.4	7.8	17.1	9.5	0.2	4.7
	1995	67.2	4.7	36.3	9.0	158.3	11.2	85.6	21.3
	1997	64.6	5.9	28.6	10.5	192.6	7.5	85.2	31.5
Venezuela	1980	29.3	7.5	1.4	10.8	31.1	8.0	1.5	11.5
	1985	19.6	3.9	0.9	7.3	17.7	3.5	0.8	6.6
	1990	16.3	6.7	0.4	3.0	32.3	13.4	0.7	5.9
	1995	39.1	3.9	2.8	23.4	122.1	12.0	8.7	73.2

Source: UNCTAD, based on Economic Commission for Latin America and the Caribbean (ECLAC), *Directorio sobre Inversión extranjera en América Latina y el Caribe 1993: Marco Legal e Información estatistica* (Santiago: ECLAC) and UNCTAD FDI/TNC databases and information from the United Nations Population Division.

2. Implications

The question arises as to whether Brazil could gain future advantage by attracting more FDI in services. Does the lag behind neighbours suggest catch-up possibilities? To answer that question, two distinctions need to be made. The first issue is whether a service is traded or not. For non-traded services – such as domestic insurance – the implications are primarily in terms of the effect of increasing efficiencies and thus the international competitiveness of customers, whether local or foreign firms. If a service is traded across borders, such as reinsurance, there is an additional factor to be taken into account: the creation of access to international markets and the dynamic resource base globally defined.

The second distinction to be made is whether a foreign affiliate adds more value than could be expected from local firms. In the non-traded sector, the possibilities for creating domestic advantage can be high, especially if there are non-equity forms of resource transfer available, as in franchising. For internationally traded services, the issues are more complex. In telecommunications, for example, many of the crucial resources require a scale of operating that only a few global firms can command. And even these are being forced into alliances so as to be able to develop the next generation of technology and gain better market access. Nonetheless, there are activities in the telecommunications business that do not require such international linkages. Establishing an appropriate domestic/global balance of efficiency and dynamic connectedness to emerging world-best standards has important derivative consequences for an economy as a whole. The international competitiveness of domestic manufacturers increasingly depends on the supply of adequate business services. For example, it will be difficult for local firms to become integrated into global TNC networks if the quality and costs of communication are significantly below worldwide standards.

Manufacturing firms' service requirements are becoming increasingly salient in the quest for competitiveness. Thus, though services-sector firms were, with the sole exception of a French supermarket operator, specifically excluded from this study, a further discussion of service industries and their impact on Brazil's overall national infrastructure is deferred to chapter III. The executives polled in the survey held views that mirror those suggested by other studies. Together, the evidence points to a need to focus on building service efficiency to support the attractiveness of Brazil for manufacturing investment. Inward FDI in services has a role to play here, a topic picked up in chapter IV. The development of industrial clusters critically relies on the support of an appropriate range of local world-standard services.

E. The shift towards FDI in capital- and technology-intensive manufacturing

1. Pattern

To identify shifts in the composition of manufacturing FDI, the manufacturing sector can be disaggregated into three broadly defined categories: resource-intensive, labour-intensive and capital- and technology-intensive industries.[10] Given that developed countries and rapidly advancing NIEs account for the bulk of both inward and outward FDI in manufacturing, it is not surprising that FDI in capital- and technology-intensive industries figures most prominently among the three categories of industries. Their share of the outward manufacturing FDI stock of the nine largest home countries increased from 46 to 51 per cent from 1980 to 1990 (UNCTAD, 1993a, pp. 70-74). This trend was still more pronounced for inward FDI. Most surprisingly perhaps, the share of capital- and technology-intensive industries in inward FDI rose faster in developing countries than in industrialized ones. This increase was largely driven by investments in the Asian NIEs (and, more recently, in ASEAN countries), for example, by Japanese TNCs in the electronics and transport equipment industry. Examples include Hitachi's plans to build a semi-conductor engineering company in Singapore, as well as Toyota's production of diesel engines in Indonesia and transmissions in the Philippines. More generally, FDI patterns and international networking in the automobile and electronics industries indicate a trend towards capital- and technology-intensive industries in various Asian economies.[11]

Yet, countervailing developments in the composition of manufacturing FDI must not be overlooked. The growth in sophisticated lines of manufacturing in the Asian NIEs gave rise to a significant relocation of the labour-intensive activities in the value chain to less advanced Asian developing countries.[12] Likewise, some industrialized home countries reported large FDI outflows in labour-intensive manufacturing in the early 1990s. Although not shown in table I.13, the share of labour-intensive industries in total manufacturing FDI outflows of Japan nearly doubled from the mid-1980s to the early 1990s. The labour-intensive industries gained in relative importance in the manufacturing FDI outflows of France and Germany, while the United Kingdom reported a pronounced shift towards resource-intensive industries. These diverse developments are probably due to a combination of factors, including developments in the North Sea (for the United Kingdom), mounting pressure towards industrial restructuring in developed economies and the opening of lower-income developing countries (e.g. China) to

Table I.13. The industry structure of manufacturing FDI outflows of major home countries,[a]
1987-1990 and 1994-1997

(Millions of dollars and per cent)

Home country	Total manufacturing outflows		Resource-intensive industries		Labour-intensive industries		Capital/technology-intensive industries	
	Millions of dollars		Per cent					
	1987-1990	1994-1997	1987-1990	1994-1997	1987-1990	1994-1997	1987-1990	1994-1997
France	7 075	6 261	41.2	25.4	9.5	21.3	49.2	53.2
Germany	5 948[b]	11 891	24.4	3.5	3.0	19.5	72.6	77.0
Japan[b]	13 352	18 441	17.8	15.6	18.2	17.8	64.0	66.6
United Kingdom	15 198	18 360	46.4	62.6	37.3	29.5	16.4	7.9
United States	13 644	31 071	33.6	24.6	1.8	2.1	64.6	73.2
Memorandum:								
FDI inflows of Brazil	1 552	1 888[d]	11.2[c,e]	36.8[d]	–	5.8[d]	18.4[c,f]	57.4[d]

Source: UNCTAD, FDI/TNC database.

Notes: Resource-intensive industries include the manufacture of food, beverages and tobacco, wood and wood products, coke, petroleum products and nuclear fuel, non-metallic mineral products and basic metals and metal products. Labour-intensive industries include the manufacture of textile, leather and clothing and other manufacturing industries. Capital/technology-intensive industries include the manufacture of chemicals and chemical products, rubber and plastic products, machinery and equipment, electrical machinery and apparatus, and the manufacture of motor vehicles and other transport equipment.

a   Annual average for the periods, 1987-1990 and 1994-1997, respectively.
b   Based on notification data.
c   Annual average for the period, 1984-1986.
d   Annual average for the period, 1996-1997.
e   Metal products only.
f   Motor vehicles only.

FDI. Nonetheless, FDI in capital- and technology-intensive industries clearly remained the most important category of manufacturing FDI outflows in all major industrialized home countries, except for the United Kingdom.

The share of capital-and technology-intensive industries in total inward manufacturing FDI stock has traditionally been fairly high in major Latin American host countries. In 1980, chemicals, machinery and transport equipment accounted for more than half of the manufacturing FDI stocks in a number of the region's economies (table I.14). This can be attributed at least partly to import-substitution strategies. Under these strategies, TNCs often established local production facilities in order to supply local markets. Recent moves towards

Table I.14. The industry structure[a] of inward FDI stocks in the manufacturing sector of Latin American countries, 1980 and most recent year

(Percentage and dollars)

Host country	Resource- intensive industries			Labour-intensive industries			Capital/technology-intensive industries				Memorandum: FDI stock in manufacturing per capita of population (dollars)
	Sub-total	Food[b]	Minerals and metals	Sub-total	Textiles[c]	Other manu-facturing	Sub-total	Chemi-cals[d]	Machi-nery	Transport equip-ment	
Argentina											
1980	22.5	9.8	12.7	23.5	4.8	18.8	54.0	19.0	11.4	23.6	119.4
1992	20.5	8.8	11.7	12.8	2.8	10.0	66.8	24.3	12.9	29.6	244.1
Brazil											
1980	20.8	7.7	13.1	13.1	3.6	9.5	66.0	24.2	23.8	18.0	106.9
1997	30.4	14.0	16.4	11.9	4.3	7.6	57.7	25.1	19.4	13.2	166.6
Chile											
1980	56.2	31.8	24.4	9.5	1.7	7.9	34.3	24.1	10.2	..	24.7
1992	27.8	19.8	8.0	34.4	4.9	29.5	37.8	26.7	11.1	..	92.0
Colombia											
1980	17.6	10.4	7.2	18.4	5.3	13.1	64.0	38.5	25.4	..	28.3
1997	27.8	21.0	6.8	14.4	4.0	10.4	57.8	36.8	21.0	..	111.3
Mexico											
1980	..	..	..	..	..	..	..	..	..	94.2	
1995	..	..	..	..	..	..	..	..	..	316.2	
Peru											
1980	34.8	26.4	8.3	11.7	7.8	3.9	53.5	27.6	20.1	5.7	17.8
1985	34.5	26.3	8.2	11.4	6.7	4.7	54.1	28.4	19.3	6.5	20.2
1997	..	..	..	..	..	..	..	..	..	..	51.0
Venezuela											
1980	34,8	23.5	11.3	10,8	4.3	6.5	54.5	24.7	29.7	..	65.5
1995	34,0	17.5	16.5	13,8	1.3	12.5	52.1	20.7	31.4	..	182.2

Source: UNCTAD, based on Economic Commission for Latin America and the Caribbean (ECLAC), *Directorio sobre Inversión extranjera en América Latina y el Caribe 1993: Marco Legal e Información estatistica* (Santiago: ECLAC), and UNCTAD FDI/TNC databases and information from the UN Population Division.

a   For the classification of industries, see table I.13.
b   Including beverages and tobacco.
c   Including leather and clothing.
d   Including rubber and plastics.

trade liberalization led to opposite changes, depending on the country. In Argentina, for example, trade liberalization served to intensify the importance of these industries in inward FDI, yet trade liberalization in Colombia and Venezuela appears to have had the opposite effect. Much depends on the domestic context of competitiveness and the ability to absorb technological change.

There is growing evidence that TNCs are internationalizing their research and development (R&D) to support the creation of specialized networks. One recent study (Kuemmerle, 1997) of such trends in the electronics and pharmaceuticals industries indicated that laboratories located in foreign markets have a strong relationship with the more general locational strategies of the firms involved. Another study has suggested that gaining access to the technological absorptive capacity of host countries has, for some, become an important motivation for FDI, and is not necessarily a consequence of other decisions (Wesson, 1993). Such evidence reinforces the importance of technological clusters in determining both the general attractiveness of a country for investors, and the dynamic effects for efficiency enhancement and development (Porter, 1990).

As technological capacity grows in importance as a determinant of FDI, the attractiveness of a country to high-technology investors is measured by the strength of its educational system in terms of human capital formation, and by the installed base of technological infrastructure. While available measures can be indicative of relative capabilities (table I.15), they do not by themselves provide an index for measuring investment motivation. Besides, the measures are averages and thus obscure many factors of interest to potential investors. For example, in countries like Brazil, which has great disparities in income, the averages do not indicate the absolute amount of trained manpower, or the capability of the best schools. What such indices do suggest, however, is that serious deficiencies can discourage FDI; investors would have to spend proportionately more on developing firm-specific skills than elsewhere.

A further implication of the trends towards more FDI in high-technology is the impact on the creation of new industrial districts that have spin-off effects. Technology clusters, such as Silicon Valley, were first created around the needs of the emerging electronics industry, and later, had a direct effect on biotechnology, with its needs for software resources. These clusters are becoming an important feature of the emerging industrial landscape (Enright, 1993). They have, in turn, been one force in the trend towards more specialized networks of production, as TNCs invest only part of their value chain in any one cluster (Harrison, 1992). Suffice is to say, the growing importance of high technology clusters adds weight to the argument that host country Governments could pay more attention to the social and educational policies that are needed to foster the creation of new clusters if they wish to increase the inflow of high-quality FDI.

In Latin America, Brazil stands out in two respects. First, the share of capital- and technology-intensive industries in total manufacturing FDI stock was the highest as early as 1980 (66 per cent). Second, although the share has shifted more towards resource-intensive industries, these industries still make up more than half of the inward FDI stock in manufacturing (table I.14). However, the persistently high share of capital- and technology-intensive industries obscures the important fact that the absolute FDI stock in manufacturing expanded significantly less in Brazil than in neighbouring countries during the 1980s and early 1990s. In per capita terms, the stock increased by a factor of only 1.6 in Brazil in 1980-1997, compared with other Latin American countries. These indicators also suggest that Brazil has historically been able to attract high-technology investment but recently has had difficulty in maintaining that position.

Table I.15. Education, local skills and R&D in Brazil, in international perspective: survey results[a]

Item	Brazil	Other Latin American countries[b]		NIE-4 [c]	Industrialized countries[d]
Education					
1. Average years of schooling	3.6	5.0	(Argentina: 6.3)	7.4	8.7
2. Primary and secondary education system	3.7	4.4	(Chile: 5.1)	6.7	7.1
3. Compulsory education	3.5	4.2	(Argentina: 5.2)	6.9	6.9
4. Educational system	3.5	4.5	(Chile: 7.2)	6.3	5.3
5. Math and science education	4.1	4.9	(Argentina: 5.4)	6.7	7.1
Local skills and training					
6. Supply of skilled labour	4.9	5.8	(Chile: 7.0)	5.7	7.0
7. Scientists and engineers	5.6	6.1	(Chile: 7.3)	6.1	8.3
8. Technical training	5.0	5.3	(Chile: 8.2)	6.2	6.2
9. Employee training	5.4	5.3	(Mexico: 5.9)	6.4	7.3
10. Retraining	6.3	6.8	(Peru: 7.2)	7.3	6.8
R & D					
11. R & D at the firm level	6.2	6.3	(Peru: 7.0)	7.5	7.2
12. R & D in key industries	4.3	4.8	(Chile: 6.7)	5.7	6.8
13. Basic research	5.0	5.2	(Chile: 7.2)	6.7	7.2
14. Financial resources	5.3	5.3	(Chile: 6.0)	6.3	7.3
Technological infrastructure and technology transfers					
15. Technological infrastructure	4.7	5.3	(Chile: 8.7)	6.8	7.7
16. Sourcing of technology	3.8	5.0	(Chile: 7.5)	5.8	6.7
17. Cooperation between companies	4.0	4.8	(Chile: 6.5)	5.8	6.3
18. Research cooperation	5.0	4.6	(Chile: 5.3)	5.7	7.0
19. Cross-border ventures	7.9	8.4	(Argentina: 9.6)	7.4	9.3
20. Strategic alliances	7.2	7.3	(Chile: 8.8)	7.3	8.0

Source: World Economic Forum, *The Global Competitiveness Report 1996 and 1998* (Geneva, WEF).

[a] Survey results are scaled from 1 (strongly disagree) to 10 (strongly agree). Items 1, 2, 5, 7, 9, 18 and 19 are from the World Economic Forum (1998) and were originally scaled from 1 (strongly disagree) to 7 (strongly agree). Items 3, 4, 6, 8, 10-17 and 20 are from the World Economic Forum (1996) and were originally scaled from 1 (strongly disagree) to 6 (strongly agree). The criteria are as follows:
1. The average number of years of schooling in the labour force is sufficient enough for your country to compete in the world economy.
2. The primary and secondary education system in your country offers rigorous training in language, math and sciences.
3. The level of compulsory education that majority of people receive is superior to that of foreign competitors.
4. The educational system meets the needs of a competitive economy.
5. The school system in your country excels in math and basic science education.
6. Skilled labour is easy to get.
7. Your country has a large pool of competent scientists and engieneers.
8. Secondary and technical training systems are well targeted to your firm's needs.
9. More employers in your country have well-developed training programs for employees.
10. Employees are generally receptive to learning new skills or a new profession.
11. R & D spending of your firm is likely to increase in real terms over the next two years.
12. R & D in key industries is often ahead of foreign competitors.
13. Basic research supports long-term economic and technological development.
14. Lack of sufficient financial resources does not usually constrain technological development in your firm.
15. Technological infrastructure is developed faster than in your competitor countries.
16. Sourcing of technology by domestic companies is superior compared to international competitors.
17. Technological cooperation is common between companies.
18. Research collaboration is very close between universities and industries.
19. Cross border ventures can be negotiated with foreign partners without government imposed restraint.
20. Strategic alliances are common between domestic and foreign firms.

[b] Average of Argentina, Chile, Colombia, Mexico, Peru and Venezuela (best performer).
[c] Average of Malaysia, the Republic of Korea, Taiwan Province of China and Thailand.
[d] Average of France, Germany, Japan, the United Kingdom and the United States.

2. Implications

The indicators discussed above provide some clues as to how Brazil might benefit more from TNC activities in capital- and technology-intensive industries in the future. In the past, the Government of Brazil promoted capital- and technology-intensive manufacturing largely in isolation from international markets. While the participation of TNCs was welcomed, the large and protected domestic market – rather than the competitive international market – served as the major stimulus for FDI in sophisticated industries. This did not encourage firms to upgrade the technological standards of their operations to the best of global standards.

An example of how differing circumstances and motivation affect reinvestment behaviour is provided by the automobile industries in Brazil and Mexico. Prior to the recent economic reforms in Brazil, automobile TNCs were primarily motivated by import substitution. As a result, the integration of their affiliates in Brazil into the regional or global strategies of their parents was considerably less advanced than in the case of Mexico. For example, the share of transport equipment and machinery in Brazil's total exports increased only modestly, from 17 to 21 per cent, during the period 1980-1993 (UNCTAD, 1995b, p. 134). By contrast, this share soared from 4 to 49 per cent in the case of Mexico.[13]

More recently, however, these differences in motivation and behaviour have diminished. Brazil's share of the world output has increased dramatically, spurred by a combination of factors: the growth of internal demand; the liberalization of policies; and the creation of MERCOSUR. Together, these factors have encouraged automobile investors to take a more sanguine view of the possibilities of creating internationally linked production strategies. They have also spurred a catch-up in the TNCs' local technological capabilities as a central means of competing, not just within the MERCOSUR, but also worldwide. These shifts are described in more detail in chapter III, for they are an important illustration of investors' sensitivities in these industries to the combination of local demand conditions and the policy regime.

More generally, the high share in total inward FDI of capital- and technology-intensive industries could be taken to suggest that Brazil is enjoying favourable access to world markets as well as to technological and managerial innovations. Further support for that conclusion may be drawn from Brazil's structure of manufactured exports. It indicates that firms have developed competitive capabilities, especially in manufactured goods other than (capital intensive) chemicals and (skill intensive) machinery and transport equipment. The share of "other" in total manufactured exports increased from 45 to 54 per cent in 1980-1993 (UNCTAD, 1995b, table 4.1).

However, in these highly competitive industries, past strengths do not necessarily guarantee future gains. Competition from clusters of specialized resources in other countries can change the "rules of the game", as can shifts in TNCs' choices as to where to locate their R&D facilities. Though market forces push the locational strategies of domestic and foreign firms in the direction of making best use of their firm-specific assets,[14] they need to draw on various tangible and intangible inputs (including skilled personnel, technology, information, finance and training) to become competitive. The Government can play a crucial role in promoting a general climate for competitiveness by providing appropriate incentives for firms to undertake the task of developing firm-specific capabilities, and by strengthening or creating factor markets and institutions that provide the inputs that firms cannot generate in-house.

Assistance in promoting local R&D is one such incentive that can help in the creation of technology clusters. Here, competitiveness should not be measured in relation to the performance of other Latin American countries, but in relation to the world's best standards. In this respect, it appears that R&D in Brazil lags behind industrialized countries, Asian NIEs and the best performer in Latin America (mostly Chile) (table II.15). If investors believe that Brazil has a technological infrastructure that is rather poor by international standards, they are likely to consider this an obstacle to investment in an emerging cluster. The same applies to the freedom of firms to access technology through outsourcing and technological cooperation. These could all be areas of specific priority for specialized public investment in education and human capital formation to complement the existing strengths in engineering.

F. The resurgence of TNCs in the primary sector

1. Pattern

The relative importance of the primary sector in worldwide FDI has been declining as a share in the outward FDI stock of major developed home countries, from 25 per cent in 1975 to 9 per cent in 1997 (UNCTAD, 1993a; UNCTAD, 1999). In absolute terms, however, FDI in the primary sector has grown considerably: the inward stock in developed countries increased from $86 billion in 1988 to $141 billion in 1997, while the inward stock in developing countries tripled during this period to reach more than $37 billion. The outward stocks of the developed countries rose from $129 billion in 1988 to $286 billion in 1997. Moreover, FDI patterns tend to understate the degree of internationalization in the primary sector. For one, low-equity and non-equity forms of TNC engagement have gained prominence, as various developing countries have sought to assume ownership control over their natural resources, especially during the 1960s and 1970s. Second, some large commodity importers have relied on long-term contracts with suppliers of raw materials, rather than investing in commodity exporting countries.

The sectoral breakdown of FDI outflows of major home countries suggests the following (table I.16):

- Agriculture has played a marginal role in outward FDI. In 1997, agriculture accounted for only 3 per cent of the total FDI outward stock in the developed countries. Finland and Japan account for over 82 per cent of the total outward stock, of which only Finland has any significant share of its own total stock (16 per cent).

- Mining and quarrying figured more prominently than agriculture, but not much more. The relative importance of mining and quarrying was highest in the case of Japan. Nevertheless, Japanese FDI in this field was modest, accounting for 3.5 per cent of total FDI outflows between 1995 and 1998 (table I.16).

- In several home countries, FDI patterns in the primary sector were clearly dominated by the oil industry. Pronounced fluctuations in United States FDI outflows in the primary sector were largely due to the unevenness of oil-related flows.

Related to the limited role of FDI in the primary sector is that flows to this sector are typically characterized by large short-term fluctuations. Nevertheless, developing countries may derive substantial benefits from FDI in renewable and non-renewable resources. In addition to fiscal revenues flowing from FDI concessions and positive externalities, such as the transfer

Table I.16. The share of the primary sector in FDI outflows of major home countries, 1985-1998[a]

(Millions of dollars and per cent)

Home country	Primary sector, value of FDI outflows (millions of dollars)	Share (per cent)			
		Primary sector, total	of which:		
			Agriculture, hunting forestry and fishing	Mining and quarrying	Petroleum
France					
1985-1990	868	5.2	0.1	0.0	5.1
1991-1994	837	5.4	0.0	0.2	5.1
1995-1998	260	0.9	0.0	0.2	0.7
Germany					
1985-1990	211	1.5	0.0	1.2	0.3
1991-1994	142	0.7	0.0	1.1	-0.4
1995-1998	-376	-0.7	-0.6	-0.1	0.0
Japan[b]					
1985-1990	1 230	2.4	0.4	2.0[c]	..
1991-1994	1 192	3.1	0.7	2.4[c]	..
1995-1998	2 020	3.9	0.4	3.5[c]	..
United Kingdom					
1985-1990	3 924	12.8	0.8	-12.1[c]	..
1991-1994	927	4.0	0.5	3.5[c]	..
1995-1998	6 305	13.4	-1.2	14.6[c]	..
United States					
1985-1990	-287	-1.0	0.1	-0.3	-0.9
1991-1994	2 178	3.9	0.0	1.2	2.6
1995-1998	3 915	4.2	-0.1	1.3	3.0
Memorandum:					
FDI inflows of Brazil					
1985-1990	18	0.8	-0.1	0.9	..
1991-1994	91	2.2	1.0	1.2	..
1996	111	1.4	0.5	0.3	0.6
1997	456	3.0	0.7	2.2	0.1

Source: UNCTAD FDI/TNC database.

[a]   Annual average.

[b]   Based on notification data.

[c]   Including petroleum.

of technology and managerial skills, FDI may share the risk ensuing from volatile commodity markets, raw material-saving technological progress and huge financial outlays for investment projects (e.g. in oil and mineral extraction).

Latin American countries have made use of the potential for FDI in the primary sector in varying degrees. Per capita inward FDI stock in the primary sector in the mid-1990s ranged from more than $600 in Chile to $10 or less in Mexico, Venezuela and Brazil (table I.17). Given Brazil's vast endowments of natural resources, the primary sector accounts for a strikingly small share in total inward FDI stocks. Moreover, the share of mining declined from 2.9 per cent in 1985 to 1.3 per cent in 1997. By contrast, neighbouring countries attracted substantially more FDI in this sector, particularly Chile, and more so, Bolivia and Ecuador. However, this trend may have turned in 1997, as the extraction of ores attracted $338 million more than the existing capital stock in 1995 (Banco Central do Brazil, 1998).

Table I.17. The role of the primary sector in the inward FDI stock of Latin American countries
(Percentage and dollars)

| Host country | | Percentage in total inward FDI stock | | | Memorandum: |
		Primary sector, total	Agriculture	Mining, quarrying and petroleum	FDI stocks in the primary sector per capita, in dollars
Argentina					
	1980	14.9	2.1	12.7	28.3
	1985	14.4	2.0	12.4	31.1
	1990	14.9	3.6	11.3	40.3
	1992	10.1	3.6	6.5	46.6
Bolivia					
	1980	67.2	..	67.1	52.7
	1985	71.6	..	71.5	71.8
	1990	71.4	..	71.4	87.5
	1994	75.8	0.0	75.7	133.1
Brazil					
	1980	3.7	0.9	2.8	5.4
	1985	3.8	0.9	2.9	7.2
	1990	2.9	0.7	2.3	7.3
	1993	2.4	0.7	1.7	7.3
	1997	1.9	0.6	1.3	7.7
Chile					
	1980	48.4	2.9	45.5	38.6
	1985	44.4	3.9	40.5	87.1
	1990	55.5	2.2	53.3	267.0
	1995	58.9	2.7	56.1	609.0
Colombia					
	1980	6.1	1.1	5.1	2.4
	1985	33.5	0.6	33.0	25.4
	1990	45.9	0.6	45.3	49.3
	1995	28.8	1.3	27.4	51.5
	1997	19.9	1.2	18.7	60.2
Ecuador					
	1980	27.9	2.1	25.8	25.2
	1985	24.9	2.9	22.0	26.9
	1990	24.9	2.9	22.0	33.2
	1994	50.8	2.1	49.1	123.1
Mexico					
	1980	5.1	0.1	5.0	6.3
	1985	1.9	0.04	1.9	3.7
	1990	1.9	0.3	1.6	6.9
	1995	1.7	0.4	1.3	10.0
Peru					
	1980	43.3	0.7	42.6	22.4
	1985	36.2	0.6	35.6	21.4
	1990	37.9	0.4	37.5	22.9
	1995	20.1	0.2	19.9	47.4
	1997	18.3	0.1	18.2	54.7
Venezuela					
	1980	1.8	1.8	0.0	1.9
	1985	2.5	2.4	0.1	2.3
	1990	5.0	4.9	0.1	9.8
	1995	3.2	3.1	0.04	9.9

Source: Directorio sobre Inversión extranjera en América Latina y el Caribe 1993: *Marco Legal e Información estatistica* (Santiago: ECLAC), and UNCTAD, FDI/TNC database and information from the UN Population Division.

2. Implications

Though declining in relative importance, the primary sector continues to offer important possibilities for growing inward FDI in Brazil as a resource rich country. The extent to which opportunities can be exploited is likely to depend on the Government's perception of, and policy response to, overall trends and changing TNC attitudes. For example, the re-engagement of TNCs in the primary sector of developing countries after the nationalizations of the 1960s and 1970s indicates that fair dispute settlement is particularly important with regard to FDI in natural resources. Another issue concerns the development of complementary local skills. This factor will increasingly shape the chances of countries such as Brazil to attract FDI in the primary sector, especially with regard to the possibilities of encouraging higher value-added investments in processing and marketing. Such incremental investments have to compete with the processing capacities installed elsewhere. Yet, as host countries help to upgrade local facilities and infrastructure, the economic arguments for preserving older capacity can be eroded.

In designing a strategy for attracting FDI, the heterogeneity of the primary sector has to be taken into account. The dominance of non-renewable resources notwithstanding, the example of Chile's attractiveness in agribusiness indicates that there are profitable niches for FDI in the renewable resources segment too. The chances for inducing FDI in the exploitation of non-renewable resources vary according to specific world-market conditions, cost considerations, the pace of raw material-saving technological progress (especially with regard to biotechnology and genetic engineering) and industry specific TNC strategies (e.g. a preference for non-equity engagements in certain areas). Put differently, some resources attract FDI more than others. In the case of Brazil, iron ore appears to be among the attractive resources, as witnessed by considerable foreign investor interest in acquiring stakes in Companhia Vale do Rio Doce, the world's largest producer of iron ore. The example of this large State-owned company also indicates that privatization can induce FDI in the primary sector, even though, in this instance, a local consortium won the day.

The heterogeneity of the primary sector raises the question of whether the Government should adopt a selective approach to promoting FDI in specific segments of this sector. While targeting may help to attract FDI where it is most urgently needed, selectivity involves risks unless the Government has special knowledge of world-market prospects for particular raw materials. Moreover, the effect of selective targeting will vary markedly between investment to exploit resources themselves and investment in processing. One study, which compared the market structures for aluminium and tin, showed how uncertainty and transaction costs of all kinds affect both location and the preference for vertically and wholly TNC-owned structures. Whereas aluminium has for long been dominated by a few vertically integrated large firms, the tin market worldwide has remained much more fragmented. A single host country acting independently has seemingly little power to change such fundamentals in the structure of the worldwide industry.

One alternative is for the Government of Brazil to adopt a generally favourable attitude towards FDI and leave it up to TNCs to choose specific investment projects in the primary sector. For such a strategy to succeed in inducing FDI, the stability and credibility of the relationship between the host Government and TNCs is likely to play a critical role. This applies especially to the primary sector, in which projects frequently require high capital investments.[15] In this context, the legal framework and the tax regime deserve particular attention. With regard to the former, transparency is a major issue, and as for the tax regimes, previous studies seem to suggest that one based on royalties, allowing for income tax credits against tax liability in the

TNC's home country (and including some form of super-profits tax), is best suited for deriving economic benefits from FDI in the primary sector.

G. SMEs as TNCs

1. Pattern

Until not long ago, TNCs were considered as being only large enterprises. Today, the overwhelming majority of some 60,000 parent corporations (UNCTAD, 1999) are SMEs. Like large firms, SMEs are affected by liberalization and the pull and push factors of globalization. In particular, market niches are no longer protected from international competition. Small firms too increasingly need to acquire a portfolio of locational assets to remain competitive in today's world economy. Furthermore, SMEs are often linked to TNCs as suppliers of intermediate inputs, and follow them to their foreign production bases.

After becoming TNCs, SMEs remain relatively small. They have, on average, 3.2 foreign affiliates per parent firm, whereas large TNCs have, on average, 60 affiliates (table I.18). However, there are strong differences in the geographical pattern of foreign activities of SMEs. Almost one third of Japanese SME affiliates were located in developing countries in the 1990s (UNCTAD, forthcoming), parallel with the high clustering of Japan's FDI in East and South-East Asia, especially in the mid-1980s and 1990s. Small firms tend to prefer neighbouring countries for FDI in order to contain transaction costs.

In contrast to Japan, SMEs from western Europe and the United States have their affiliates located primarily in developed countries. Developing countries host less than one tenth of SME affiliates from western Europe and less than one fifth from the United States. This is significantly below the proportion of affiliates of large TNCs that they host (table I.18). Again, geographic proximity is a good explanation, together with trade linkages and transaction costs. Small firms often seem to rely on their foreign trade partners for locational initiatives and support, and often enter into joint ventures with them. Thus, SMEs trading more with developed countries are likely to establish more affiliates there.

From the perspective of host developing countries, the contribution of foreign SMEs to employment creation, technological development, and managerial and marketing know-how can be significant, even though SMEs account for a small proportion of total FDI inflows. They tend to be relatively labour intensive, and prefer greenfield investments when they establish

Table I.18. The geographical pattern of FDI by SMEs of selected home countries, 1986-1987

Home region or country	Number of foreign affiliates per parent company		Developed countries' share in number of foreign affiliates (Per cent)		Developing countries' share in number of foreign affiliates (Per cent)	
	SMEs	Large TNCs	SMEs	Large TNCs	SMEs	Large TNCs
Western Europe	3.6	105.0	92.1	77.0	7.8	22.9
Japan	3.7	15.1	46.6	56.6	52.3	42.9
United States	2.5	51.6	82.6	67.6	16.9	32.2

Source: UNCTAD, 1993b, p. 51.

production bases abroad, thus creating more jobs than is the case of FDI through the acquisition of local companies. Moreover, SMEs tend to rely more on indigenous than expatriate personnel (UNCTAD, 1993b, p. 27) and they have a preference for joint ventures rather than becoming a fully-owned subsidiary of a large TNC. This can enhance the diffusion of technical and managerial know-how in host countries. Small firms also have stronger backward linkages, which implies that they are less burdensome for the balance of payments of host countries, and contribute more to local capacity building.

In their home economies, SMEs generally account for more than 95 per cent of all enterprises, and for more than half of all employees, value added and sales in manufacturing and trading sectors (ibid., p.11). But the share of SMEs in outward FDI of these countries is rather small. In the United States, SMEs accounted for 24 per cent of all TNCs in 1982 and 28 per cent in 1988. At the same time, only 3 per cent of the assets of all United States foreign affiliates were owned by SMEs in 1988 (ibid, p. 66). In the United Kingdom, only 1 per cent of the book value of total outward FDI was attributed to SMEs in 1981; however, it is difficult to know whether this low share has risen since then owing to the lack of data. Yet SMEs are likely to be a rich source of FDI in the future, and can be expected increasingly to engage in FDI in order to maintain their competitiveness in a globalizing and liberalizing world economy.

2. Implications

There are two principal implications. First, SMEs should not be neglected in efforts to attract FDI. Because Brazil's large domestic market and its membership in the MERCOSUR are attractive to larger TNCs, regulatory practice and administrative behaviour might inadvertently tend to discriminate against foreign SMEs (UNCTAD, forthcoming). Second, SMEs are often looking for market niches, and their chances of finding them are likely to increase if growing markets lead to more diversified demand patterns. The problem, however, is the cost of obtaining accurate information about such specialized potential. Often, the early investments abroad by SMEs are prompted as much by personal contact and chance as by a considered review of all possible alternatives. Thus, Brazil can help alleviate such information asymmetries by providing easy access to relevant information about investment opportunities in the country.

This could be done by a business promotion agency such as SEBRAE (Brazilian Support Service for Small Business), as well as by embassies and consulates. Brazilian institutions could intensify their cooperation with investment promotion agencies and various organizations in developed countries that support FDI by SMEs in developing countries.[16] In addition, cooperation can be sought from UNCTAD's Entrepreneurship Development Programme (EMPRETEC), which aims to promote and develop entrepreneurship in small and medium-sized operations, UNIDO's Programme on Plant Level Cooperation for Technology Transfer to Small and Medium Enterprises, and the World Bank's International Finance Corporation (IFC). Such cooperation may help to disseminate information about Brazil as an interesting host for SMEs.

An interesting question is whether Asia's experience with Japanese SMEs can be repeated in the case of United States and European SMEs in Brazil and the rest of Latin America. East and South-East Asian countries attracted high amounts of equity investment from Japanese SMEs during the 1970s, 1980s and early 1990s, and these SMEs played a role in the "Asian miracle". They were welcomed as investors, particularly because they were willing to accept local partners in the Asian host countries. The internationalization efforts of Japanese SMEs found strong support both from Japanese promotion agencies and the Government of Japan, which instituted special FDI promotion agencies targeting SMEs (the Japan Small Business Corporation and the Small Business Finance Corporation of Japan). Moreover, Japanese outward investors seem to have obtained greater support through Japanese economic aid (Agarwal, 1986). The Japanese trading companies – the *sogo soshas* – contributed to the internationalization of Japanese SMEs by undertaking market research, identifying local partners and organizing financial support. Japanese TNCs also encouraged their local SME suppliers to follow them to foreign production bases in East and South-East Asia, thereby providing the latter with dependable buyers for their products abroad.

In order to repeat the Asian experience, the United States and the EU would have to match the Japanese efforts to promote FDI by their SMEs in Brazil and other Latin American countries. This will mean additional promotional efforts. The preferential arrangement negotiated by the EU with MERCOSUR could also help. But it is an open question whether European home countries are prepared to give Brazil the same priority as Japan did in the case of its Asian neighbours. While European countries are aware that SMEs need greater promotional support, their present attention seems to focus on Asia (European Commission and UNCTAD, 1996), and they already have association agreements with several countries in Central and Eastern Europe as well as in the Mediterranean region. As these countries compete with Latin America, the EU may not find it useful to change the configuration of its international economic relations. As far as the United States is concerned, it attaches less importance to the promotion of outward FDI by both small and large TNCs. Small firms based in the United States had traditionally invested more in Latin American countries than in other developing areas, but more recently, they have invested more in Asian countries (UNCTAD, 1993b, p. 65). Thus, Brazil will most likely have to increase its promotional efforts for attracting FDI from SMEs.

H. Sequential and associated investment

1. Pattern

An important subset of FDI consists of sequential and associated investments. Sequential investments refer generally to reinvested earnings, which accounted for an average of 3.5 per cent of annual FDI inflows during 1990 and 1994 but shifted dramatically during 1995 and 1998 to an average of almost 21 per cent (figure I.1). Countries with large outward FDI stock tended to have a much higher share. In the United States, about 43 per cent of FDI outflows were reinvested earnings during 1990 and 1994, and about 54 per cent during 1995 and 1998. An initial favourable experience in a host country can act as a powerful inducement for a TNC to extend its first investment. It is typically easier for host countries to persuade investors to keep a greater portion of earnings as reinvestments – or to add new investments – than to induce initial investments. One reason is that, once established, a foreign affiliate typically has its own life. Local managers who are producing attractive returns can become strong advocates of further investment, especialy if they are local nationals, as it is in their career interests to do so. A second reason, discussed further in chapter II, is that TNCs have to overcome barriers of both economic and "psychic" distance[17] before they make an initial investment in a host country. If the initial learning experience is good, then re-investment to support success can appear less risky than a new start in another country.[18]

These arguments show that it is imperative for public authorities not to regard inward FDI as a one-off affair. The greatest gains can come many years after the initial investment. In the past, sequences of investments used to be those of progressively deepening the investment relationship, from, say assembly to full manufacture. There is much evidence today that the

Figure I.1. Components of FDI inflows, 1990-1998

(Per cent)

World [a]

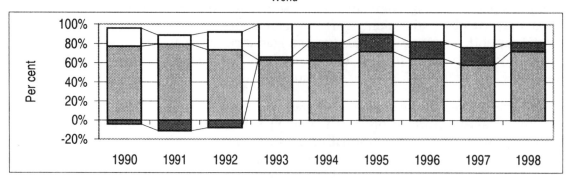

Developed countries [b]

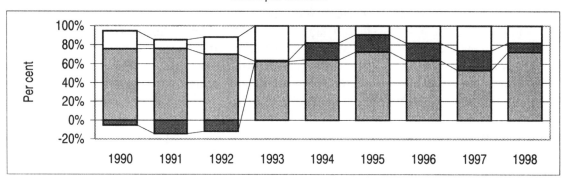

Developing countries [c]

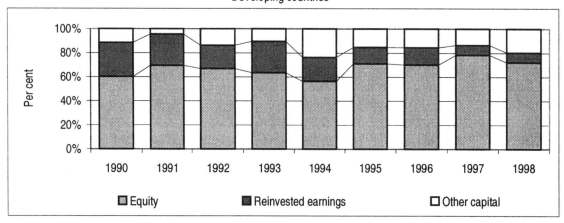

☒ Equity   ■ Reinvested earnings   ☐ Other capital

Source: UNCTAD, based on IMF, *International Financial Statistics,* May 1999, CD-ROM.

Note: Figues are based on 30 countries for which the data on each component of FDI inflows are available throughout the
         period.
a   Including two economies in Central and Eastern Europe: Estonia, for which data starts in 1992, and Poland.
b   Including: Australia, Finland, Germany, Iceland, the Netherlands, New Zealand, Switzerland, the United Kingdom and the
         United States.
c   Including: Antigua and Barbuda, Barbados, Botswana, Dominica, Fiji, Grenada, Guatemala, Kazakhstan, Malta, Mexico,
         Namibia, the Netherlands Antilles, Panama, Saint Lucia, Saint Vincent and the Grenadines, Senegal, Sri Lanka, Swaziland,
         and Trinidad and Tobago. 1996 data are not available for the Netherlands Antilles and Trinidad and Tobago. 1997 data are
         not available for Antigua and Barbuda, Dominica, Fiji, Grenada, Netherlands Antilles, Saint Lucia, Saint Vincent and the
         Grenadines, Senegal, and Trinidad and Tobago. Data for Kazakhstan are not available prior to 1995.

importance of such sequences is diminishing as barriers to FDI are becoming lower, and as firms find novel ways to deploy their knowledge base in more specialized ways (UNCTAD, 1996b, chapter IV). Nonetheless, the importance of the local knowledge base and of an installed system remain important in influencing new forms of investment and new sequences.

Even the FDI associated with privatization should not be regarded as a one-off transfer (see section I). For example, after the unification of Germany, German investors in chemical plants in eastern Germany found that they had to make a stream of further investments to bring the facilities up to the standards of the western part of the country and to deal with problems of earlier neglect of environmental standards. Similarly, investors in privatized telecommunications assets can find – and indeed are often required – to invest further to extend and upgrade the networks they have acquired. Chile's sale of Chile Telecommunications Company (CTC) is a case in point as will be discussed later.

During the 1990s, TNCs in Brazil reinvested an average of less than 3 per cent of their retained earnings (table I.19). While this ratio is below the world average, it should not be interpreted as evidence that Brazil has been relatively successful in inducing sequential FDI. There is some evidence, shown in chapter III, to suggest that the relatively high ratio is the statistical consequence of the reluctance of new investors to engage in Brazil, while some traditional investors merely maintain their market position. In this context, it should be noted that the amount of reinvested earnings in Argentina, for example, was more than five times higher than in Brazil.

Moreover, cross-country comparisons of reinvestment ratios are flawed by several factors. In the case of Asia, for instance, FDI is coming mainly from new investors. Reinvestment ratios are bound to be lower in these cases because initial rates of return are generally low due to start-up costs. In the United States case, many foreign affiliates reported large losses in 1992, largely because they had to conform with new accounting standards. Low or negative rates of return of

Table I.19. Reinvested earnings in FDI inflows in Brazil and selected regions and economies, 1990-1998

(Millions of dollars and per cent)

Host economy/region	FDI inflows (millions of dollars)				Share of reinvested earnings (per cent)			
	1990-1992	1993-1995	1996-1998	1990-1998	1990-1992	1993-1995	1996-1998	1990-1998
Brazil	1 384	3 074	20 921	8 460	19.6	4.1	1.3	2.6
Developed countries	78 067	100 783	227 690	135 514	-12.3	12.7	14.6	9.0
United States	31 208	53 212	130 538	71 653	-44.7	6.7	11.2	2.0
Developing economies	9 109	16 927	42 509	22 848	23.7	18.4	9.6	13.6
Africa	208	120	219	182	-29.1	-13.9	37.4	0.8
Asia and the Pacific	138	536	1 484	720	15.2	7.0	3.8	5.3
Latin America and the Caribbean	8 709	16 140	40 536	21 795	24.9	18.8	9.5	13.9
Argentina	2 886	3 825	6 919	4 543	17.0	20.2	9.1	13.9
Mexico	3 930	8 296	10 752	7 659	29.6	21.4	23.6	23.8
World	87 557	120 319	273 667	160 514	-8.4	13.7	13.7	9.7

Source: UNCTAD, FDI/TNC database.

Note: Annual average. Minus sign denotes losses of foreign affiliates.

foreign affiliates in the United States also reflect the recent nature of much FDI in the United States, which has often been undertaken through acquisitions. In many acquisitions, initial returns are low due to restructuring costs and write-offs. Many investors accepted such short-term costs in order to gain access to the large United States market and to seek technological efficiencies (Fahim-Nader and Zeile, 1995, p.119). And finally, the recession of the early 1990s had a negative impact on the profitability of foreign affiliates.

"Associated investments" are of two basic types. The first and more important type takes place when suppliers of components and services follow their clients abroad. This type figured prominently, for example, in the case of FDI by Japanese automobile TNCs in the United States and the United Kingdom. Until 1990, 184 Japanese component makers had followed automobile TNCs into the United States. By 1993, this number was estimated to have increased to 300 (Madeuf, 1994, p. 50). These suppliers accounted for 46 per cent of the sourcing of Japanese automobile TNCs in the United States. They usually belong to the car-makers' network of suppliers in Japan, often to the same group of firms known as *keiretsu*.

In the case of the United Kingdom, which hosts important Japanese car-makers (Nissan, Honda, Toyota and Isuzu's joint venture IBC), several component suppliers from Japan as well as other countries (e.g. Bosch from Germany) followed the initial Japanese automobile FDI (UNCTAD, 1995a, pp. 234-236). However, associated investment by input suppliers appears to be less significant in the United Kingdom and other European host countries than in the United States. By mid-1991, Japanese car-makers had only 60 joint ventures, or had acquired firms in Europe to manufacture automotive components (Madeuf, 1994, p. 50), as compared to a multiple of this number in the United States. Arguably, this difference is mainly because competitive component suppliers were more readily available in Europe. Moreover, Japanese firms appear to have feared opposition from local suppliers in Europe to a larger-scale influx of Japanese component-supplying firms. This may have motivated them to prefer joint ventures to wholly-owned subsidiaries in Europe.

Associated investments often feature prominently in the aftermath of a process of privatization that pulls in new firms. For example, Volkswagen's investment in the Czech Republic was followed by nearly 100 joint ventures started by suppliers. Similarly, General Motors' FDI in the Hungarian automobile industry attracted numerous related investments by firms that are suppliers to General Motors in its western markets. Likewise, Ford's and Fiat's investment in Poland, and Suzuki's in Hungary, have been followed by investments by some of their international suppliers (UNCTAD, 1995a, p. 103).

Because of the pull-through effect in the wake of a flagship, scale is less important than in stand-alone investments: the flagship investor provides the data and the incentives needed to offset the information asymmetry and risk factors (discussed in section G) for public policy mechanisms. Thus, associated investments are often undertaken by SMEs, which, as was discussed before, offer many advantages to developing countries. For example, Volkswagen's assembly plant in China is supplied by more than a hundred SMEs which were earlier supplying it with various inputs in Germany. The same possibility applies to supplying firms in Brazil, as they can be pulled abroad by the large inward investors. Though most of the firms polled in the survey done for this study did not accord much weight to this factor, experience elsewhere suggests that the pull-through effect can be important and can apply to Brazilian firms associated with foreign TNCs as well.

However, there can be wide differences in the pattern of investments associated with backward linkages of initial FDI. The pattern depends on the investment strategy, the stage of investment projects, the mode of entry (merger and acquisition or greenfield), the FDI regime of the host economy, the availability of local supply, and the type of industry. In the case of the iron and steel industry, for example, the propensity to attract associated FDI appears to be lower than in the automobile industry, as the number of components is smaller in the former industry. Furthermore, backward linkages need not be confined to one particular host economy if that is part of an integrated economic area (see chapter II).

Finally, in this catalogue of countervailing trends is the effect of policies that many TNCs are now trying in order to reduce their number of suppliers. Volkswagen, Xerox and many others are seeking new sources of efficiency by developing closer relationships with a few key suppliers. These relationships often involve taking on component suppliers early in the design process for new finished products and building adjacent facilities so as to gain the advantages of such systems as just-in-time supply. The implication is that fewer local suppliers may grow in association with inward investors, but that those chosen to do so are more likely to be required to internationalize their operations simply to maintain their local contracts.

The second major type of associated investment is when rivals match each other in foreign markets. Especially in industries characterized by oligopolistic competition, firms try to counter any market advantage that a front-runner may score from its entry into a particular host country. Hence, an initial investment may induce FDI by competing firms in the same host country. For instance, the entries of United States firms into foreign markets were bunched in time (Knickerbocker, 1973), which is consistent with the view that rival firms followed the FDI of the leading firm. The type of associated investment, however, now seems to be less important than it was in the 1960s and early 1970s. The evidence on strategic choice, shown in the next chapter, indicates that, in a world of scarce managerial resources, TNCs often deliberately build networks of investment that differ in location from their main oligopolistic rivals.

In sum, many initial investments have a multiplier effect in terms of bringing with them sequential and associated investments. As in the case of initial investments, the size of this multiplier effect primarily depends on the overall investment climate. This implies that a host country has to review its investment conditions continuously to maintain its international locational competitiveness.

2. Implications

All host countries face the question of whether to promote greater rates of reinvestments by relying on transparency and market mechanisms or by resorting to specific interventions and incentives. The evidence is mixed, making for difficult policy choices.

The argument for transparency is that Governments should rely on the positive power of the attractiveness of their markets: both in the short- and long-run, FDI will flow to those territories which offer the greatest prospects for growth and profits. The negative power of, for example, intervening by restricting profit repatriation can be evaded by TNCs, some argue, through transfer pricing of intra-firm trade, which accounts for about one third of world exports (UNCTAD, 1995a, p. 193). In the longer run, reinvestments are likely to be higher if foreign investors are confident that profits can always be transferred unrestricted.

Although true in theory, the argument does not necessarily apply in practice. Much of the FDI flow in south-east Asia has been accompanied by various regulations that have impeded the associated flows of re-investments. Moreover, the recent growth of FDI in the Brazilian automobile industry provides an example where incumbent investors can be encouraged to re-invest their earnings under conditions of local content rules and Government intervention in trade.[19] Though such regulations have provoked complaints by investors, the lure of new sources of growth has prevented complaints from being translated into action.

The central issue in this debate is the extent to which intervention inhibits the creation of longer-term competitiveness and the possibilities of export-creating resources, not merely import-substituting ones. The major challenge for Brazil is thus to finds ways to deploy its positive power to improve the international competitiveness of local suppliers through skill formation, tax breaks for prospective domestic suppliers, and incentives to foreign affiliates to develop local supplies.

A related challenge in many countries concerns rival investments. In their negotiations with foreign investors, public authorities should not grant new entrants the luxury of monopolistic or quasi-monopolistic positions through protection against potential investments by competing firms (UNCTAD, 1997a). Firms often try to negotiate exclusive rights in the markets of host developing countries that are not quite open for trade and investments. The past experience of countries that granted such exclusive market positions – often in the framework of their import-substitution strategies – shows that they not only hinder rival investments but also render domestically produced goods internationally less competitive.

Such a danger may arise in developing countries only in a number of exceptional cases related to privatization projects in the services and mining sectors, requiring direct negotiations between foreign investors (should they be permitted to, and decide to, participate in such projects) and the Government. Otherwise, entry into most host countries does not involve negotiations with the Government (box I.4), including in privatization projects in the manufacturing sector, which are handled through auctions by a specialized institution acting on behalf of the Government.

Box I.4. Investing in Brazil

Direct negotiations between foreign investors and the Government are not required for investing in Brazil. There is no screening system in the country, with thresholds that impede investment. The usual procedure is to open a Brazilian company and to pay in the capital established in the by-laws. Once the by-laws are registered with the commercial registry, a taxpayer number is obtained and the company can start its operations. Capital sent from abroad is registered with the Central Bank only for statistical purposes. That is how the majority of investments take place. If a company is to operate as a concessionary of public services, such as telecommunications, or if it wins a bid to sell goods or services to Governmental agencies, a foreign-owned company will be subject to the regulatory agencies and/or bidding legislation just as any Brazilian company. Competition laws are enforced by a special Council (CADE); it has been very active in the recent past, reviewing mergers and acquisitions and enforcing antitrust legislation.

Source: UNCTAD.

I. Privatization programmes can fuel FDI inflows

1. Pattern

As mentioned in section D, FDI inflows may be spurred by allowing foreign investors to participate in the privatization of State-owned enterprises. Moreover, promoting foreign participation in privatization can, though not always, offer the host country a number of associated benefits.[20] The involvement of TNCs can serve to increase the selling price of State-owned assets (Odle, 1993, p. 21). More importantly, though, it can provide a source of better technology and managerial, marketing and organizational skills. Especially in industries characterized by rapid technological change, local companies may find it difficult to stay competitive by pursuing self-reliant strategies. The telecommunications industry is a case in point. On the one hand, an inefficient telecommunications infrastructure hinders a country's competitiveness. On the other hand, local companies are often constrained in financing complex technologies and managing rapid product and process change. Hence, by linking privatization and FDI, developing countries can benefit from the capital, technological and managerial resources to which TNCs have access in order to modernize and expand existing facilities.

Despite the fact that privatization often involves local companies with obsolete technologies that incur losses and have to be restructured, TNCs are, in general, interested in acquiring such enterprises, especially in service industries such as telecommunications, transportation, banking, insurance, energy production and distribution. Enterprises in these and other industries frequently enjoy monopoly or nearly monopoly positions and, by acquiring them, TNCs also acquire their markets and good prospects for profitability after their restructuring. This, together with the fact that many TNCs are competing with each other to acquire a privatized company, puts Governments in a better position to benefit from FDI, provided of course that they take advantage of their bargaining position. Great care has to be taken to ensure that public monopolies are not replaced by private foreign monopolies which exploit this position in the host country.

Privatization can also bring other disadvantages. For example, some privatization programmes in Africa and Asia have been characterized by "crony capitalism" (Stopford and Strange, 1991), with consequent negative repercussions throughout the society and economy. The implication is that industry, competition policy and sectoral regulations need careful consideration in any privatization process. A further problem can arise when there is no guarantee that, without specific requirements, the investment will be more than a one-shot affair. In this case, the benefits from sequential investments are lost. In practice, however, such a danger is rather low, and FDI related to privatization does not cease after the purchase of a domestic enterprise by foreign investors (see above discussion). Yet further negative effects can arise when efficiency-seeking investors reduce employment. Thus, in general terms, privatization as a means of fostering competitiveness and faster development needs to be assessed carefully at both the sectoral and firm levels. Gains and losses can only be assessed realistically by a broad review of the impacts across the whole political economy (Vernon, 1988).[21]

Privatization-related FDI flows were clearly of greatest importance in post-socialist countries throughout the process of economic transformation. The sales of State assets accounted for a high share of FDI inflows throughout the transformation process, varying from country to country depending on the privatization programme. The share probably reached its peak in Hungary during 1995, but because of voucher privatization programmes, the process has been somewhat delayed in other countries. However, it rapidly accelerated in Bulgaria, Croatia and Romania during 1999. Not surprisingly, privatization was less important for FDI flows into developing countries, in which the role of State-owned enterprises, though significant, was less pervasive than under conditions of central planning in central and eastern Europe. FDI related to privatization constituted probably less than one-tenth of total FDI inflows to all developing countries in 1989-1994 (UNCTAD, 1996a).

But this figure masks remarkable differences across regions. The share of FDI from privatization in total FDI inflows in 1989-1994 was probably less than 5 per cent in East Asia while it may have been about 12 per cent in Latin America (ibid.).

Substantial inter-country variations in privatization-related FDI indicate that the potential to attract FDI through privatization can in some countries be higher than regional averages suggest:

- Chile was the pioneer in privatizing State-owned companies in Latin America. A far-reaching privatization programme was implemented in 1985, which included the Chilean telephone company and the national airline, LANCHILE. During much of the period, 1988-1995, Chile had already moved beyond a stage during which privatization contributed significantly to FDI flows (UNCTAD, 1995a, p. 70).

- Privatization programmes in the 1990s accounted for a large share of FDI inflows into Argentina, Peru and Venezuela. About 50 per cent of the FDI inflows into Argentina came from the sale of State assets between 1990 and 1993 (ECLAC, 1995, p. 82). While the various privatization programmes involved practically all sectors, the focus was on telecommunications, air transport, electricity and financial services. The sale of Peru's largest telecommunications company, for example, accounted for 30 per cent of the country's total FDI inflows in 1997 (ibid, p. 126). Argentina encouraged foreign investors to participate in privatization by allowing external debt titles to be used as a means of payment.

- Until, not long ago, FDI played a much more limited role in privatizations in Mexico and Brazil. While Mexico implemented one of the most comprehensive privatization programmes in the region, it maintained sectoral restrictions on foreign participation (IADB-IRELA, 1996, p. 49).[22] Privatization in banking, for example, was restricted almost exclusively to local investors. In Brazil, privatizations initially took place in the steel and petrochemical industries. However, this country lagged considerably behind its Latin American neighbours in implementing a consistent privatization programme (UNCTAD, 1995a, p. 70; *The Economist*, 1996, p. 9). Furthermore, until the mid-1990s the privatization of State assets to TNCs remained marginal "mainly because of constitutional restrictions on foreign ownership" (IADB-IRELA, 1996, p. 47). Since 1995, the privatization programme has accelerated and FDI has become a driving force of FDI inflows into Brazil, maintaining these inflows at a high level even during the financial crisis.

Privatization in Latin America has primarily been driven by economic motives, which can be divided into *proximate* and *enduring* factors (Ramamurti, 1992). Among the former, the need for fiscal consolidation, and thus a reduction of subsidies granted to inefficient State-owned firms, figured prominently. As concerns the latter, various Governments aimed at a better allocation of scarce resources by reversing the excessive use of State-owned enterprises for which an economic justification did not exist (or that had failed to overcome market failures at reasonable costs). FDI can help to achieve these aims, both directly through the sale of State-owned enterprises to foreign investors, and indirectly through post-privatization capital inflows.

The wave of privatizing State-owned enterprises may have passed its peak in many Latin American countries. Taking Latin America as a whole, FDI related to privatization began to slow in 1993 (ibid., p. 49). However, as discussed earlier, this form of FDI does not cease with the completion of a privatization programme. The Latin American experience indicates that the sale of State-owned enterprises to foreign investors is frequently just the first stage of a process involving substantial post-privatization FDI, sometimes several times larger than the original investment (UNCTAD, 1995a, pp. 77-78). Sequential FDI for rationalizing and modernizing privatized enterprises has been especially prevalent in telecommunications and energy (IADB-IRELA, 1996, pp. 53-55). For example, when Chile sold its telecommunications company, CTC, to Australia's Bond Corporation in 1987, the new owner invested $400 million per year from 1988 to 1994, doubling the number of telephone lines and introducing more advanced telecommunications services. Likewise, the reinvested earnings of firms that foreign investors acquired through privatization have resulted in additional FDI in the years following the initial purchase. Finally, privatization tends to improve the climate for FDI in less obvious ways, as it signals a Government's seriousness about economic reform and may reduce uncertainty about the sustainability of the reform process. It also provides Governments with opportunities to impose budget constraints on enterprises, notably by ending the subsidization of non-competitive firms. This eases the fiscal burden and contributes to macroeconomic stability, which in turn improves the prospects for attracting FDI on a regular basis. These general arguments suggest that countries which restrict foreign participation in privatization programmes may also compromise somewhat their chances to attract regular FDI.

As a latecomer, Brazil stands out among Latin American countries in having a great potential for FDI that may be tapped through privatization and liberalization in the coming years. By the end of 1994, Brazil had only privatized $6 billion worth of State-owned assets, compared with over $20 billion in Mexico and $16 billion in Argentina (UNCTAD, 1995a, p. 70). At the same time, Brazil hosted 28 of the 50 largest Latin American public companies (ranked by sales). Since mid-1995, President Cardoso's new policy has increased the pace of privatization considerably. The sale of State-owned assets accounted for over $2.6 billion, or about 25 per cent of total FDI inflows, in 1996 and another $5.2 billion or 28 per cent in 1997 with a further $6.1 billion, or 21 per cent of FDI inflows in 1998. The pace appears to have picked up in 1999 with the sale of State assets amounting to $8.8 billion or almost 29 per cent of the total FDI inflows (Banco Central do Brazil, 2000).

Privatization in Brazil may have suffered from insufficient political backing in the past (IADB-IRELA, 1996, p. 49). The first wave (in the petrochemicals, steel and fertilizer industries) was stalled by the restructuring of State-owned firms prior to their sale (Porter, 1995), but the process has gathered momentum, even though the sale of certain large State conglomerates remains politically contentious.

2. Implications

If Brazil is to make best use of its potential to attract FDI through privatization and reap the associated benefits, several issues deserve attention. A first set of questions refers to the timing of privatization. Most importantly, there is a need to evaluate whether State-owned enterprises should be restructured prior to sale. Government revenues may increase if the efficiency of State-owned enterprises earmarked for privatization is improved through restructuring. However, the price effects of restructuring have to be weighted against the Government outlays required for restructuring. The opportunity costs of Government-financed restructuring may be large, considering the substantial post-privatization FDI related to the modernization of inefficient enterprises in other Latin American countries. Moreover, international experience suggests that TNCs "are frequently not impressed with the enterprise restructuring efforts of Governments prior to privatisation ... The reason is that the TNC that wins the bid has not only its own conception of what needs to be done to make the enterprise viable, but also its own understanding of how the newly privatised enterprise fits into its transnational network ... The end result is that the TNC may acquire the pre-rehabilitated asset at a relatively low price" (Odle, 1993, p. 23). Just how much of an implied subsidy is obtained by this means depends critically on the extent of the post-acquisition restructuring programme. It should be noted, however, that some TNCs prefer to buy assets that have already experienced a good deal of the pain of rationalisation; they thereby avoid the political costs of being seen as an asset-stripper or "job destroyer". The timing question cannot easily be answered, for much depends, as with the valuation of the assets, on the extent of the need to build new skills that are integrated with the parent company's international system rather than being managed on a local, stand-alone basis.

The high indebtedness of many State-owned enterprises may constitute another obstacle to privatization. For example, owing to its high level of corporate debt the State-owned electricity company, ELETROBRAS, is considered to require restructuring prior to sale. However, the Government may avail itself of another option under such conditions, namely: debt-equity swaps, which can help avoid further delays in its privatization (UNCTC, 1991). Various TNCs and creditor banks have shown an interest in the capitalization of debt in other Latin American countries, partly because of the resulting indirect price discounts on the assets earmarked for privatization.

Debt-equity swaps may speed up some sales, but they involve heavy discounts. In Chile, for example, such swaps accounted for 75 per cent of reported FDI inflows during the latter half of the 1980s, at a discount of 46 per cent (French-Davis, 1990). Is such an implied subsidy for inward FDI worthwhile? It is not clear whether Chile benefited appropriately in all cases. A case-by-case review would be needed to be sure of the real return obtained by the implied subsidy. Part of the issue is precisely the same as for the cost-benefit assessment of inward FDI that takes the form of the acquisition of a local entity. If the transfer is purely financial, without a change in the economic prospects of the venture involved, a subsidy is worthless. Worse yet is a situation in which the acquired asset is financed by local debt. If, however, the purchase prevents a firm from failing, or leads to efficiency gains or the exploitation of new capabilities, a subsidy can be an appropriate inducement. The same is true with privatization. A subsidy is only worthwhile when there are real gains for the host economy. There is thus an effective market test. Where a secondary market exists for the debt of State-owned entities, the Government can decide whether the implied subsidy is worth the potential gain. It can be a test of political resolve to resist market pressures for a quick sale and impose performance requirements as a condition of the sale.

To gain the potential efficiencies in services and infrastructure, policies towards restrictions on foreign ownership as regards some of the firms earmarked for privatization are important. Surveys show that executives see Brazil as improving the regulations that allow TNCs to acquire control of a domestic company, but these regulations were less open than in Chile and Argentina as of early 1998.[23] Such findings suggest that the existing policies are no impediment to the planned sales. However, further improvements may be desirable with regard to investment protection, for which Brazil received a lower ranking than most of its neighbours.[24] Compared to other locations in Latin America, it was also considered difficult to acquire corporate control in a Brazilian company (see also box I.2 in the case of CVRD), to employ foreign skilled labour and to negotiate cross-border ventures. The approval of constitutional reforms in 1995, by which discrimination against foreign capital was forbidden in principle, represents a major step towards overcoming such concerns.

As emphasized earlier, privatization alone does not guarantee economic efficiency, and may cause unemployment and social disruption in the short term. However, a detailed discussion of how to deal with the social consequences of rapid privatization is beyond the scope of this study. When the Government retains a controlling stake in privatized companies in order to moderate adverse social consequences, reduced private investor interest is a possible result, especially if TNCs consider substantial restructuring to be necessary for the prospective affiliate's integration into global strategies. Efficiency gains are most likely to be achieved in industries in which privatization and FDI inflows lead to more competition. However, in some service industries (e.g. telecommunications, electricity), privatization-induced FDI may replace a State monopoly with a foreign-owned private monopoly. Depending on the specific circumstances, it is necessary to evaluate whether deregulation may induce competition also in these service industries, and in which areas Government regulation remains necessary. A related issue concerns performance requirements and binding obligations imposed on the buyers of State-owned enterprises to undertake modernization, not to increase prices, and to keep or create jobs. While the economic and social objectives of the Government may be easier to achieve in this way, possible trade-offs should be taken into account. In particular, selling prices may be lower. Moreover, the enforcement of commitments may prove to be rather difficult in a rapidly liberalizing world of trade and investment relations.

All these arguments can be combined into two general issues. One is that the potential for greatly accelerated FDI in privatization in Brazil is quite considerable. The other is the associated effect of spurring FDI by firms in other industries. The importance of this effect in creating an attractive investment climate is underscored by the evidence, shown in chapter III. Both experienced investors and those who have not yet invested in Brazil have pointed to the need for an acceleration of an "open" privatization regime. This, they have argued, would be one of the strongest possible signals of the Government's serious intention to transform the economy. But whether or not particular State-owned firms should be privatized is entirely up to the Government.

J. Growing interlinkages between FDI and trade

1. Pattern

The close link between trade and FDI is demonstrated by the high and growing shares of intra-firm trade in total trade. Though there is great variation from one country to another, the trend shows a steady increase. For example, the share of intra-firm exports was 42 per cent of total United States parent exports in 1996, up from 28 per cent in 1983 (UNCTAD, 1999). The causality of the relationship is, however, ambiguous. On the one hand, FDI can follow trade once a certain market share has been achieved through exports. The reasoning that physical proximity between producers and their customers has become increasingly important under conditions of "global localization" (Oman, 1994) also implies that FDI replaces trade. Furthermore, FDI (and international investment cooperation in non-equity forms) provides a means to jump over protectionist fences. For instance, Brazil appears to have been the largest recipient of market-seeking FDI among developing countries prior to the foreign debt crisis, mainly because import-substitution policies had hindered trade. Likewise, some of the recent

Asian FDI in the EU is said to be motivated by fears of a "fortress Europe" (Chia, 1995). All these arguments suggest that FDI flows can be, under certain conditions, and to a certain extent, a substitute for trade flows.

The traditional sense of substituting investment for trade is now being challenged by increasingly globalized production and marketing. Both FDI and trade have expanded faster than world production since the 1970s. Booming FDI in services appears to be complementary to trade in manufactures. It should also be noted that the service sector's share in global FDI flows increased, in spite of the increasing tradability of various services. Moreover, globalization means that declining communication and transaction costs allow for the fragmentation of production processes. The liberalization of trade and FDI regimes, along with technological improvements, enables firms to choose more freely the modality (e.g. FDI, trade, licensing, subcontracting, franchising) they prefer to serve international markets and organize production.[25] TNCs slice up the value chain and capitalize on the tangible and intangible assets available throughout their corporate systems to maximize overall efficiency.

Efficiency-seeking FDI that optimizes gains from integrating geographically dispersed manufacturing and service activities within corporate systems – is one hallmark of contemporary TNC adjustment to the changing economic environment. The fragmentation of value-added activities influences the sequence of internationalization. To the extent that TNCs convert their collection of foreign affiliates into integrated production systems, the process of internationalization "can be speeded up either through a faster progression from one step to the next, or through leapfrogging directly to FDI" (UNCTAD, 1996a, p. 98). Moreover, "the sequence can begin anywhere within a TNC system, i.e., no longer only in the home country. Innovation and production can be undertaken by a foreign affiliate and the sequence starts from there" (ibid.).

These developments are the product of specific changes in corporate strategy. For the reasons discussed in chapter II, each firm has to choose its own developmental path and create its own capabilities and configuration of assets. The growing range of technical possibilities means that there is increasing *divergence* in the choices made – another reason why the associated investments of oligopolistic rivalry are decreasing.

Developing countries can benefit from these processes of fragmentation, notably from outsourcing of labour-intensive and standardized segments of the production process. Rather than replacing trade with developing countries, the recent boom of FDI in developing countries will then lead to intensified trade relations. Rising FDI tends to be associated with higher exports of capital goods by the investor country. At the same time, global sourcing stimulates exports of intermediate inputs by developing countries to the investor country.

Empirical findings indicate that complementarities between FDI and trade have dominated substitution effects, although the latter remain important in some specific conditions:

- While developing countries have attracted a rising share of world FDI inflows, at the same time they have increased their share in world exports of manufactures. Comparing 1984 and 1994, the share of (non-oil) developing countries in inward FDI flows nearly doubled from 21 to 39 per cent. All developing countries, which accounted for one eighth of world manufactured exports in 1984, contributed nearly one quarter to world manufactured exports in 1993 (Gundlach and Nunnenkamp, 1996a, table 1).

- Correlation analyses based on bilateral trade and FDI relations of Germany, Japan and the United States with both developing and developed countries support the view that trade and FDI flows are complementary to each other. It is particularly noteworthy that FDI is not only positively correlated with exports of investor countries to host countries, but also with exports of host countries to investor countries (Gundlach and Nunnenkamp, 1996b). Thus, the issue is no longer whether trade leads to FDI, or FDI leads to trade, rather, trade and FDI flows appear to be simultaneously determined by globalization strategies. That is, firms decide where to produce and refer to various modalities of international activity at the same time, in order to exploit the opportunities offered by liberalization and technological progress for maintaining or increasing competitiveness.

- TNCs account for about two-thirds of world exports of goods and non-factor services (UNCTAD, 1995a, p. 193). This underscores that FDI and non-equity forms of international investment cooperation[26] are intertwined with trade in the process of globally converting inputs for global markets. About half of TNC exports are intra-firm exports. This share is particularly high in intermediate products and industries such as transport equipment and electronics (ibid., p. 197).

All this suggests that the international division of labour is pushed forward by different mechanisms at the same time. FDI "complements trade in enabling countries to gain from international specialisation" (UNCTAD, 1995a, p. 192). It not only helps developing countries in getting access to resources to strengthen their production capabilities, but also in penetrating world markets with goods and services in the production of which developing countries enjoy a comparative advantage.[27] The local presence of foreign affiliates provides developing countries with better opportunities to become involved in the increasingly important intra-TNC system of "markets". Yet, cross-country analyses have shown that host countries have to meet various requirements in order to benefit from the current trend towards globalized production and marketing, which is reflected by complementarities between FDI and trade.[28] The subsequent section deals with some implications of these studies for economic policy making in Brazil and then turns to the issue of policy coherence.

2. Implications

Brazil's economic policies should be examined in the light of the increasing options available to TNCs for choosing where to locate and how to internationalize their operations. Does the new international environment – offering, as it does, additional corporate opportunities – increasingly constrain the Government? It is too simplistic to infer that national powers are in unavoidable decline. On the contrary, they seem as strong as ever, though perhaps in a different way.

Public policy can play an important role in maximizing the benefits that Brazil could reap from inward FDI. There are two kinds of power at issue. One is the positive power associated with increasing the attractiveness of the country to existing and potential investors. The other is the negative power associated with influencing investors to conform to certain standards and performance requirements. Both have their place, as the foregoing discussion has indicated.

In terms of the positive power of Government, empirical analyses suggest that several policy areas are particularly important: macroeconomic stability, investment in physical and human capital, infrastructure and openness:

- Successful stabilization after Plan Real restored Brazil's attractiveness for FDI has led to a dramatic increase in the rate of inward FDI. The data shown in chapter III underscore the importance of the need to retain stability to reduce perceived investment risks relative to other locations. A review of tax policies may reveal further possibilities to promote investment, and thereby improve the availability of complementary local factors of production.

- Brazil's competitive disadvantages with respect to human capital formation and infrastructure constitute another challenge. For example, investment in communication and transport systems appears to be all the more necessary as globalization is driven by dramatically declining information and transaction costs on a worldwide scale. Taking into account the constraints that macroeconomic stabilization imposes on public spending, the Government may be left with two options: to utilize more private financing of infrastructure; or to review spending priorities.

- Worldwide liberalization and deregulation represent a major element of the new international environment within which the Government of Brazil has to act. Maintaining consistency of purpose – both domestically and within the MERCOSUR framework – is an essential part of adjusting to conditions where the domestic and international economy are more directly connected. Policies of openness have to be balanced against the need for policies for specific sectoral development.

Given that FDI and trade are increasingly intertwined, policies in these areas are obviously related to each other. This raises the question of policy coherence. For instance, a policy of investment openness may not attract export-creating investors when restrictive import policies are maintained. Large market size confers power on host countries to continue to attract FDI inflows (Gundlach and Nunnenkamp, 1996b), but the evidence of chapters II and III suggests that power applies mainly to import-substituting FDI. Where export-creation is desired, open trade policies are becoming more important. This is of particular relevance for countries such as Brazil, whose attractiveness for FDI in the past was largely based on large and protected local markets.

The protection of local producers in Brazil could make it difficult to become competitive by international standards. This would negatively affect the chances of local input suppliers to enter the vertically integrated production chains of TNCs, and subcontracting with foreign affiliates would probably remain underdeveloped. Under such conditions, TNCs would tend to source less in the host country than they would if input supplies were available at competitive terms. The consequence is that the import content of the foreign affiliates tends to rise, thus reducing the income benefit from a rise in net exports and other spillover benefits that accrue within the production chain. Over time this decline in competitiveness can also have a detrimental effect on Brazil's balance of payments.

Apart from the lessons of international experience offers, more specific issues related to policy coherence emerge from the business community's assessment of FDI and trade policies in Brazil. The trend towards a simultaneous, rather than a sequential, determination of trade and investment policies adds urgency to the tests of policy coherence. The calculations made by major and experienced TNCs take into account these and other policy interactions. One direct consequence is a heightened desire for control over all aspects of the operations of export-oriented foreign affiliates; typically this desire is translated into policies favouring equity ownership. It is thus also from the perspective of becoming involved in global production and trade networks that the perceived difficulties of foreign investors in ensuring corporate control in Brazil are a relevant issue. Less discretion with regard to ownership restrictions may induce more export-oriented FDI in the relevant industries. It has, however, to be noted, that the issue of sensitivity over control is not always tied to demands for ownership; there are other means within structures of contracts in alliance agreements that help preserve control of crucial resources without requiring the cash exposure and risks of ownership.

Another important issue is that of trade openess. As one survey revealed, Brazil was considered by the international business community to be less open to trade than the Asian NIEs, the developed economies and several Latin American neighbours (table I.20). Import tariffs were perceived to be high by international standards and, together with quotas, to impair companies' international competitiveness. Furthermore, the real exchange rate was widely believed to be misaligned, and its negative impact on exports was considered to be significant at the time the survey was done.

Table I.20. Trade policy indicators of Brazil in international perspective[a]

	Brazil	Latin American competitors[b]		Asian NIEs[c]	Developed countries[d]
Executive opinion survey					
1. Trade policies	6.5	6.7	(Chile: 8.2)	7.7	7.0
2. Protectionism	6.5	7.3	(Peru: 9.0)	6.8	7.3
3. Regional trade integration	6.5	5.8	(Chile: 7.3)	6.7	6.7
4. Export position as a priority	6.6	5.9	(Mexico: 8.4)	8.1	7.0
5. Tariffs and quotas	6.0	6.9	(Mexico: 7.9)	6.6	8.3
6. Exchange rates and exports	4.1	5.1	(Mexico: 6.6)	7.7	6.0
7. Exchange rate volatility	7.4	6.7	(Argentina: 9.3)	4.9	6.1
Other indicators					
8. Average tariff rate	13.6	8.7	(Mexico: 5.1)	7.2	3.3
9. Misalignment of real exchange rate	3.0	27.5	(Argentina: 5.0)	47.3	19.6
10. Capital account restrictions	3.5	4.2	(Argentina and Peru: 5.0)	4.2[e]	4.7

Source: World Economic Forum, *The Global Competitiveness Report* 1996 and 1998 (Geneva, WEF).

[a] Survey results are scaled from 1 (strongly disagree) to 10 (strongly agree). Items 1 to 3 are from the World Economic Forum (1996) and were originally scaled from 1 (strongly disagree) to 6 (strongly agree). Items 4 to 7 are from the World Economic Forum (1998) and were originally scaled from 1 (strongly disagree) to 7 (strongly agree). The criteria are as follows:
1. Trade policies support international activities of your company in the long-term.
2. National protectionism does not prevent foreign products and services being imported.
3. Your country's integration into regional trade is sufficient.
4. Your country's export position is perceived as a national priority.
5. Existing import tariffs and quotas help your firm's international competitiveness.
6. The exchange rate policy of your country is favorable to export expansion.
7. Exchange rate is expected to be stable in the next two years.
8. Unweighted average rate (in per cent) for the latest available year.
9. Ranking as of 1994; for the calculation of the index underlying the ranking (ranging from 1 for the best performer to 48), see appendix 1 in the source.
10. Index as of 1995, ranging from 5.0 (rank 1) to 2.0 (rank 46); for the calculation of the index, see appendix 1 in the source.

[b] Average score of Argentina, Chile, Colombia, Mexico, Peru and Venezuela; in parentheses: best performer within this group.
[c] Average score of Malaysia, the Republic of Korea, Taiwan Province of China and Thailand.
[d] Average score of France, Germany, Japan, the United Kingdom and the Unites States.
[e] Excluding Taiwan Province of China.

From all this it follows that the issue of a mutually supportive FDI and trade policy remains on the agenda. Brazil's ability to enhance its share of globalized production and marketing will increasingly depend on its attractiveness for efficiency-seeking FDI. The evidence from interviews undertaken for this study (and discussed in chapter III) confirms that, for investors, policy coherence has a critically important influence on their choices of location.

K. Conclusions: the emergence of international integrated production systems and the competitive position of Brazil

International production has become an integral and important part of the world economy (UNCTAD, 1996a, chapter IV). The most notable feature of this process is the growing number of TNCs, their affiliates, their home and host countries and the complex integration strategies they increasingly are pursuing. Moreover, even though most TNCs are still based in developed countries, there is a clear trend towards a diversification of home countries, with developing countries accounting for a rising share in total FDI outflows (section A). At the same time, more and more countries have emerged as hosts to inward FDI, or have recently restored their attractiveness for foreign investment (section B). Newly emerging host countries include economies in Asia and Central and Eastern Europe, while FDI inflows have recovered in various Latin American countries.

The creation of internationally integrated production systems is being driven by various forces. Two of the most important are technological developments and policy liberalization. As regards the former, progress in information and communication technologies has made it possible for companies to process vastly more information at dramatically reduced costs and has made many information-related services tradable. This has rendered it easier to manage and coordinate widely dispersed production and service networks. As regards policy liberalization, the worldwide trend in this respect constitutes a force that has fostered globalized production and marketing. Multilateral trade liberalization proceeded during various GATT rounds and received another push with the conclusion of the Uruguay Round; in addition, trade liberalization was pursued at the regional level in the context of several integration schemes, and various developing countries implemented trade policy reforms unilaterally. While many service industries have remained more regulated than manufacturing industries, some first steps towards liberalization have been taken in this sector as well. Last but not least, various countries have opened up towards FDI by removing FDI restrictions unilaterally and strengthening standards of treatment, and by regional agreements for liberalizing capital flows.

As a result, the international division of labour is pushed forward by different mechanisms at the same time. International trade is growing faster than global output of goods and services, and FDI is growing faster than both. Furthermore, FDI has been complemented by non-equity arrangements ranging from such traditional means as licensing to innovative forms of inter-firm cooperation with regard to R&D activities. Growing economic interdependence of countries at the production level is the result. Markets are increasingly contested by a growing and more complex range of international economic transactions. Firms that remain purely national in scope are being threatened more directly in almost every industry, for there remain few safe havens in protected home markets.

This does not mean, however, that national borders are diminishing in importance, either for citizens or for TNCs. Perhaps paradoxically, the multiple sources of dynamism in the globalizing world economy have led to a divergence of national policies that mirror the divergence of corporate strategies in the same industries (as will be shown in chapter II). Far from creating pressures for convergence and homogenization, the divergence of the past decade confounds the expectations of microeconomic theory that there is one best way to operate in a given market. Multiple approaches can coexist to the advantage of all concerned.

The evidence for this coexistence of alternative and successful policy approaches is shown vividly by the multiple development policies adopted by high-growth economies. Some of the Asian NIEs based their development on the promotion of indigenous capabilities. For decades, they emphasized the need to strengthen the technological and human capital capacity of their domestic enterprises and institutions. They used the promise of their growth to strike advantageous deals with foreign firms, mainly in the form of trade in capital goods and licensing in technology. These policy mixes came in many varieties – where Japan and the Republic of Korea, for example, emphasized the need for large-scale domestic champions, Taiwan Province of China emphasized networks of small-scale enterprises. These policies proved to be enormously beneficial during the period of catching-up. More recently, however, they seem to have run out of steam in Japan, and even the Republic of Korea is now considering reform of its *chaebols* so as to give foreign firms greater access to both the domestic market and the technological clusters in the country.

By contrast, some Asian economies, such as Singapore and Malaysia, based their growth on extensive use of TNCs' resources. Their trade and investment policies were liberal and permitted TNCs to integrate their local operations into global networks at minimal cost. Incentives were employed to target preferred firms and to condition their behaviour towards national policy goals.

In both types of policy, the importance of dynamic local actors cannot be over-emphasized. The issue therefore is of inward FDI being *complementary* and not a *substitutive* for local investment. Not only are TNCs important for shaping the course of development, they also have a role in creating dynamic comparative advantages for the host economy. Purely passive policies towards inward FDI are likely to attract TNCs only in areas of static comparative advantage. For the sorts of reasons advanced earlier, the lack of local dynamism can quickly erode historic advantages, especially those based on natural endowments. The future is being established on the basis of *created assets*, in the formation of which both firms and public policy have important roles to play.

Most TNCs have already adjusted, and are continuing to adapt, to this shifting balance of forces, as chapter II will explain. The increasing number of options offered by the liberalization of trade, FDI and technology flows have permitted many TNCs to fragment their investments as they internationalize different parts of the value chain at different speeds. Potentially, all parts of the production process are subject to FDI (and non-equity arrangements) in a globalizing economy. Relocation and outsourcing are shaped by the created dynamic advantages of host countries. In order to strengthen firm-specific competitive capabilities, a TNC based in the EU may decide to undertake R&D in an affiliate located in the United States and to source standardized inputs from affiliates located in Asia or Latin America, or vice versa.

To the extent that TNCs are able to integrate their production systems in such ways, the activities of foreign affiliates become less restricted to serving the local markets of host economies. When this happens, the power of local market size as a magnet to attract new investment declines (UNCTAD, 1996a, p. 97). Instead, such investors accord more weight in their decisions to such factors as cost differences between locations, the quality of infrastructure, ease of doing business and the availability of complementary local skills. Furthermore, they are giving preference to locations capable of being connected to the global economy and characterized by stability, transparency, predictability, internal dynamism, the supply of strong human capital and consistent policies that recognize the increasing importance of strong complementarities between international trade and FDI and the policy coherence this requires.

Under these circumstances, regionalization needs to be seen as a complement, and not as an alternative, to globalization. This implies that if regional integration is pursued in isolation from world markets, the chances of member countries to become part of global production networks will remain limited.

The assessment of global trends and their policy implications reveals various options for Brazil to increase the inflow of FDI in ways that will further its policy goals; many of these options are also available to other developing countries. The strong recovery of such flows in 1996 and thereafter indicates that the markets are recognizing the extent of the internal reforms and the enhanced growth potential of the country. Nonetheless, FDI inflows appear to be still below Brazil's absorptive capacity, considering the country's relative position prior to the debt crisis, its vast endowment of natural resources, domestic market potential, and the emergence of regional networking within the MERCOSUR. Further FDI may be attracted in all sectors.

- Global FDI in natural resources has been on a declining trend in relative terms, but TNCs are expanding their engagement in absolute terms (section F). The interest of firms in renewable and non-renewable resources can be rejuvenated through a favourable tax regime and the stability of contractual relations.

- FDI can contribute to upgrading service industries, including telecommunications, transportation and other business services, once State monopolies are abolished and foreign participation is allowed (section D). The benefits of more efficient services spread into manufacturing industries, most importantly into those industries with global system options and less reliance on local market size as inducements to invest.

- In the manufacturing sector, one challenge is to strengthen and reinvigorate the competitiveness of existing capital- and technology-intensive industries that were developed behind protectionist walls in the past. For some industries, policies designed to enhance the ability of firms to link their Brazilian affiliates more directly into global corporate systems are appropriate. For others, dynamism requires less direct integration and greater local supplier capability and complementary local skills and technological capabilities (section E). Another challenge is to create a policy framework that recognizes the variety of new international needs for Brazil's already sophisticated industrial base and to build on existing strengths and international relationships. Given the importance of attracting into the country investors whose objectives are consonant with the country's development goals, there is a need to recognize firms' fundamental strategy choices as well as the sectoral dynamics.

The privatization of State-owned enterprises is an effective vehicle for increasing FDI inflows (section I). The goal, however, is broader than investment stimulation; it is to create substantial economic gains for the nation. To that end, specific privatization programmes need to ensure that the actions taken will infuse dynamism in ways that both meet social objectives and provide a continuing inflow of capital and technological resources. The options for Brazil to tap this potential include restructuring inefficient State-owned enterprises, and using debt-equity swaps to overcome the problem of high indebtedness faced by some of them. Both options, however, must be used carefully to avoid high costs. Furthermore, well-managed privatization programmes may also support the credibility of the whole reform process and thus improve overall investment conditions.

Small and medium-sized enterprises from both developed and developing countries represent another source of FDI (section G). The share of SMEs in global FDI flows is likely to increase, an opportunity that can be seized by providing SMEs with information about investment opportunities through host and home country agencies and international institutions. The goal should be to lower transaction costs, which tend to be especially burdensome for SMEs, and to address the information asymmetries that often condition SMEs' choices of location (UNCTAD, forthcoming).

The final implication for Brazil is that there is no "one best way" to deal with TNCs. Firms, even in the same industry, can respond quite differently to the same macroeconomic and policy conditions. Where some may be attracted by changes, others may be unaffected. Where some may respond in ways that are beneficial to Brazil, others may attempt to minimize their exposure of assets and transfers of key technologies. Because firm-specific advantages are crucial to competitiveness, TNCs are attempting to develop their own value-adding networks in ways that make them hard to copy. Any official promotional effort, therefore, has to be based on a growing appreciation of how firm-level strategy choices are made by managers responding to more than the structural economics of their industry.

Notes

[1]   To calculate the increase of FDI in real terms, the World Bank's gross domestic investment (GDI) deflators of the 24 developed countries were used. Between 1972 and 1996, dollar-based prices increased in these countries, on average, four times. This implies that the average FDI outflow per country was approximately $6 billion at 1972 prices.

[2]   Table I.1 includes only countries with FDI outflows of more than $50 million on an annual average during 1990-1998. The total number of developing countries and countries in transition investing abroad increased from 17 in 1980 (IMFa, 1984, excluding South Africa) to 56 in 1995 (UNCTAD 1996a, annex table 2).

[3]   These numbers must be treated with some caution, especially those for Hong Kong (China) and Taiwan Province of China which together account for half of the total for developing economies. They also include some investment flows that represent Chinese savings being re-routed through Hong Kong (China) in order to gain better investment treatment. They include investments from developed countries in foreign affiliates in these economies to gain access to the internal Chinese market.

[4]   UNCTAD database.

[5]   However, a great deal of caution is necessary when evaluating these figures because a significant proportion of intraregional outward FDI went into tax-haven countries in the 1990s. See footnote (b) to table I.2.

[6]   The link between market dynamism and FDI can also be seen in developed countries; during recessions, FDI flows to these countries typically decrease.

[7]   One must be careful when interpreting various indicators. While each of the specific indicators suggests that improvement facilitates more inward FDI and that deterioration is an inhibitor, the relative importance of each indicator varies. For example, investment guarantees may be less important than the ability to have complete control over foreign affiliates.

8   The average share of services in GDP increased from 59 per cent in 1980 to 65 per cent in 1998 for the developed economies (World Bank, 1999).

9   For further details, see UNCTAD (1995a) and Nunnenkamp (1996, p. 8).

10 The classification of industries is according to UNCTAD procedures; for details, see note in table I.13. It should be noted that the range of factor intensities may vary considerably within particular industries. For example, certain segments of the electrical and electronic equipment industry, which is classified as capital- and technology-intensive, may be as labour-intensive as certain segments of "other manufacturing".

11 For a more detailed discussion, see UNIDO (1996).

12 For details, see Agarwal et al. (1995a, chapter B.III); European Commission and UNCTAD (1996, chapter I), and UNIDO (1996).

13 It must be emphasized that these data are not wholly comparable because of the proximity of the United States to Mexico, the associated security issues and the related investments in *maquiladora* facilities.

14 For this definition of competitive advantage and a more detailed discussion of the role of Governments in boosting national competitiveness, see European Commission and UNCTAD (1996, chapter II). The impact of strategy on firms' choices of specialization is discussed in chapter II.

15 For a detailed discussion, see Wälde (1993).

16 For a list of these institutions see UNCTAD (1993b, pp. 155-157).

17 Psychic distance is defined as factors preventing or distubing the flows of information between economic actors. These factors include language, culture and socio-economic and political systems. The term was first used in W. Beckermann, "Distance and the pattern of intra-European trade", *Review of Economics and Statistics*, vol. 28, 1956. The term as used in this study has the same meaning as in F. Wiedersheim-Paul, *Uncertainty and Economic Distance – Studies in International Business*, Upppsala, Alnquist and Wicksell, 1972.

18 Barlow and Wender (1955) argued that foreign earnings are like gamblers' dollars, and a company is much more willing to take a chance with them than with new FDI. See also Penrose (1956), who presented a historical analysis of the subsidiary of General Motors in Australia.

19 Decree 1761 of December 1995 stipulates that local producers have to meet the 60 per cent local content requirement to qualify for reduced tariffs on imported inputs. Imports of capital goods and other inputs have to be matched with purchases of domestically produced goods, and imports should not exceed a given ratio of exports (EIU, 1996, pp. 20-21).

20 For a detailed evaluation, see Odle (1993).

21 Some clues about the methods needed for such analyses are provided by Jones and Vogelsang (1990).

22 According to IADB-IRELA (1996, p. 47), Latin American privatization programmes accounted "for at least 25 per cent of total FDI flows to the region from 1990 to 1995".

23 For a summary of relevant survey results, see Nunnenkamp (1996, pp. 16-18).

24 *The World Competitiveness Yearbook* indicates that Brazil has improved its ranking from 30 out of 47 in 1997 to 20 in 1998. Argentina ranked second and Chile ranked fifth in the 1999 survey.

25 For a detailed discussion, see UNCTAD (1996a, part II) and Nunnenkamp and Agarwal (1994).

26 Complementarities also prevail between FDI and non-equity forms of international investment cooperation; for a detailed analysis, see Nunnenkamp and Agarwal (1994, pp. 27-43).

27 UNCTAD (1995a, chapter 4) provides a detailed account of the opportunities that TNC activities offer to developing countries and UNCTAD (1999, chapter 7) discusses the role that TNCs can play in transferring technology.

28 For details, see, for example, Sachs and Warner (1995), Gundlach and Nunnenkamp (1996c); Nunnenkamp (1996) and UNCTAD (1999).

CHAPTER II

STRATEGIES OF TRANSNATIONAL CORPORATIONS

The review of the patterns of FDI in chapter I suggests that corporate strategies are being transformed in response to the changing complexities of the world economy. Transnational corporations are agents of many of these changes, but they are also critically affected by the changes others make and thus need to adapt to them. TNCs are being buffeted by unprecedented turbulence in the "rules of the game", and many are being forced to compete on the basis of innovations in their strategies.

One immediate consequence of this turbulence is that many models, which explained much of the competitive behaviour in the past, now need serious modification if they are to capture some of the new dynamic of change. For instance, it has long been asserted that large scale and high market share provide market power and thus protection from predatory attack. Yet many famous market leaders disappeared in the 1990s – PanAm, Dunlop, RCA were notable casualties. Many other market leaders found it extremely difficult to maintain their competitive positions. In the United States, IBM, General Motors and Westinghouse are major examples of leaders that have suffered from abrupt declines or even elimination of all profits. In Europe, AEG and Philips have had similar problems, while in Japan, market leaders, such as NEC, Ricoh, Hitachi and Matsushita have suffered profit declines and have been forced to adopt new policies of reconstruction and re-positioning of their strategies. At the same time, many other market leaders have increased their strengths both absolutely and relative to many powerful competitors: ABB in Sweden, GE in the United States and Royal/Dutch Shell in Europe are exemplars, though they too have made many important adjustments in both strategy and organization during the 1990s.

This chapter aims to provide an overview of the forces that shape TNC behaviour and to illustrate the range of their responses to various challenges in the environment. The diversity of these responses is an important feature of today's strategies. This diversity has important implications for Governments dealing with TNCs. Since there is no *one* TNC strategy or response to the same opportunity, challenge or even to the same piece of information, there can be no *one* prescription for how to deal with TNCs. Therefore, to deal effectively with these firms, government officials and/or negotiators need to understand individual TNC strategies. And the key to such understanding is to know the mechanisms of the inner workings of firms: how market forces are interpreted in individual corporate behaviour, how managerial perceptions are shaped and decisions made, what are the most important problems firms face in today's world, etc. This chapter discusses seven issues that shape TNC behaviour, providing helpful and rich insight for Governments dealing with TNCs. An overview of these issues, including their implications for host countries, is provided after the introduction for those readers who prefer to read only the highlights rather than spend too much time studying the details of the entire chapter. Since, in distinction from chapter I, the issues discussed in this chapter are parts of the whole – strategies of TNC – it is not possible to draw implications for Brazil and other host countries for every one of them. Wherever it was possible, the discussion of implications is integrated with the discussion of issues rather than being separated into individual sections as was the case in chapter I.

While it is difficult to suggest, after the following analysis, generalized implications for governments dealing with individual TNCs – for, as mentioned earlier, individual dealings should be "custom made" and depend on individual strategies – it is possible to draw such implications at the policy level; this is done in section C of this chapter.

The discussion is based on two primary sources. One is the general publicly available literature on the changing strategies of TNCs of all types. The other is part of the results of the survey of TNCs' views that was undertaken specifically for this study. These results are in two parts: the views of TNCs with great experience of operating in Brazil, a group of 32 firms with an average Brazilian experience of over 30 years referred in the tables as "TNCs established in Brazil" or "investors"; and the views of investors who have developed important international positions but not in Brazil as of 1996, referred to as "TNCs not established in Brazil" or "non-investors" (box II.1). In this chapter, the responses from both groups are mainly shown in combined form, for the focus is on their world-wide strategies, where little difference was observed. That commonality of view is an important part of the background for interpreting the data shown in the next chapter, where differences, born of different experience, familiarity and understanding of how to operate in the Brazilian environment produce sometimes quite strikingly different views.[1]

Box II.1. The sample of TNCs and its limitations

The views of TNCs that constitute the empirical base for the report, discussed in this chapter and, especially, in chapter III, were collected by means of interviews with chief executives or their appointed representatives (see annex 1 for the list of interviewed TNCs). The interviews were based on a questionnaire (annex 2).

As regards the 32 TNCs established in Brazil, or "investors", about one third of them had had a presence in Brazil since before World War II; about one third had been there for 36 to 50 years; and the remaining third for periods between 20 and 35 years. Eleven have headquarters in the United States, 15 in Europe and 6 in Japan. With one exception, they operate in manufacturing industries, and three of them have significant raw materials interests.

The sample of TNCs established in Brazil has a number of important biases. First, it is skewed towards the experienced investor. Given the well-known effects of learning after the first investment in any country, this bias could influence perception. To deal with that problem, a

/...

A. Overview: seven themes

Seven themes dominate the discussion in this chapter. First is the *drive for growth* and its impact on all the resources of a firm. Intensifying global competition has made the drive for growth an imperative in the eyes of most executives. The dynamics of the market are such that standing still seems no longer feasible, if indeed it ever was possible. Moreover, the quality of the needed growth means that fewer and fewer industries can remain both profitable and efficient on a purely domestic basis. Yet this drive for growth has produced a curious paradox.

On the one hand, as noted in chapter I, there are more firms entering the world FDI market from more home countries, sectors and industries. This may result in competition for attractive investment sites or projects and thus may benefit host countries as, for example, when rivals bid up the prices of privatized assets. However, on the other hand, this competition encounters limits, as the drive for growth, combined with the growing requirements for greater levels of skills, quality and competence generally, have caused leading TNCs to become acutely aware that management itself has become a scarce resource. Few TNCs operate throughout the world; Coca-Cola and perhaps Microsoft are two examples of the few exceptions. Even large firms, such as British Petroleum, have withdrawn from some markets in order to focus their

---

(Box II.1, concluded)

second, roughly comparable, sample of about 25 firms was developed to canvas a range of opinions among chief executives of important TNCs that had limited or no investments in Brazil. These data were gathered by telephone interviews, based on a shortened version of the main questionnaire.

A second important bias is in terms of the industries represented. The focus is on the manufacturing sector and, within it, on automobiles, chemicals, electrical machinery, electronics and a range of consumer goods. Not covered are service industries which are among the most rapidly growing industries for FDI worldwide. Given their importance in Brazil's programme of privatization, they have been among the most important industries attracting new FDI in the second half of the 1990s; their omission from the study means that the opinions reported here understate the potential for FDI growth. When services were mentioned, this was done in the context of what manufacturers would like to see by way of greater service support.

A third bias in the sample is in terms of the home countries covered. The TNCs surveyed are all from the principal developed countries and do not include firms from developing countries. Third World TNCs are, however, discussed briefly in chapter I.

It should also be noted that the aggregate totals in some of the tables presenting the results of interviews do not align with the number of companies interviewed. This is because, in some cases, no answer was received to some of the questions or because, in other cases, more than one answer was received to a given question (e.g. one from the corporate perspective and one from an individual business unit's perspective).

And, finally, it has to be kept in mind that the interviews took place in spring 1996 and that, since that time, there have been many changes in a rapidly reforming economy. In particular, a number of concerns of foreign investors have been taken care of by legislative changes or economic measures. In spite of that, the text relating to these concerns has not been removed from the interview material because it is part of the catalogue of issues which matter to foreign investors in any host country. But in every case, the change in Brazil has been noted in either the text or an endnote.

Source: UNCTAD.

---

efforts on a more limited set of countries. Precisely the same effect has been driving the policies in many large corporations to slim down their product portfolios (Markides, 1996). Thus, the growth in numbers of potentially competing TNCs does not have to heighten the level of competition in any one host country market and bid up prices they are ready to pay in any one privatization project. In general, TNCs do not need to lower their expectations as regards what they consider an optimal investment climate and they do not need to be prepared to carry greater risks. Much depends on the rules of decision-making employed by firms to make these critically important choices of focus.

The *nature of managerial choice* is a second theme of this chapter. In part, firms make choices based on their experiences; hence the importance of the sequential nature of investment, mentioned in chapter I. In part they also make choices based on their expectations of risk (both economic and political) and likely managerial difficulty. Thus, issues of how attitudes are shaped to form these expectations and views become an important part of the information flow that crosses the desks of all senior executives. It is not clear any longer, for example, that priority in these choices is always accorded to the largest markets for a firm's output. Given the economic significance of TNCs in the growth of developing countries, where TNCs as a whole increased their share of domestic capital formation from 2 to 10 per cent between 1985 and 1997 (UNCTAD, 1999), the determinants of the information that create favourable views become a critical part of any effort to promote more inward investment and to deal with TNCs.

The third theme concerns processes for *assembling new resources* to create new sources of firm-level competitiveness. There are many related issues here. One is the question of the specialization of the activities of any one foreign affiliate. The trend towards specialization was noted earlier, but to understand its significance one has also to understand the consequences for managing growing complexity in the corporate networks that are being built. Another key issue is that of gaining access to immobile resources. Even in a globalizing world, many critical resources, especially those in specialized "clusters", remain localized. Access to these immobile resources cannot always be gained by FDI, especially where there are regulatory barriers as in telecommunications, thus spurring the development of alliance contracts of various forms. Another spur to alliances is the growing realization that few, if any, firms can command the high ground on all the technologies needed for all stages of their operations. Cooperation with others may be possible and, under many conditions, even more desirable than traditional forms of hierarchical control (Stopford, 1995).

The fourth theme is the *managerial desire for control*. As a means to help deal with the growing complexity of their operations, managers are re-emphasizing the central importance of control. By control, they do not mean necessarily equity ownership, as contracts may provide a sufficiently strong alternative. But the need for unambiguous control may conflict with the desirability of forming alliances. Thus there is tension among these two and other themes in the development of global strategy.

These tensions and ambiguity provide a fifth theme, namely the need for *consistency in policy development over time*. The sheer dynamic of the market can act to erode positions of strength very quickly, as noted earlier. Changing policies for focusing resources or outsourcing functional activities can have quite different effects at headquarters levels and in the local affiliates. What may seem both rational and consistent at the global level may be impossible to interpret at local levels, creating another form of paradox, namely that a growth policy for world markets may erode strength in some national markets. The important example of General

Electric (GE) in Brazil is discussed to indicate both the severity of the paradox and to underscore the fact that TNCs are seldom internally monolithic.

Sixth is the fact that firms in the same industries can, and do, take *contradictory strategic positions*. There is considerable evidence now available, to show that the structure of an industry accounts for only a small proportion of a firm's profitability (Rumelt, 1991). The implication is that managerial choice matters more than industry structure and that, in a dynamic market, there is no single best way to operate in a given market. In dynamic markets, the race is to accumulate resources faster than others. These races can be won by speed and innovation over extended periods, as well as by strength at the start. Where strength has bred complacency and inertia, David has the opportunity to beat Goliath. Consequently, conventional frameworks used to analyse competition need to be enlarged to recognize that it is "not exclusively a battle between the large and the small, or the well resourced versus the impoverished, all playing by the same set of 'rules'. Competition is also a contest among strategies" (Baden-Fuller and Stopford, 1994, p. xii).

The strategy a firm adopts is influenced by its initial resources and also by its ability to learn and accumulate new resources of all kinds. Because these processes reflect the internal abilities of many people, the "time-path" for strategy can take quite different forms. For example, at some point in time Microsoft announced a series of clear strategic priorities for its investments in the future "networked society". These involve growing complexity in users' PCs and in the control protocols for gaining access to the worldwide web. These policies were entirely consistent with Microsoft's capabilities and methods of operation at that time. By contrast, Oracle was attacking the same target with an entirely different philosophy and strategy. Instead of complexity for the user, Oracle was betting on simplification, with high-speed switching and relational database capabilities being developed in the infrastructure of the system. This infrastructure would, they estimated, be managed by several competing firms rather than solely by Microsoft in Microsoft's alternative concept. These two combatants were basing their strategies on quite distinct assumptions about how the system could be developed, as well as on quite distinct assets and levels of ambition and confidence (Lane, 1996).

Finally, in this list of seven themes that depict the driving forces in the evolution of firms' strategies is the *problem of organizational resistance*. Whereas the need for change in strategic priority may be well understood in the planning forum, it may be quite another thing to make the change happen in practice. Communicating the need and the details of the way forward to thousands of managers takes a great deal of time. Besides, there can often be resistance, especially from those who feel they will be losing power and influence. In these respects, the organization of TNCs resembles any large bureaucracy. The important question for interpretation of the data, however, is that the delay function – or "hysteresis" as it is called later on to signify the link to engineering control systems – means that views from chief executives do not always match the current reality. Furthermore, central views can imply promises of future action. However, there is strong evidence that when TNCs are competitively weak in their industries or are losing out in the race to accumulate new resources, they are unable to deliver on their promises.

Policy makers and negotiators need to be aware of these factors, so as to be spared later surprise and disappointment. For example, in response to a prolonged and heated debate in Parliament in the United Kingdom, Chrysler reportedly made twelve "binding" promises about future performance when it acquired the Rootes Group in 1964. However, they were not honoured, as Chrysler lacked both the resources and the strategic capability to implement their entry plan. The Rootes group was then sold to Renault and Chrysler withdrew from the market.[2] A more thorough review of all these features of strategy, strategic choice and competitive strengths to deliver on the promises made both to employees and to outside bodies might have led to a different outcome. The dynamics of the international market need to be captured in any assessment of a firm's investment plan.

A guide through the detail that follows may serve to focus attention on key issues for policy makers. There are four aspects of firm-level behaviour that raise policy issues:

- The imperative of growth means that managers regard strategy as a form of "arms race", in which they are assembling new resources to provide corporate scale. Scale advantage at the level of the plant or national affiliate is being complemented and on occasion superseded by the competitiveness of the system as a whole. This trend adds an urgency to the assessments of national attractiveness for investors. Firms are looking for locations that hold out the promise of future adaptability and upgrading of skills and resources to meet rising international demands. Firms are also becoming more selective about where they operate, for few firms have the resources needed to compete in all possible countries. Thus, attractiveness is being measured not just in terms of the traditional factor costs, but also in terms of the relationships they can establish with local firms and local public bodies.

- Growth is increasingly associated with the specialization of the asset bundles firms are assembling in networks of growing complexity. It is also associated with structures of alliances as a way to expand the resources under command faster than would be possible on a go-it-alone basis. Location attractiveness is thus being measured as much in terms of local contributions to resource strengthening as it is in terms of the size of the local market. Because investments are made for both supply and demand reasons in an environment in which cross-border transactions are growing, supply is being de-linked from the markets. Nations cannot rely solely on the size of the domestic market as the primary magnet to attract investors. Moreover, the growth of alliance structures challenges many conventional notions about competition law and the provision of skills and support services needed to manage both competitively and in cooperation with others. A particular feature is the need to pay attention to the development of small firms, both local and foreign. They can become critical players in helping to create an environment conducive to dynamism and growth.

- The growing complexity of these specialized networks is strengthening managers' desires for greater control (either through equity or through contract arrangements) of the operations so as to optimize activities across borders. Despite managers' general (often rhetorical) desire for liberalization of regulations, most accept the need for regulations of some sort. The issue has become one of transparency and predictability of policy.

- The strategic role of the State can be reassessed in terms of "triangular bargaining" that involves host countries, local and foreign firms, and on occasion, foreign governments. The new demands of competition heighten the need for the State to provide key resources in as stable a manner as possible, and to do so over time in consistent ways that match the needs of changing competition. Part of the new role for the State as "orchestrator" of resources is to assist in making general resources, such as education, more than a commodity easily matched by other countries. The challenge is to create specialized support services. In this connection, support for the nurturing of clusters of related resources to create new poles of growth at a local level can become a priority. The needs are not the same as those for traditional infant-industry support nor for large complexes, but for market-friendly infrastructure within which firms can develop more easily.

B. Strategies of TNCs

1. The imperative of growth

The economic forces described in chapter I combine to create a world in which TNC strategies are being re-engineered to permit accelerated growth. If the decade of the 1980s was a period of refocusing, asset specialization and gaining new internal efficiencies, then the 1990s has been a decade of expansion, resuming the trends of the 1960s and 1970s.

Many leading TNCs now regard their global strategies as a form of strategic arms race in which they are attempting to accumulate new resources faster than their rivals. Their strategies take a wide variety of forms:

- Firms see new ways to gain scale advantages, where they exist, for their key activities. To this end, they seek ways to specialize their resources and retain control over the resulting cross-trades.

- Firms seek new resources that allow them to achieve critical scale in local markets and at the same time retain an ability to respond to local differences.

- TNCs seek new abilities to become "insiders" in each of their key territories and to build a quality of intelligence that helps provide a competitive edge in their local dealings with government and the private sector.

- Firms seek to command the key technologies required or, by alliances, gain access to those needed to complete the range. They also seek new abilities to create new technologies faster than others, as, for example, in the pharmaceutical industry where leading firms are moving, directly or indirectly, into genetics.

The critical resources are both tangible in the form of cash and physical equipment and intangible in the form of skills, technologies, brands or control systems. Of particular importance for the purposes of this volume is that the competitive advantages being sought are economies of scale at the *corporate* level rather than at the *factory* level. An example is the importance of the global reservation system for international airlines. The scale of this system can give more competitive power than the scale of the route system. American Airlines' acclaimed SABRE system has earned the corporation more money than flying aircraft in seven out of the ten years from 1985 to 1995.

Where corporate scale is important, it confers on leading TNCs a greater power than hitherto. The effect is more than merely the power of "deep pockets" (though this too is important), as the acquisition boom by foreigners in Brazil (see chapter III) and other host countries demonstrates. The effect is that it allows complex combinations of resources that smaller firms cannot achieve. These combinations can lower total system costs and/or create new products and services.

Achieving all these advantages is extremely difficult as some of them are seeming opposites. Gaining scale by integrating activities across borders can impede the flexibility of the local affiliates to respond rapidly to changes. Thus, a key feature of the new corporate strategic race is the ability of firms to develop and extend managerial competence to manage the increasing complexity of their world operations. As one executive in the survey stated: "We are being held back by the difficulty of finding and training enough managers for these new tasks. It is very frustrating that our internal constraints on growth are now greater than the constraints of our markets".

2. Configurations of networks

To help deal with the imperative of growth, TNCs need to build an architecture of communications and control. They also need to choose among a variety of quite different types of configurations of assets. Some of the more complex configurations can be managed by only a few of the most experienced and capable TNCs. Indeed, the internal ability to manage complexity, or to find novel ways to simplify the tasks, can be a prime determinant of market strategy. According to one executive: "We are developing new forms of management and new skills as a specific investment. We are, in effect, buying options for future asset configurations. It is hard to deal with these things, for they lack the clarity of, say, one of our refineries, but we know that these options are at the heart of our future competitiveness".

The alternative configurations of the international networks can be considered as falling into three basic categories:[3]

(a) Stand-alone strategy

In a number of TNCs, the affiliates in different host countries have a great deal of autonomy and their link with the parent company is restricted to issues of ownership, technology transfer and the supply of long-term capital. The affiliates develop independent links with the various segments of the host economy (such as local suppliers and subcontractors), hire local managers and workers, and are responsible for most of the value-added chain in their output (figure II.1).

Figure II.1. Stand-alone strategy

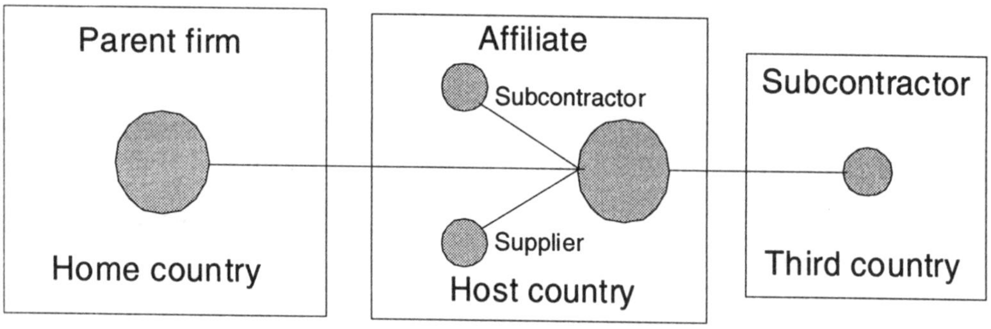

Source: UNCTAD, 1993a, p. 119.

There are different reasons why TNCs have *stand-alone affiliates.* First, if there are trade barriers and limits on the movement of resources, or there is an absence or high cost of the appropriate technology in the host country, the parent firm might be forced to allow the setting up of a stand-alone affiliate. For example, in the manufacturing sector, if the import of materials and components is difficult or expensive, and the host country has the capacity to provide most of the inputs, a TNC might be willing to set up a stand-alone affiliate. In the services sector, given the non-tradability of most services and the greater need to cater to differing tastes, stand-alone affiliates are quite common. Second, such affiliates could evolve over a period of time gaining greater independence as a result of such factors as: changes in host Government policy, major political events, or the increased competence of the affiliate, reflected in its profitability.

(b)   Simple integration strategy

In a number of industries, especially those that are mainly cost driven, there is a strong trend in international production strategies towards *outsourcing* (figure II.2). This entails transferring some of the value-adding services to locations that offer locational advantages. The parent firm might exercise control either through direct ownership of the affiliate or it might enter into non-equity arrangements with various local firms in the host country. Of the non-equity arrangements, subcontracting is the most common, with subcontractors usually specializing in the labour-intensive parts of the value chain. As subcontractors cannot often stand alone, they are functionally linked into the parent firm's value chain. This entails a certain degree of integration into the corporate functions of a TNC; the nature and extent of the integration depends on the role of the outsourced production in the parent firm's value chain.

Figure II.2. Simple integration strategy

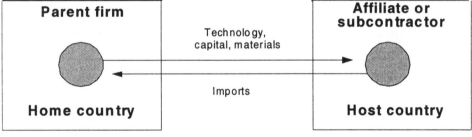

Source: UNCTAD, 1993a, p. 120.

The factors that play a critical role in the adoption of such strategies are the lowering of trade and economic barriers to investment, as well as low transport costs relative to the value of the outsourced output. In the context of a liberalizing global economy, in which technology is rapidly reducing the cost of transporting goods, there is tremendous scope for outsourcing production. This is reflected in the dramatic growth in the labour-intensive manufacturing plants in emerging markets, especially China; these markets offer substantial savings in labour costs.

Such strategies are common in the low-cost, price sensitive manufacturing industries – such as clothing, shoes, toys and sports-equipment – where there is a need to cultivate low-cost suppliers so as to maintain a competitive edge. On the other hand, in the high-technology industries, the adoption of such arrangements is a function of the technological strengths of the host country. Increasingly, the distinctive feature of these industries is to focus on cost-considerations based on technological specialization. The growth of the semiconductor industry in Asia is an example of such a strategy. Initially, the firms in the region concentrated on the functions at the lower end of the value chain, with the parent firms retaining control over the technology that was the major source of firm-specific advantages. Over the past decade, however, local firms have moved up the learning curve, and are now seeking to attract the more sophisticated stages of the process, so as to become competitors in world markets. The advances in technology and communications have made services more tradable and this has allowed firms in the services sector to adopt simple integration strategies. The use of firms in Bangalore, India, by TNCs to write software and process data is an example of this strategy.

(c) Complex integration strategy

A complex integration strategy is characterized by the functional integration of different processes and different locations into the parent firm's value chain. This entails locating the various functional activities of the firm where they can be performed most effectively, as long as they fulfil the firm's overall strategy. While each element of the value chain may not be integrated to the same degree into the parent firm's value chain, each operation is judged by its contribution to the parent firm's value chain (figure II.3).

The changes in the world economy have been the driving force behind the adoption of complex integration strategies by TNCs (table II.1). Of the various changes, increased competition, advances in information technology and growing consumer demand are the most important. Increased competition is forcing TNCs to seek continually new ways of gaining competitive advantages, especially by cutting costs. Growing consumer demand, along with

Figure II.3. Complex integration strategy

Potentially all functions

Parent firm

Affiliate or subcontractor

Home country

Host country

Market

Affiliate

Goods and services

Third country

Host country

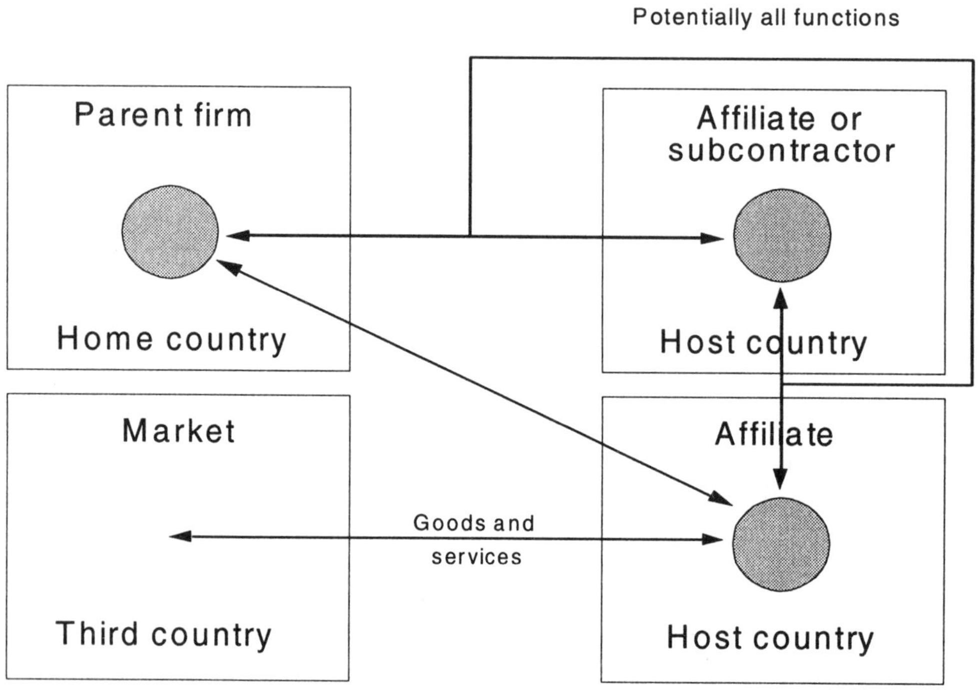

Source: UNCTAD, 1993a, p. 123.

the convergence of consumer taste, to some extent, and the increasing cost and quality consciousness of these consumers, is forcing TNCs to pay close attention to the different elements of their value chain. The ability of TNCs to meet such rising demand and expectations in the face of increasing competition is mainly through advances in technology. The advances in telecommunications have dramatically increased the capacity to process information, at the same time reducing costs. This facilitates easier coordination and integration of the various parts of the value chain. The fact that these developments in technology are no longer confined to the developed countries means that TNCs can nurture centres of innovation and excellence in R&D at various locations, even in developing countries. These advances have helped pioneer integration between suppliers and subcontractors in low cost centres of production, while, at the same time, ensuring product quality and constant innovation. It also allows long-run cost savings through the adoption of shorter product development schedules and just-in-time inventory management.

While technological changes have allowed some firms to adopt complex integration strategies, there are costs involved in coordinating such a structure. This is especially true in the context of issues like control, organizational learning and the transfer of best practice between the various units. The situation could be exasperated if there is a conflict of interest between the various units that form the integrated structure. In the best interest of the firm, it has to learn to strike a balance, at minimum cost, between integration and responsiveness to the needs of its customers.

The nature of specialization within these complex networks varies considerably, depending on where a TNC feels it is most able to achieve scale benefits *and* sufficient responsiveness. For many consumer goods companies (such as Unilever and Johnson & Johnson), scale is being created at the level of the regional plant. Unilever has drastically reduced the number of its plants to serve Europe as it has abandoned a country-by-country approach and begun to build a regional network. For others, like GE, Hoechst and United Technology, scale is achieved by building plants large enough to serve world markets. Such an approach requires an extreme form of the locational choice processes discussed later. For yet others, scale is gained by product specialization. Toyota, for example, has announced moves to have its major assembly plants specialize in the production of a particular model of automobile. Thus, the Avalon is assembled only in Kentucky, requiring dealers in Japan to order the product from the United States.

Table II.1. Strategies of firms

Form	Types of intra-firm linkages	Degree of integration	Environment
Stand-alone, e.g. multi-domestic	Ownership, technology	Weak	Host country accessible to FDI; significant trade barriers; costly communications and transportation
Simple integration, e.g., outsourcing	Ownership, technology, markets, finance, other inputs	Strong at some points of value chain, weak in others	Open trade and FDI regime, at least bilaterally; non-equity arrangements
Complex international production, e.g. regional core networks	All functions	Potentially strong throughout value chain	Open trade and FDI regime; information technology; convergence of tastes; heightened competition

Source: UNCTAD, 1993a, p. 117.

The coordination costs can escalate rapidly as such networks are being developed. Thus, much management attention is shifting to new dimensions of choice and new ways to expand managerial capacity to handle complexity.

In many cases, these complex networks have a further dimension of specialization. They can emphasize the integration of production and consequent trade in goods and services within regional groupings, such as the EU, ASEAN or MERCOSUR, where transaction costs are low, and, simultaneously, develop global networks in the intangibles, such as control systems, brand management and (increasingly) R&D.[4] Ford and Volkswagen have such networks within Western Europe and North America, with only relatively minor interregional flows of products. The same applies to the Thomson/RCA television business with its European, North American and Asian supply hubs. Yet, neither Toyota resembles Ford, nor does Matsushita resemble Thomson. The precise configuration of a network is determined more by firm-specific factors than industry ones. Public officials need to be aware of the variety of approaches that can be taken by firms within an industry.

These trends in general strategic priority and network configuration have important implications for Brazil in terms of the need for a trading regime that permits a carefully managed flow of intermediate and finished goods, as well as services. Strategies of complex integration depend on a firm's ability to optimize its total supply system across national borders. Impediments to such optimization seriously weaken a country's attractiveness to those investors who depend on an internationally calculated low-cost position.

The more complex the strategy of integration becomes, the greater is the need for stability in both the regulatory climate and the macroeconomic environment. Indeed, some of the managers interviewed went so far as to say that stability was more important than complete freedom to manage the transfers. "We can usually work out how to survive profitably, provided we are sure the necessary investments in the systems will be allowed sufficient time to show their worth", was a common sentiment. The stabilization plan is thus a critical component in the total armoury of weapons to boost attractiveness. Stability in the exchange rate is also critical. The views of investors on these matters, as reported in chapter III, reflect the growing importance of openness and stability.

3. Managerial choice

(a) Products, technologies and markets

To make any one of these networks operate effectively, TNCs face a myriad of specific choices. At the risk of oversimplification, these can be grouped into three, interrelated categories.

- One is the series of decisions about the limits to the product range, the extent of adaptation of products and services to differing national demand patterns and the location of supply for components and finished products and services. Where Boeing and Microsoft may choose to concentrate on a few global products, Unilever may decide in favour of many different products, some developed specifically for one country. These choices are driven by industry characteristics, but, as chapter I emphasized, firms seek differentiation and may choose quite contradictory product strategies. For example, Whirlpool, which specializes in white goods, emphasized standardization of its range of brands across borders, while Electrolux had a broad range of international and local products supported by over 40 brand names, some of which were used only in a single country. These choices, in turn, have an important bearing on where the supply is to be located.

- A second set of choices affects the range of the underlying technologies and competencies that are regarded as central to defining a firm's competitive advantage. Technologies and other resources deemed not to be central to the firm's mission are often outsourced. In part, the decisions are conditioned by relative costs, but they are also affected by managers' perspectives on the development trajectory anticipated for the future evolution of the industry and the firm's desired position in that future. These perspectives also condition choices of location of supply.

- A third set of choices concerns the markets to be served and the means of serving them. A critical issue is the extent to which a firm's customers are national or international. If they are purely national, then the choices have much to do with market size and its prospects for growth. If, however, they are international, then the choices become more difficult. For example, the British firm, International Paints, the world leader in marine coatings, has to balance the competing demands of international customers (fleet owners) and the national demands of the shipyards. Both are important, but each group has different influences on the location of supply and service capabilities. Such factors exercise pressure from the demand side of the market for TNCs to build networks in their sales and service functions akin to the networks of supply discussed in chapter I.

It is the impact of these factors on the choices of location – both for supply and market service – that is of specific concern here. The need for choice in today's competitive battle was summed up by the chief executive officer (CEO) of a United States consumer goods company who said, "In the past, bigger was better. We aimed to reach every customer worldwide. Now, we have learnt that we must become more focused on where we want to go. We know we cannot be everywhere. Our past mistakes in some countries and the difficulties of managing diverse international businesses have taught us that".

The challenge of managing the resulting complexities in the networks for all functions and activities across borders is at the heart of why choice is so important in the management of TNCs. To the extent that these complexities have been increasing and changing more rapidly, the traditional measures of attractiveness of any one country are being altered in both form and emphasis.

(b) Choice of territory for FDI

For convenience of discussion, the choice of territory for new investment or reinvestment can be considered also to have three primary variables. Other important features of priority locations are discussed later in this chapter. The primary variables of choice have to do with the economics of market growth; with the problems of developing managerial behaviour capable of coping with economic and "psychic" distance; and with the sequence by which a network is extended both within territories and across new borders.

(i) Perceptions of market growth

The importance of the growth potential and size of the market was clearly highlighted in the survey (figure II.4). The majority of firms from the United States, the EU and Japan emphasized that in a global economy, their strategy was, to a great extent, driven by optimizing the potential for rapid growth, by choosing territories that were either large or growing rapidly, and preferably both.

Owing to the size of its market, including the Brazilian market, its dynamism and relatively open FDI regime, Latin America was in the 1970s the most important host developing country region.

When, as a result of the debt crisis in the early 1980s, the region lost its dynamism, it lost

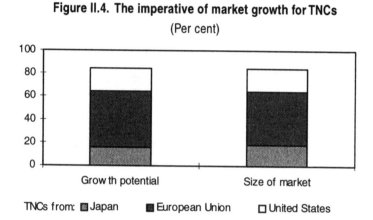

Figure II.4. The imperative of market growth for TNCs

(Per cent)

TNCs from: ▨ Japan   ■ European Union   ☐ United States

Source: survey data, corporate responses (all interviewed TNCs).

Note: The question asked was: "What are the factors that make a difference in choosing countries outside your domestic market in which to invest?" The per cent number indicates the percentage of TNCs that cited each factor (e.g. growth potential) as the factor that made the greatest difference.

its position among host regions to Asia, and especially to South, East and South-East Asia, which grew rapidly during the 1980s – 6.2 per cent per year during 1980-1991, compared to Latin America's 1.6 per cent (UNCTAD, 1994b, pp. 438-442). Since 1986, FDI inflows, and since 1988, FDI stock in Asia have been consistently and increasingly higher than those in Latin America. In 1996, FDI stock in Latin America and the Caribbean ($316 billion) was only two thirds of the stock of South, East and South-East Asia, while in 1985 it was one fifth higher (UNCTAD, 1997a).

Although, by the mid-1990s, growth (and growth prospects) for the Latin American region greatly improved, and distance to Asia in many respect was reduced or even vanished, the majority of the TNCs included in the survey still considered that the Asia/Pacific was by far the region of the world with the greatest growth potential for their products. Yet there was an important difference in emphasis for some. Those firms already highly experienced in Brazil were much more likely to expect the most rapid growth (for them) to lie in Latin America; (Japanese managers emphasized Asia more than the others, but not significantly) (figures II.5A and II.5B).

These differences in perspective illustrate an important common feature of international investment: investors tend to favour what they know and to regard territories they do not know as risky. Responses were from TNCs with wide global coverage but not in Brazil. Though it might be thought that the differences were due to a more limited global perspective, there is no evidence to this effect.

More generally, investors give preference to territories that have features in common with the home country; the challenge of complexity in the system is thereby reduced. In this case, it could be that the lack of investment is due to a fear that there might be pronounced differences: a lack of knowledge is strongly associated with fear of negative possibilities.

Fear can act to slow down the pace of adjustment to new market possibilities. It is possible that the group of non-investors are reacting just as United States investors did to Asian opportunities. They were slow to invest in the growth dynamic of Asia, in part because of regulatory obstacles discussed earlier, and in part because they did not find the economic arguments compelling enough to switch away from the earlier concentration in Europe and Latin America. Only when these arguments became strong did the switch in relative emphasis occur.[5] United States investors reacted more quickly than Europeans, as will be discussed later. Part of the reason is that they were being more directly

Figure II.5. Countries with the greatest growth potential in the global economy in the 1990s
(Per cent of TNCs' responses)

A. According to TNCs established in Brazil

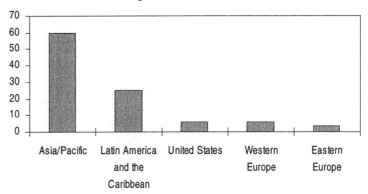

B. According to TNCs not established in Brazil

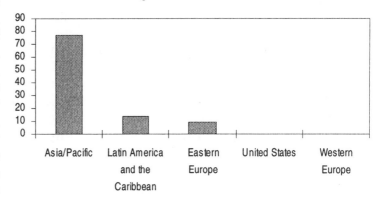

Source: survey data.

Note: data at product level.

threatened in their home markets by Asian imports, and partly because they had some earlier experience in the region due to their component supply bases (Encarnation, 1992). That early experience was limited to a few, but their investment behaviour may well have induced some of the bandwagon effects associated with oligopolies (Knickerbocker, 1973).

(ii)   Economic and "psychic" distance

To explain why such differences can exist, a short digression into three features of managerial behaviour is needed. The first issue is that of handling complexity. In reaching decisions on investment, managers are confronted with complex and often conflicting data. Board members cannot comprehend all the issues and therefore have to rely on their staff to filter and simplify the information. The difficulties lie in the filtering, for the dynamism of the world economy, the multiplicity of growth opportunities, the transition in development strategies and firms' resource limitations challenge known rules about decision-making. Investment decisions, therefore, are subject to varying degrees of internal politics: TNCs are not monolithic in their behaviour as sometimes portrayed. Final choice can seldom be made on grounds of economic rationality alone. The decisions are, more often than not, based as much on perceptions as they are on any factual evidence.

The second behavioural issue concerns how managers find out what is going on around the world. There is considerable evidence that perceptions of the attractiveness of entry possibilities to any one country or region is shaped by two related factors. First, the "economic" distance of an investment site from the home country or from the international network already established. The concerns here are in terms of transaction costs and differing rules and regulations. Where there are equally strong arguments in favour of investment in two projects and when there are resource limitations requiring a choice, economic rationality argues in favour of choosing the investment with the lesser costs both of addition to the network and of the transaction of daily business. For these sorts of reasons, most TNCs have evolved their international networks by first going into neighbouring countries entailing the shortest "economic" distance.

But economic calculation alone cannot capture the full set of costs. There are further costs in terms of adjusting behaviour to fit in with foreign cultures, socio-economic and political practices and norms. This cost has been labelled "psychic" distance. Managers' ideas about a foreign country, especially before the first operations there have been established, are heavily influenced by the media and government communications. Just as with "economic" distance, "psychic" distance has influenced how firms internationalize. Many United States firms have concentrated their European investments in the United Kingdom where language and legal adjustments are minimal. The fact that they started investing in Asia earlier than European firms did may have been induced not solely by the economic reasons mentioned earlier but also because of the ethnic diversity of their own domestic workforce. This has provided them with options to cross cultural barriers more readily than the Europeans. For example, leading United States TNCs, such as IBM and Motorola, routinely entrust their negotiations in China to United States citizens who are also ethnic Chinese. Taking advantage of these internal human resources can greatly reduce the perceived costs of "psychic" distance. These problems of "psychic" distance seemingly deter many Japanese firms from considering Brazil, in spite of a large number of Brazilians of Japanese descent (see chapter III).

The third behavioural issue has to do with the problem of adjusting policies and practices. This difficulty, a form of internal friction in the managerial system, is labelled *"hysteresis"*. While many of the firms interviewed identified Asia as being the most attractive growth area for future investment, they have, in practice, not yet started to invest there (figure II.6). Emerging practice can, and often does, lag behind observations of opportunity and changes in general policy. The European data in figure II.6 need careful interpretation. The survey data referred to intentions to invest in Asia, not actual practice; a study (European Commission and UNCTAD, 1996) showed the relatively low FDI from European TNCs into Asia.

Historically speaking, European TNCs have underestimated the growth potential of the dynamic Asian economies – a form of "psychic" gap. While Japanese and United States TNCs used Asia as a low-cost production base for their home markets, European firms preferred using neighbouring countries for this purpose. This meant that the trade and FDI involvement of EU TNCs in Asia was often below the critical mass beyond which a virtuous cycle of increased trade and investment can come into being and make a compelling argument for a shift in investment priority (ibid., p. 59). It should be noted that these problems of both economic and "psychic" distance, combined with information asymmetries, have made the smaller European investors even slower to invest in Asia (ibid., p. 82). It is very likely that many of the non-

Figure II.6. Main regions in which all interviewed TNCs were likely to invest in the second half of the 1990s

(Per cent of TNCs' responses)

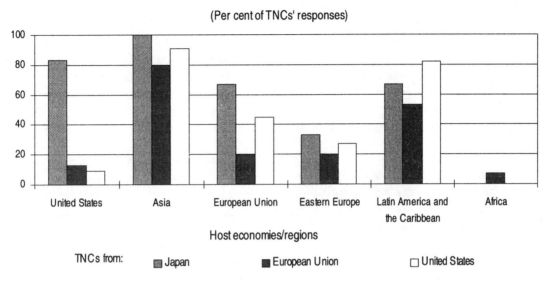

Host economies/regions

TNCs from:　▨ Japan　　■ European Union　　□ United States

Source: survey results, based on corporate responses.

investors in the sample will experience the same sense of delay between realizing the new Brazilian opportunities and actually investing there. Moreover, the need for assistance for smaller firms, discussed in chapter I, may be even greater than might be suspected from looking solely at economic data.

Further evidence of delayed adjustment or *hysteresis* is provided by the surveyed firms' statements on the speed of their investments in greater specialization. All the TNCs agreed that specialization had been an important feature of competition in their business for some years. Yet about half of them also stated that they had either made little progress in re-configuring their international networks or that the process of change had started in earnest only during the previous year or so.

This delay reflects in part the difficulty of changing everything at once. Efficiencies gained during the 1980s had retarded implementation of the new growth-oriented strategies until the 1990s: only then could some observers legitimately claim that most TNCs were little more than national companies with international operations, and continued to be dominated by their home market nationalities in strategic and organizational terms (Hu, 1992). The evidence of the survey is that the organizational picture was changing rapidly and that national authorities needed to be acutely aware of the dynamics of this processes.

The twin challenges of overcoming economic and "psychic" distance at the time of entry, and of rapidly developing mechanisms for linking new affiliates to global networks, have historically caused many TNCs to develop their location strategies in reasonably predictable sequences. United States-based TNCs have typically started in Canada – geographical proximity – and then explored other English-speaking territories such as the United Kingdom (Vernon and Davidson, 1979). Similarly, United Kingdom-based TNCs for long concentrated their investments in the English-speaking world (Stopford and Turner, 1985), and Japanese investors in Europe have given preference to the United Kingdom because of greater familiarity with the legal system and the language relative to the rest of the EU.

(iii)   Sequential investment

These cautious step-out sequences have been accompanied by preferences for re-investment discussed in chapter I. Indeed, nearly half of the TNCs sampled, with experience in Brazil, regarded local learning effects as very important (table II.2). Only nine firms claimed that reinvestment decisions were taken without explicit reference to accumulated experience of local conditions. The importance of local learning increases as investors attempt to become insiders in each major territory of operations. If, as one investor stated, "the first investment is successful, we are more likely to begin a stream of investments that will, among other things, create goodwill among government officials who can see us demonstrating our commitment to their country".

Such internal learning clearly exercises a bias on how investors weigh the various factors that together make up a case for investment. The implication for a host country is that it would do well to encourage small investors to enter its territory as early as possible. As investors grow internationally, they are likely to put a disproportionate amount of their continuing investment into those countries in which they have had early favourable experiences. Not only will assistance in making the investment help in creating a favourable sense of cooperation, but the early nurturing of fledgling operations will also have long-term payoffs. These practices apply equally to domestic as to foreign start-ups in many countries, such as Denmark, and have proved effective (Levie, 1994). In some cases, the policies also include tax incentives that foster the provision of "informal" capital, as in Sweden (Landström, 1992). For a foreign investor, the converse is that bad initial experiences make reinvestment less likely and heighten the forces that create the hysteresis effect.

Table II.2. The effect of local experience on criteria for FDI
(Number of responses)

Not important	Some effect	Very important
9	9	13

Source: survey results, based on responses of TNCs established in Brazil.

(c)   Strategies of market entry

These influences on the sequences of investment and local learning effects have a strong impact on how TNCs calculate their strategies of entry into each priority market and the required ownership structure. In the context of a global strategy that requires complex integration, conventional thinking about the determinants of entry now needs serious modification. Such thinking focused on the following determinants of FDI (Dunning, 1993):

- economies of scale;
- dynamics of supply capabilities and flexibility of production processes;
- import barriers and/or export incentives;
- behaviour of competitors;
- a firm's own experience; and
- cross-border transport and administration costs (part of economic distance).

There is now need for a re-evaluation of how the scale of the market influences decisions; where in the value chain the critical economies of scale lie (at unit or corporate levels); the effect of splitting up of the value chain in investment sequences working at different speeds; the valuation of incentives; the imitative effects of oligopolistic rivalry; and the need for control.

Many of these issues were discussed in chapter I in terms of the simultaneous determination of trade and investment decisions and the development of internal networks. The changes in oligopolistic rivalry are due to the emergence of new competitors with different priorities, different calculations of risk and different structures of economic and "psychic" costs. For example, General Motors is reported to have considered and rejected the possibility of investing in Poland. However, when Daewoo made the same analysis, it came to the opposite conclusion and invested. General Motors then re-examined the market and changed its mind. Clearly, the Korean investor had perceived opportunity where the United States one had not; its "new" calculation changed the other's procedures and weightings among the variables.

Perhaps the most fundamental change, however, concerns the issue of control, particularly as it affects decisions about ownership. A TNC can choose to establish a wholly-owned subsidiary in a foreign market, either by setting up a new operation or by acquiring an established company in the host country, to promote its products in the host market. A particular form of complex specialization is when a foreign affiliate is accorded the mandate to manage the entire spectrum of developmental activities for part of the corporation's product line. Such "world product mandates" are growing in popularity in electronics, for example, for they constitute one means of reducing the complexity of the total system. However, they also represent the stewardship of fundamental competitive advantages. Thus, TNCs are usually unwilling to share ownership of such mandates. There are, to be sure, exceptions, such as the alliance between GEC in the United Kingdom and Siemens in Germany for the development of a complete line of communications switches. Here, the argument turns on the relative advantages of pooling resources, an issue discussed in the next section. In other cases, the call for specialization may apply only to one function, such as the manufacture of specific product lines or components which can be exchanged with other foreign affiliates as part of an integrated global production system. Even here, a TNC often finds it difficult to share ownership because of the coordination costs. These networks – or "architectures" – of intense specialization permit a TNC to maximize location-cost economies and, at the same time preserve its ability both to take advantage of global scale, where appropriate for specific activities, and still maintain flexibility to respond to local differences. But these advantages have to be balanced with the inherent costs and risks associated both with investments in countries in which there might be cultural, economic and political problems, and with the currency trade risks inherent in systems dependent on extensive cross-border integration.

One alternative to wholly-owned assets is the joint venture, either with a minority stake, an equal or a majority stake. Joint ventures give a TNC access to a local partner's knowledge, share the development costs and reduce the risks associated with such investments. In a number of countries, joint ventures are the only acceptable form of investment for the host Government. But inevitably there are problems associated with losing control over its technology to its venture partner (especially if the TNC is the minority partner). Furthermore, the different perspectives, abilities and time-scales of local partners may make it difficult to manage global strategic co-ordination effectively and adjust sufficiently rapidly to change. For these reasons, many TNCs have used joint ventures more in strategies of simple integration than in those requiring great complexity and the periodic demands of immediate system-wide adjustment when operating conditions change in one part of the world.

As is discussed later in this chapter, most TNCs are increasingly requiring unambiguous control in order to maintain or create the ability to gain economies of scale from integrating or coordinating activities across borders. Although some firms adopt a step-by-step approach, and gradually increase their investments and commitments in a country or region based on their learning curves, others choose to bypass some of the steps and instead set up a fully-owned subsidiary, especially if they feel that they have to respond to moves by competitors.

The trends identified in the survey suggest that equity participation is becoming less important than control. At a basic level, the need for managers to feel "in control" is well illustrated by Suzuki's actions in Spain. Suzuki is reported to have abandoned its $500 million assembly plant in southern Spain on grounds of undue local intervention. Local officials were, reputedly, making it so difficult to integrate the Spanish operation into the growing European network that the costs of staying in business there began to outweigh the benefits of harnessing capacity elsewhere in the region.[6]

The trends also suggest that control can be exercised by means of contracts and various forms of alliances. There are many tensions in the struggle for control. Many executives maintain that alliances are inherently unstable because of the limits to the ability of cross-border contracts to cater to all eventualities requiring change in operating arrangements. Others are more sanguine. Both categories of opinion are united, though, in the insistence that the primary objective is to retain the ability to maintain some form of control over the operations. Under these circumstances, understanding the dynamics of control in its various forms thus becomes critical for government officials; equity stakes are not always so important as other, often invisible, sources of power and influence.

4. Accumulating resources through alliances and other cooperative ventures

In the race to accumulate new resources, the question always arises as to whether it is better to grow organically, to buy assets, or to enter into an alliance of some kind.[7] This is sometimes known as the "quality-of-growth" argument.

Because many of the fundamental considerations of the choice between build or buy are well known, they will not be discussed at length here. Many TNCs grow by both means, recognizing that building can be slow and also that creating value after a merger can be difficult. The current boom in mergers and acquisitions (M&As) worldwide (see chapter III) seems inspired by the strength of the world's stock markets forgetting that more than half the mergers in the previous boom failed (Haspeslagh and Jemison, 1991).

An important shift in the quality-of-growth argument in recent years has been the rapid escalation of the use of alliances as a means to accelerate growth and gain access to resources that are both difficult (maybe impossible) to create and in any event are not for sale. Indeed, the trend towards alliances has become so strong that, according to one estimate, they accounted for about a quarter of all new cross-border ventures started during the period 1987-1992 (Harbison and Pekar, 1993), and they have continued to strengthen since then (UNCTAD, 1999). These developments are taking place against a backdrop in which alliances have a high failure rate with only about half proving successful, as with acquisitions. Moreover, only about one in seven alliances survives for more than seven years.

Given the poor chances of success, the question arises as to why managers persist in such seemingly risky and unwise activities. There are three basic reasons:

- When an alliance succeeds, the gains can be enormous, just as when a large acquisition succeeds and transforms the fortunes of the acquirer. The risk is often justified by the prospect of such a reward.

- Abandoning an alliance is not necessarily a sign of failure. The partners may both have a temporary need for collaboration and have worked out from the beginning the mechanisms for divorce when the mutual advantage has ceased to exist. For example, Honda has claimed that its alliance with Rover in the United Kingdom was a temporary convenience during the period when it was building up its presence in the United States at great expense. The alliance with Rover permitted Honda to build a presence in Europe with much less asset exposure than would otherwise have been possible. For its part, Rover gained access to Honda's design and assembly technology. When Honda had reached critical mass in North America, it could afford to go it alone in Europe and no longer needed Rover's resources. Meanwhile Rover, then State-owned, had internalized most of the lessons it learned, which resulted in a spectacular renaissance of its fortunes and made it a desirable takeover target for BMW of Germany. The alliance had served its purpose.[8]

- Managers believe that control over an operation can be maintained, not by legal contract, but by a deep relationship bred of mutual dependency. The strongest alliances, many claim, are those in which both parties (or all parties, if it is a constellation of partners) will suffer if one party pulls out of the arrangement. This mutual dependency is more far-reaching than mutual gain. The fact that the exit of one party hurts all others acts as a powerful deterrent to quitting and a powerful inducement to find ways to resolve disputes effectively in the mutual interest. Equity goes beyond reciprocity because equivalence of benefits among parties also includes sociological indebtedness (Blau, 1964). Thus, under such conditions of mutual dependency, one typically finds managers learning about how to develop new forms of working relationships with managers in other legal entities. These are new skills which may provide another dimension to the human resources base that could affect the competitiveness of the enterprise. Instead of competing on the basis of seeking dominance, alliance skills require new behaviours that emphasize harmony, balance, equity and mutual support as a means of achieving shared goals and maximizing joint value. Many managers find these skills hard to acquire.

The intensification of business competition has spurred the development of alliances in a variety of different forms. In this section, terms such as "cooperative venture", "strategic alliance" and "international joint venture" are used interchangeably (although they stand for differing arrangements). What is important is that they all fall under the category of "co-operative" business relationships, often in stark contrast to the traditional black-and-white definition of competitors. "Cooperative ventures" can be defined as a host of joint collaborative arrangements between TNCs to pursue a common goal (Morris and Hergert, 1987). They include such forms of alliances as licensing, joint ventures, R&D partnerships, joint marketing, consortia and countertrade agreements.[9]

Cooperative strategies are formalized through a variety of agreements which can be classified into two major categories: investments entailing an equity participation of the parties to an arrangement; and non-equity involvement in such agreements such as licensing, R&D collaboration, joint marketing, and supplier agreements. Many of the non-equity agreements apply only to specialized activities, not to the enterprise as a whole.

There is a steep learning curve to make alliance management effective. Often an alliance develops in stages. The so-called "first cooperate, then compete" strategy occurs when companies feel that they are not ready to compete in a particular area and therefore decide to cooperate instead, until they reach a common standard. Such cooperative moves are part of a firm's business strategy. The next mode, "cooperate while competing" occurs when, on the whole, firms compete but they decide to cooperate in a particular area in order to learn from each other and to overcome each other's weaknesses. The last mode, "cooperate among themselves and compete with others" involves companies establishing alliances and other networks or groupings just to compete with third parties.

The underlying rationale for strategic alliances is not new – business enterprises have long entered into joint ventures, licensing, franchising, equity ownership and other forms of alliances. What has changed is the reasons why companies enter into strategic alliances. Sincethe Secon World War until the 1970s, most alliances were formed either to hedge risk, especially political, and to gain access to markets. For example, a number of TNCs engaged in joint ventures with local partners in developing countries as a means of reducing political risk. The rationale was that a strong local company with sufficient clout and contacts would help reduce post-colonial resentment and forestall expropriation or other forms of political risks. Additionally, a number of countries were reluctant to give access to their domestic market unless there was some form of local involvement. This was either mandated by law or through other barriers to investment. Both these factors continue to play a role in the formation of strategic alliances. For example, the formation of various regional trading blocs (e.g. the European Community), coupled with the continuation of a host of non-tariff barriers in important markets, has led to the pursuit of strategic alliances to obtain market access. Even where there are no regulatory barriers, some alliances are designed to gain access to immobile resources within specialized clusters or specialized infrastructure. For example, all serious investors in microprocessors need to have a significant presence in Silicon Valley in order to tap the myriad sources of innovation there (the implications of these developments for the "strategic role" of the State are discussed later in section C).

With globalization, other factors are influencing the formation of strategic alliances. The global market is characterized by rapid technological change emanating from various sources. This has effectively shortened product life cycles and increased the financial risks in any new investment. Strategic alliances are "a means to expand product lines, make the company more competitive in existing markets, and to reduce the investment and time it takes to bring good ideas to our customers".[10] They play a critical role in pooling corporate knowledge, amortizing fixed costs and coping with the turbulence and uncertainty caused by discontinuous change, thus exploiting markets and/or technology and helping to define future industries. For example, Ford and Nissan, and General Motors and Isuzu were involved in co-designing and co-producing small cars for the United States markets (Goldhar and Lei, 1991).

Evidence from the survey supports these general arguments. Almost all of the companies included in the survey had developed alliances of some kind. In many cases, however, these were restricted to a few product areas with especially stringent resource needs, technology and capital. In addition, some investors had distribution alliances, a form of outsourcing. About 40 per cent of the TNCs surveyed used alliances in some developing countries. Despite the increasing number of alliances, traditional forms of equity-linked control remain the dominant means of entry into markets and the development of complex production networks.

There is an issue of timing in the interpretation of these data, as seen in the case of IBM. During the 1980s, IBM stated that it was opposed to the idea of alliances, in part for fear of creating "free-riders" out to exploit IBM technology. However, since mid-1990, IBM, like many others, has changed its policy and entered into over 600 alliances, viewing them as a means of accelerating growth in activities that would otherwise be hard to develop. For IBM, many of these new alliances are in areas of technology or market development peripheral to its main business and thus might be considered as a series of options for future development without risking loss of control in the meantime. Many of the firms surveyed were in similar positions of transition.

Licensing is, as expected, common in its usage, though a few United States investors stated forcefully that they "did not like doing it". Usually such statements reflected the long-standing fear that licensees might get a free ride on the licenser's technology and compete unfairly in the future. In the main, though, the sentiment was that licensing was a convenient alternative to investment when the economic situation dictated against asset exposure for a TNC. In some cases, licensing was seen as a positive competitive weapon, notably when applied to the use of a brand. Brand licensing and the construction of dealerships were means to trade assets with local investors and create a much stronger local market position than would be possible for either party independently.

The rapid growth of alliances has three implications for developing host countries:

- Alliances need a strong base in the law of contracts and the building of the trust that bind together the partners involved. Given the need for control (discussed later in this chapter), stability and reliability of the contract regime are essential. A transparent legal system and efficient dispute-settlement mechanisms are thus important ingredients of attractiveness.

- When groups of legally separate commercial entities act together, they can exercise a degree of competitive power together that far exceeds the importance of any one of the legal entities acting independently. Commercial law, and especially its anti-trust provisions, need to be applied carefully to take account of this new competitive reality.

- Alliances provide an additional non-equity form of resource transfer across borders. In some cases, an alliance may do no more than create new possibilities of access to foreign markets; but in others, where there is a constellation of partners (rather than simply two or three partners), the network can act to train and develop the less well equipped members.[11] In most cases, these arrangements are "invisible" to national or regulatory authorities. To the extent that they provide additional resources for growth and development, they should be encouraged and included specifically in promotional efforts.

Recognizing that business networks and alliances can provide large pay-offs, the Government of Australia initiated in 1995, a $25 million programme to promote the development of better inter-firm linkages and to train managers in the acquisition of the new skills needed to overcome the difficulties of making cooperative ventures work. This programme was modelled on earlier versions in Norway, Denmark, Spain and other places, including the State of Oregon in the United States. One particular objective of the initiative was to take more advantage of the fact that alliances with foreign firms had been assessed as being especially helpful in promoting firm-level performance and competitiveness (Bureau of Industry Economics, 1995). Developing host countries would do well to investigate such experience from other countries.

5. The imperative of control

As suggested in the previous section, participation in equity and management control are not the same thing. The investors interviewed were unanimous about the need for management control. The only exceptions were two firms (amongst the investors) with respect to their natural resource investments. For both manufacturing and service investments – and despite the growth of alliances – the dominant preference was for 100 per cent equity or a strong majority of the equity to assure control. This preference applied especially to assets and activities that were considered of central importance to the global strategy. For peripheral operations, the demands for equity control were muted or absent.

Indeed, among all the firms surveyed, only 9 per cent were prepared to relax this requirement (table II.3), but most of them limited that flexibility to countries considered to be of low strategic significance. The two exceptions both actively seeking local partners and willing to act as passive investors if necessary were both processors of natural resources. In commodity-related businesses, such policies are reasonably common, but were not strongly represented in this study due to the composition of the sample.

Table II.3. The imperative of control over strategically important assets
(Per cent of responses)

Management control essential	Management control **not** essential
91	9

Source: survey results based on responses of all TNCs.

One frequently cited rationale reflected the development of more specialized networks of international production mentioned earlier. As one machinery maker put it: "We have developed an integrated business in which, for cost control and overall efficiency, we can make and cross-ship from anywhere. Because we can now adapt quickly to changes in demand, exchange rates and regulations, we cannot afford to share control with any local partner whose interests do not match our global scope". Equally important for others was the traditional rationale of needing to defend the brand name and not risk any diminution of quality and brand value.

A few firms went so far as to say that host country requirements for local partners was a specific barrier to entry. One executive went so far as to say, "Management control is so essential for the maintenance of efficiency in our international system that we would not invest in any country where we thought we would not be able to achieve and maintain control". Another attributed a firm's refusal to invest in one country primarily to its inability to negotiate a protocol for *management* control.

Most of the surveyed firms, however, indicated that, though such policies had been common in the past, they had given way to a position where minority positions were acceptable, provided several conditions were met. First, that regulations requiring a local majority holding did not interfere with the unambiguous agreement among partners giving ultimate control and the resolution of disputes to the foreign investor. A second condition, mentioned several times, was that a minority position was acceptable provided that the articles of incorporation gave the TNC the right to buy majority ownership later. A third condition was that, though local nationals could hold top executive positions, national regulations had to permit the head office to maintain ultimate control in cases of dispute.

This demand for control challenges earlier research that suggests that European and Japanese firms are more open to joint ventures than United States firms. This survey did not reveal any differences by national origin. In part, the reason is that most research has concentrated on ownership, not on control. As shown above, the two are different. One chemical firm described its mix of foreign affiliates as wholly-owned, majority-owned and minority-owned, but claimed that "we have management control in all". A consumer goods manufacturer echoed these sentiments: "size of ownership is not necessarily important, provided management control is secured; we are a management company, not an investment house".

A further factor of importance to those negotiating the terms and conditions of entry concerns the possibility of changing ownership and control requirements over time. Many firms mentioned that they might be prepared to enter a country without managerial control, but only if they were assured this was a "stepping stone" to eventual control.[12]

The growth of strategic alliances is forcing some of the firms interviewed to reconsider their policies. As one said, "We are having to choose now between our desire to have unambiguous control and tightly integrated operations across borders and our desire to use alliances to accelerate our ability to grow and command a broader range of technologies". There were many similar indications that changes in the form of control were likely, but that the need for control of decisions remained undiluted.

The very low utilization of franchising among the surveyed firms is another illustration of the desire to maintain control, primarily through equity shares. Though franchising is common in such activities as fast foods and sporting goods, the particular sample of firms interviewed was concentrated in industries in which franchising is generally rejected as a means of servicing markets.

Natural resource investments have a different dynamic in terms of control. Sometimes a mine or plantation is owned by a consortium, membership of which is a necessary condition for access to the output. Where the primary strategic objective was that of gaining access to reliable supplies of raw materials, the demand for control was seen to be of less importance than the need for a contract guaranteeing security of supply. This is linked to the general notion of attractiveness in terms of stable supply conditions. For example, in some industries, consortia of buying firms have been formed to provide a guarantee of the scale of demand needed to justify investment in the minimum efficiency of scale facilities. An example for Brazil is in the pulp industry. Japanese investors were persuaded to collaborate in the development of a large-scale pulp mill. Membership of the consortium was desirable as it gave access to a supply stream that was difficult to get elsewhere. If a consortium can outperform the market, then collective FDI confers advantages on the investors.

These findings provide an important modification to the general statements, often repeated in official publications, that TNCs are becoming prepared to consider looser, more federal network arrangements. Though the survey generated a great deal of information that pointed towards a much greater degree of flexibility and accommodation to the volatility of international markets and the special needs of local markets, the desire for control persists.

Control and flexibility can go together in new management systems. Indeed the evidence that emerges from the survey is that the drive for efficiency is so strong in global markets that few can afford to compromise on the location of ultimate authority to set the rules of engagement. Basically, there are major problems associated with managing investments from a distance. The influence of the various levels in the hierarchy and regions is the determining factor. Given the subjectivity involved, and the differing structures of control, the outcome in each case is different and Governments cannot adopt general policies that are applicable across the board; the need for strategic targeting cannot be overemphasized.

6. Maintaining consistency of purpose

The sheer dynamism of the market and the existence of countervailing forces provide conditions under which maintaining a consistent balance among competing pressures has become a central challenge for TNCs. Clever strategies can become ineffective if the dilemmas are not adequately resolved, breeding confusion and allowing managers to work at cross-purposes. Part of the difficulties stem from the fact that the calculations of global strategy and, for instance, the form of specialization may make sense in some territories but not in others. Another is the sheer difficulty of communicating complex messages to large and scattered cadres of managers. Inconsistencies can easily arise between a manager in the parent firm and foreign affiliate managers, among the foreign affiliates themselves or even across corporate functions.

Inconsistencies introduced into hierarchies that are not internally monolithic have important implications for public officials. Who can provide reliable information about the direction and purpose of an enterprise? Local managers are not necessarily the best source, for they may be misinformed. They may also disagree with corporate policy and use official conversations to influence an internal debate. Though such fears may easily be exaggerated, they are nonetheless real. During the survey, several disagreements surfaced and different versions of future policy in Brazil were offered. Thus, care in the interpretation of evidence is, as always, necessary.

Part of the problem has to do with whose perspective is most important. A general issue has been the consequence of the many moves to slim down TNCs' global product portfolios during the 1980s. Their objective was to concentrate on those product lines for which corporate management felt they had or could create a comparative advantage. Yet the effect was sometimes the elimination of products that had strong positions in some national markets with a result that local assets were sold for reasons that had nothing to do with the attractiveness or otherwise of the host country. In some cases, this had a negative effect on the sequence of developments in host countries, again with no reference to local conditions. The example of GE in Brazil (box II.2) shows what can happen if consistency is lost. It also indicates the range of sophistication needed for a public official to be able to interpret data accurately from corporate sources. It is not sufficient to take a purely host country's perspective on the information; it is also essential to place local information within the context of a TNC's global position.

Box II.2. General Electric in Brazil

A study by Bartlett and Ghoshal (1989) described GE's history as follows:

"In the early 1960s, GE's Brazilian subsidiary proposed becoming a low-cost source for GE's radios in the United States. The parent company responded that GE was de-emphasizing radios and urged the subsidiary to focus instead on colour TV, which was due to boom in the Brazilian market. GE Brazil complied. After the introduction of colour TV in the mid-1960s, Japanese manufacturers streamed into Brazil, setting up plants in the low-labour-cost and tax-free northern region of Manaus. Despite its leadership position in Brazil, GE was not willing to develop the German PAL technology that had been adopted as the Brazilian transmission standard, or to relocate its plants to Manaus. By 1968, the company had decided to exit the TV business and focus on its attractive major appliances and housewares businesses.

GE had also been the first entrant in refrigeration and air conditioning in Brazil, importing products until the late 1950s, when local assembly was established. By the 1970s, with GE's Brazilian sales approaching $500 million, strong local competitors started taking share. Reviewing the detailed strategic plans that were now central to GE's decision-making process, corporate management became concerned about declining share, fluctuating demand, price controls, and aggressive competition in its Brazilian appliance business. Judging the product line and manufacturing efficiency to be vulnerable to global competition, they decided to withdraw from this business in 1981, and encouraged local management to concentrate on its strong position in the Brazilian housewares market.

In the Welch era, GE managers were forced to evaluate businesses on the basis of their global competitive position. In a last ditch effort to bring costs in line with those of Far Eastern competitors, the company launched its 'World Iron Project', a bold experiment in competition in small appliances. Brazil and two other global-scale plants in low-labour-cost countries became the company's worldwide sources for irons. But in the Welch era, unless a business was number one or two in its industry worldwide, it was divested. A couple of years after the global iron project was initiated, corporate management sold its worldwide housewares business to Black and Decker.

Over a twenty-year period, the Brazilian company's dominant position in a broad line of consumer products had evaporated. The fundamental problem was that its managers had no idea, from one year to the next, what their role was in the overall corporate strategy. The lack of commitment and consistency led to the gradual weakening and eventual abandonment of GE's consumer businesses worldwide" (p. 179).

More recently, GE has announced far-reaching plans for a new form of global strategy. Part of this repeats the concentration and scale-building changes tried our in the "World Iron Project". Part of the change, though, has been in terms of how GE manages its businesses. There have been large investments in new processes, such as "work-outs", and new forms of communication, all designed to ensure a greater degree of consistency of purpose worldwide. One consequence is that GE has located many of its operations within an intricate and complex network, making each unit more protected (at least in the short term) from variations in local conditions.

The importance and indeed the possibility of consistency and commitment to a strategic direction for growth is amply illustrated by Unilever's long-standing general philosophy. This was summed up by the then Chairperson in a speech in 1983 to employees as: "If someone were to ask me to say in one word what aspect we devote most attention to in managing this company, my answer would be 'continuity'. Rather than short-lived successes we must set our sights on profitability over the long term. The interests of a very large number of people are directly or indirectly dependent on our company's continuity" (p. 179).

His successor, Floris Maljers, expressed the same idea more colourfully in speaking of the company's enduring commitment to Brazil, despite volatile swings that had caused others to leave: "In those parts of the world you take your management cues from the way they dance. The samba method of management requires you to take two steps forward, then one step back. Companies with a short-term perspective are unable to adopt this perspective. They will either not get on the dance floor because it looks too difficult or risky -- as was the case with Procter & Gamble which has never entered Brazil, despite numerous opportunities -- or they will choose to sit down when it comes to the part that involves one step back -- as our other competitor Henkel recently did, selling its Brazilian business to us" (p. 180).

Source: UNCTAD.

7. Developing firm-specific configurations

The thrust of the argument so far is that TNCs increasingly are being propelled into finding unique and innovative solutions to the challenge of building their next-generation competitiveness. These developments are calling into question the conventional wisdom that there is a "dominant recipe" for success in an industry. They need to be clearly understood by policy makers, otherwise data on industry dynamics can easily be misinterpreted.

The search for unique, firm-specific configurations of resources means that TNCs not only see different priorities in the shifting global markets, but act differently, even in the same industry. The result is that, for example, the general tendency of greater ties between trade and FDI (discussed in chapter I) mask developments in opposite directions. These issues are discussed below to indicate the importance of understanding corporate strategy in some detail as one of the foundations for dealings with TNCs in host countries.

(a) Varying spurs to invest abroad

A more liberal trade and investment regime has made greater specialization economically more feasible for TNCs. Though all the surveyed firms talked about specialization, their motivations for doing so varied. For some, it was a case of "simply reducing total costs by specializing local output, cross-shipping and betting that obstacles to trade will not be imposed". For others, liberalization has "opened up new market segments. We are growing rapidly where we can (profitably) add new products with greater adaptation to local needs". For yet others, national borders have become irrelevant as a way to calculate market segments. As one put it, "We can now build whole new businesses by combining market niches in, say, Moscow, Saõ Paulo, Tokyo and Washington. Each is too small to be viable on a stand-alone basis. Only by low-cost combination can we make these new businesses work".

Among a range of driving forces for more FDI, industry effects (such as sensitivity to cost pressures) do not seem to play a discernible role in influencing the range of the ratings of importance (table II.4). This suggests that strategic perspectives condition how executives calculate their investments.

(b) Variety in industry "recipe"

Table II.4. Dynamic drivers of FDI

(Per cent)

Driver	High	Medium	Low
Matching competitors' actions	78	16	7
New/shifting consumer needs	75	14	11
Changes in government regulation	60	27	13
Deregulation	56	25	19
Shifting input costs/ availability of inputs	54	26	20
New technologies	48	18	34
Privatization	47	21	32
Emergence of new industry segments	36	21	43

Source: survey results, based on responses from all TNCs.

Note: Per cent refers to the number of TNCs with each score (high, medium or low) for each driver.

The generally high importance given to "competitors' actions" (table II.4) should not be taken as evidence of imitation in investment planning. On the contrary, the impact of associated investments in oligopolies, discussed in chapter I, appears to be declining. Earlier theories (e.g. Knickerbocker, 1973) that TNCs in strong oligopolies will match each other in all key markets need to be re-examined in the light of changing competitive imperatives. In the survey, less than half of the investors in high-technology industries practiced oligopoly matching (table II.5). A much lower proportion did so in low-technology industries and (as might be expected) neither of the two firms in natural resource extraction and processing felt that competitors' investments were an especially strong influence on their own choices.

These responses suggest that the need for firms to make choices of investment priority according to their own internal capabilities and resources is stronger than ever. Especially in the low-technology category, which includes many industries that are also capital intensive, the need for resource rationing is acute. Few firms, if any, can afford to be in all markets. Consequently, though the need to match competitors remains strong in many industries (semiconductors is a good example), other strategic requirements are equally important, complicating the decision-making process and underscoring the needs, discussed earlier, for clarity and consistency in making choices.

Table II.5. Oligopolistic "matching" is no longer the norm

(Number of firms)

Sector	Yes	No	Total
Natural resources	0	2	2
Low-technology	2	7	9
High-technology	6	8	14
TOTAL	8	17	25

Source: survey data based on corporate responses from TNCs established in Brazil. In some cases, the responses apply to particular product categories.

Note: the survey asked whether matching major competitors' actions in all markets was a reason for FDI.

(c) Changing ties between FDI and trade

The evidence of chapter I, that trade and FDI have become much more closely intertwined as a result of the changes in the global competitive environment, provides the general background for the data presented here. Because the impact of globalization has not been uniform across industries, it is important that the export practices of the investors surveyed is assessed in ways that add to the understanding of the range of their experiences and perspectives on such issues.

The survey asked how TNCs were developing their internal trade policies. The data collected was not comprehensive because of either restrictions of confidentiality or lack of readily retrievable information. Thus, the evidence presented here (table II.6) is no more than impressionistic. It does, however, sketch a picture entirely consistent with the earlier discussion on how strategies of specialization affect trade arrangements, and it illustrates the wide range of outcomes.

Evidence from elsewhere suggests that there should be strong industry effects, as for example in the EU.[13] However, the arguments in preceding sections about how firm strategies have been evolving within industries provide an alternative interpretation. None of the possible ways of analysing the data reveals strong industry effects. The quality of the data most probably obscures the industry effects, owing to lack of detailed evidence on the extent and direction of trade. What is striking, though, is the incidence of trade by firms in industries, such as household products, where investment is the predominant mode of servicing foreign markets.

The survey data suggest that the development of export trade from foreign affiliates has gone much further in developed than in developing countries (table II.6). To understand the data in the charts, consider first the European investors. Five companies stated that they exported

Table II.6. Ties between trade and FDI: exports by foreign affiliates

(Number of companies)

A. Exports from host developed countries

Home country of TNCs	Number of companies exporting from foreign affiliates in developed countries			
	All foreign affiliates	Numerous foreign affiliates	A few foreign affiliates	One foreign affiliate or none
Europe	5	3	1	1
Japan	-	-	5	1
United States	-	7	2	1

	Host countries from which more than 50 per cent of output was exported			
	United States	United Kingdom	Japan	Other EU
Europe	1	2	1	3
Japan	1	1	-	-
United States	N/A	2	1	10

B. Exports from host developing countries

Home country of TNCs	Number of companies exporting from foreign affiliates in developing countries			
	All foreign affiliates	Numerous foreign affiliates	A few foreign affiliates	One foreign affiliate or none
Europe	-	1	6	1
Japan	-	2	3	2
United States	-	1	9	-

	Host countries from which more than 50 per cent output was exported			
	Brazil	Mexico	Asia	Other
Europe	1	1	1	-
Japan	-	2	6	-
United States	3	1	2	3

Source: survey results of TNCs established in Brazil.

Note: figures apply to corporate behaviour, supplemented by some data for specific product categories.

from all the developed countries in which they had manufacturing facilities; three exporters from numerous, but not all, of the developed countries in which they had invested, only one European company indicated that it exported from only a few developed countries, and one had created no export trade from any foreign manufacturing affiliate. When asked whether any of those countries' operations exported more than 50 per cent of the local output – either of the whole or part of their product range – three European companies claimed that they had at least one foreign affiliate from which 50 per cent of output was exported. These firms favoured Europe and in particular the United Kingdom for their export-oriented projects.

The opposite effect might be expected in developing countries, namely more exporting. The explanation for the behaviour of the European firms has much to do with the development of regional bases of specialized investment and growing cross-shipment within the regions (see chapter I). This is one of the fundamental bases for the growth of much intra-industry trade and FDI. Given the fact that European investors have been slower than others to invest in Asia, their trade in specialized supply from such sources would be expected to be less well established.

The same arguments apply to the evidence from the United States investors. None of them claimed to export from all the developed countries where they manufacture, though seven have significant exports from numerous developed countries. One stated that it also exported from numerous developing countries. Many United States firms had created extensive networks of specialized output across Europe. Ford, for example, has a much publicized European network.

The effect of regional origin has some bearing on the outcomes, but why this should be so is a matter of speculation. The Japanese firms shared a different perspective in that none of them had created exports from all or even numerous foreign affiliates in developed countries. Their export behaviour remained centred on exports from Japan, and export supply from the rapidly growing manufacturing foreign affiliates was still in its infancy. There were, however, important exceptions in the development of exports from Asian facilities, as the discussion in chapter I indicated. Many Japanese manufacturers had created extensive, cost-reducing regional networks to serve Japan and the Asian region. The offshore plants were primarily for component production, though a few had started to open up these networks to a more integrated global pattern of finished-goods specialization and cross-shipping (Stopford, 1997b). Firms included in the survey were representative of these trends. Their specialized plants, which exported more than half of their output, were clustered primarily in Asia, and two had built *maquiladora* plants in Mexico to serve the North American market.

This highlights the fact that moves towards extensive specialization have had a pronounced impact on export development and that these trends are more pervasive in developed than in developing countries. The Asian trends – as well as the creation of the MERCOSUR in Latin America – have been acting, however, to reduce this asymmetry. It is noticeable that Brazil features as frequently among the surveyed companies as does Mexico (table II.6). This may be due to a bias in the sample, but even so it is striking, especially considering that many firms reported much of their export stream from Brazil was going mainly to countries other than the United States.

(d)   *Research and development*

Consistent with the earlier arguments about the development of global networks in intangibles, the surveyed firms reported a high frequency of internationally distributed R&D laboratories. Indeed, research for 20 out of 29 product categories was undertaken in three or more developed countries (table II.7). Only three firms had not built a foreign R&D facility for any of their product lines. In some cases, the foreign research work was focused on development, leaving the more fundamental research to be carried out in the original home facilities. Though no specific information was collected on the history of these specialized investments, there was considerable evidence that many

Table II.7. TNCs undertaking R&D abroad

(Number of countries in which R&D is carried out)

Area	None	One or two	Three or more
Developed countries	3	6	20
Developing countries	14	12	2

Source: survey results of TNCs established in Brazil.

Note: the data are based on lines of business, where applicable.

of them were fairly recent. For all the investors, a primary motivation was the need to gain access to R&D clusters and the related, immobile resources surrounding such clusters. For example, NEC and Toshiba operated telecommunications laboratories near Princeton and the Bell Labs (now Lucent Technologies); Texas Instruments had a facility in Tsukuba Science City; and most electronics firms had facilities in Silicon Valley.

Understandably, the trend was not as pronounced in developing countries. Yet half of the sample firms undertook research in at least one developing country, and three had an extensive network of laboratories. For some of the United States firms, for example, the primary driving force had been the increasing possibility of lowering total research costs, but their laboratories in developing countries were intended for development and product adaptation rather than for pure science or basic research.

Noticeable in the sample of major investors in Brazil was that eight of them had R&D laboratories in Brazil, more than reported for any other similar country. In a few cases, this reflected corporate policy to locate development work alongside all manufacturing facilities. No precise data were obtained as to the motivation for these investments, for the respondents did not seem to be aware of these. However, the impression form the evidence suggests that at least some of the eight had created the laboratories in the expectation that Brazil would become the hub for the Latin American region and the lead player in setting the pace for regional product adaptation. It was noticeable that none of the Japanese firms had located research in Brazil by the time of the interviews, but the trends suggest that they might follow the lead of United States firms and some European ones by developing more extensive networks of R&D facilities around the world.

C. The strategic role of the State

A useful framework for assessing global competition in terms of the crucial interaction between Governments and firms in a globalizing world economy is the notion of "triangular diplomacy" (figure II.7) (Stopford and Strange, 1991). In this model, State-firm bargaining is regarded as central to international economic and business interactions. The growth of global competition is conditioned more by new types of commercial diplomacy and managerial technocracy than by the traditional definitions of state power and adversarial relations with TNCs.

The competing national and international forces in the global political economy are located on the sides of the triangle (figure II.7). One side of the triangle represents the interaction between Governments that are competing internationally for the resources that will create wealth and economic growth. While earlier the focus was essentially on competition, underwritten by "beggar-thy-neighbour" and "zero-sum-game" attitudes, lately there has been a pronounced shift towards the use of cooperative instruments, such as bilateral and multilateral treaties and the creation of trade blocs to maximize the gains from interactions between Governments. Inherent in such a shift towards cooperation is a paradox. This is because, in a trading bloc, one of the countries might turn out to be more attractive as an investment site and might attract the bulk of investment, at the expense of the other countries in the bloc.

The other side of the triangle represents the interaction between Governments and firms. The nature of this interaction has changed qualitatively, especially in the context of developing countries. Until the late 1970s, primarily for ideological reasons, the rhetoric of the day cast TNCs in the role of predators that maximized their gains at the expense of the developing

Figure II.7. Triangular diplomacy

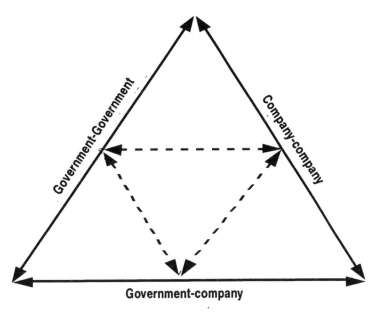

Source: Stopford and Strange, 1991, p. 22.

countries. Policy in many developing countries was, to be sure, a different and more pragmatic affair. The rhetoric, however, cannot be dismissed lightly, for it had the potential to influence official attitudes. But in the recent past, there has been a clear shift in attitudes, and TNCs are seen as a vital component in the development of the domestic economy, both in terms of internal industrial growth and the promotion of exports. The rapid growth of the South-East Asian economies (characterized by close ties between government and industry, and, in some of these countries, such as Singapore, by the critical role of TNCs in capital formation and exports) have contributed to this shift in attitude. More generally, the worldwide movement to embrace more fully market forces as a means to wealth creation has helped stimulate more favourable attitudes towards TNCs. The relationship remains marked by caution, however, because the degree of benefits associated with it is subject to various influences, including government policies.

The third side of the triangle represents interaction among firms. The global political economy is a product of competition and cooperation along the three sides of the triangle – the outcome of each influencing the other – and is dependent on the balance of power among the various actors in the economy. The fundamental point of the framework is that change on one side of the triangle affects the other two sides, but often in unexpected ways, and across industry boundaries. A good example of this is the interaction between the United States and Brazil; because of perceived market-access restrictions, the Government of the United States threatened Brazil with a Super 301 trade sanction within the aircraft industry. Brazil in turn conceded, revising its informatics law to allow information-technology transfers to Brazil. What started as a State-State dispute in one industry created changes that significantly affected the company-company relationships in another industry, namely automobile. The liberalization in informatics, which allowed the import of new production-control technologies to be deployed in Brazil enabled the production of a new generation of automobile engines sufficiently advanced in technical terms and at sufficiently low costs to create a new stream of exports from Brazil.

The recent shifts in attitudes combined with a competition for FDI has led to a new appreciation of the role of the positive power of the State to assist TNCs in building competitiveness resulting in national economic gain. By appreciating the plurality of TNCs' strategies, host Governments can focus on consistently building up those resources that are attractive to TNCs. In the context of interactions in the global economy, Governments can make strategic choices that will affect the international strategies of firms (i.e. they can cause firms to take actions that depart from their previously established strategic criteria). The Government could adopt an industrial strategy, characterized by coherence and consistency in economic policies, so as to allocate resources with intent to meet long-term economic objectives. The ability of the State to influence is a function of target specificity, policy credibility and the institutional arrangements necessary to operationalize and manage the policies. Since the Government has to focus on the overall development of its economy, it may offer incentives and disincentives to TNCs, depending on its strategic goals. In some industries, the Government might insist on local participation; in others, it might offer incentives and guarantees to promote investments and exports. The success of the Government in influencing TNCs is a function of the attractiveness of the entire package that it has to offer. For example, the very size of China's market is enough to influence TNC investment pattern, as exemplified by the fact that a number of TNCs that do not accept joint ventures in other countries are willing to enter into joint ventures there.

A Government can, in addition to creating the basic conditions that are necessary for firms to compete, adopt proactive policies that will help firms cultivate competencies that are vital in an interdependent international economy. These proactive policies need to fit into the framework of an overall economic policy. A key question is whether that policy is designed to encourage local firms to catch up with leaders at the global level, or whether it is to exploit natural advantages and galvanize existing assets into new life. The distinction is important for it has a bearing on the form of appropriate public investments. Japan's catch-up policies worked well for many years, but are less appropriate today in the defence of leadership roles and rapidly changing technologies such as digital switching in telecommunications and high definition television (HDTV). Countries, such as Australia and Canada, have employed quite different policy mixes to find new ways to capture dynamic benefits from their natural resources. Once Canada had abolished its Foreign Investment Review Agency (which many regarded as a barrier to leading-edge FDI), attention shifted to building highly specialized business and non-business infrastructures.[14]

Brazil appears to have numerous natural advantages that can be exploited by means of proactive policies. There are, for example, strategic advantages to be had from its unique possession of a large share of the world's tropical pharmacopoeia. These, surely, can be deployed to change the bargaining power with TNCs, to the advantage of both sides, just as in alliance management, the objective is to reach a win-win position, not for one party to seek to dominate the other. The installed base of capacity in chemicals and electrical machinery is another resource that could be harnessed in novel ways to create new wealth.

Such approaches differ importantly from the traditional role of government intervention in the form of infant-industry protection. There the objective has been to focus on a specific industry and to ensure that it receives protection to "grow up" before being exposed to competition. Such a focus today can be risky, for policies dependent on "picking winners" depend upon forecasts that are very difficult to make, given the turbulence of competitive rules and the demand for diversity in today's global business environment. Instead, Governments in such countries as Canada, New Zealand, Spain and Singapore move away from being primary actors and experiment to find ways to become "orchestrators" of resources.

As an orchestrator, a Government increasingly relies on firms, whether local or foreign, to take centre-stage in creating wealth. The State remains an important provider of the market-friendly assets of general education, technical skills and infrastructure. But, because every country is doing much the same thing, these general assets are becoming commodities that by themselves do not create superior wealth. For these resources to become part of durable wealth creation, they have to be turned into specialities that are hard for others to emulate (Stopford, 1997b, p. 478).

The drive to turn general resources into specialized ones is seen most visibly and most effectively in the emergence of clusters of resources, as in Silicon Valley or the City of London. These clusters have to be carefully nurtured, with public policy designed to be in harmony with market forces, otherwise expensive failures (as in some petrochemical developments) are likely to result.

Perhaps paradoxically, a liberalizing world economy has strengthened the forces that lead firms to cluster together in particular locations. Obvious examples include the entertainment business around Hollywood and specialized machinery in Baden-Württemberg in Germany. Three factors have been identified as being behind industrial clustering (Krugman, 1991):

- The congregating of a large number of firms of the same industry creates a pool of skilled workers. In industries with increasing returns, economies of scale encourage the concentration of activities in one or a few places.

- The concentration of industries spawns a greater number of specialized local suppliers, thereby providing greater variety at lower cost.

- In industries in which the flow of information is vital, and is better over shorter distances, clustering has advantages in the transmission of knowledge between firms.

Thus, central to the logic of geographical clustering is the effort to maximize the benefits from knowledge externalities or spillovers; the sharing of knowledge with others involved in R&D by a firm reflects R&D spillovers, as a firm does not pay for that information in a market transaction. In such a cluster, the cost and burdens of R&D needed to create innovation are shared by networks of regional participants, which include firms, suppliers, the regional work force, universities and research institutes, and government bodies.

This clustering of industries is one of the key factors that has led to the emergence of "poles of growth". These growth areas provide a locus of pooled talent and an environment that encourages the growth of industries that are critical to economic success in the coming millennium.

In the context of dynamic comparative advantage, the Government of Brazil (or any other host country) could play a strategic role by making a concerted effort to nurture specific locations that will attract clusters of related industries. By adopting a holistic policy, encouraging universities, research centres and local authorities to coordinate their efforts with firms, the Government can create an environment that will attract investment and self-sustaining clusters of economic growth. It should be emphasized that wealth-creating clusters apply equally to high- and low-technology industries. Italy, for example, has important clusters of specialized resources in Emilia-Romagna for textiles and ceramics that have given them great export advantages over competitors which have relied on firm-specific scale and ignored the externalities needed to create regional dynamism.

The pervasive nature of the potential for clusters has led to a growing disparity between mobile and immobile factors of production. In such a milieu, it is imperative for the Government to appreciate the factors that are critical in different points of an industry and to determine what is driving their constant changes. The problem for a number of developing countries is that they might be stuck with "wrong" factors in the context of specific industries which will prove to be a handicap in attracting investments. This problem is compounded by the constraints of the extant political economy that might stall efforts to cultivate the necessary factors for attracting investments. The challenge is to find a balance that permits skills to migrate among industries and thereby stimulates a continuous upgrading of skills and the performance levels of service providers – the key to durable competitiveness.

D. Conclusion

The liberalizing and globalizing world economy has spurred TNCs increasingly to drive for dynamic growth as the main strategic objective. To do this, they have either to exploit the locational attractiveness of different countries that are seeking FDI, and/or to enter into strategic alliances to overcome the various resource shortcomings that constrain growth. In such an environment, the strategies of manufacturing TNCs are evolving from those based on stand-alone foreign affiliates to those based on simple integration strategies, and further, towards strategies determined by complex integration and network-type linkages, leading to the emergence of integrated international production systems. While the liberalization of international transactions and the emergence of new information technologies have created an enabling regulatory and technical framework for international integrated production system, the resulting intensified competitive pressures are forcing TNCs to adjust their global and regional strategies and organizational forms to the requirements of greater efficiency.

In an integrated international production system, the role of affiliates changes: they are looked upon as a potential source of efficiency for the corporate system as a whole, and as units in intra-firm international division of labour, be it for the large-scale (and therefore more efficient) production of a material component for a final product assembled elsewhere, or a service needed for the whole network or as the leading unit holding a world-product mandate. As a result, specialization among affiliates is becoming increasingly functional: not only a component of the final product, but also any information-based function (such as the management of a regional network or services such as data processing and accounting) can be assigned to a foreign affiliate or outsourced or subcontracted to a firm controlled through non-equity arrangements.

Partly as a result of these developments, but also independently from them, TNCs increasingly need to be seen as systems extending beyond the legal limits of the traditional firm. These systems have three essential components:

- headquarters, acting as the coordinating body and the accumulator and controller of central resources, such as cash, brand names and intellectual property, that provide the benefits of corporate scale;

- the network of domestic and foreign affiliates providing goods and services; and

- with varying degrees of operational integration, the related network of suppliers of parts, components or services.

The implication of this is that each member of the corporate system has privileged access to the resources of the system as a whole, as well as to the market it represents.

As TNCs increasingly specialize their location preferences (figure II.8) and divide up the value chain (as indicated in chapter I), parts of the corporate system migrate to locations where the global competitive advantage of each activity can be maximized (Williamson and Hu, 1994). Governments need to take into account how these recent developments affect the kinds of resources needed to foster the specialized clusters that give greatest advantage to the specialized investor.

Three major factors are driving changes in TNCs' location strategies, each making it increasingly possible to separate supply from the market, not simply as it used to be in terms of an export strategy, but in complex forms of related transfers:

- The requirements for local support services for the specialist needs of particular TNC activities can be more important than the general needs of the TNC as a whole. Thus, for the design and R&D activities, the provision of appropriate local services (for laboratories and drafting offices, for example) can be more influential in the location decision than the density of demand for finished products.

- Communication and other local infrastructures for linking up the various activities of a TNC and creating the advantages of corporate scale are becoming increasingly important in location decisions.

- Firms typically need high-quality and cost-competitive support services in the form of high-quality subcontractors or shared facilities. These services may be more important in their effect on total system cost than, for example, the local costs of an assembly operation.

Figure II.8. The decoupling of TNC activities

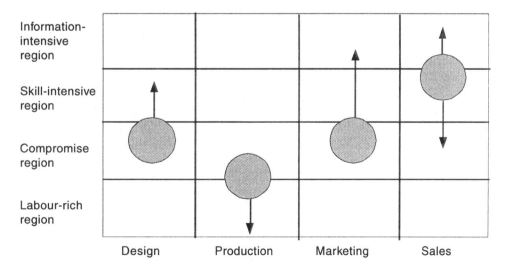

Source: Williamson and Hu, 1994.

Any attempt to understand the way in which TNCs think about the attractiveness of specific locations should include an appreciation of the shift in the locus of "power" in the context of Government-TNC interaction. In an environment characterized by intra- and inter-regional competition to attract FDI, in which resource-constrained TNCs are spoilt for choice between equally attractive locations in different parts of the world and their decisions are governed by the dictates of efficiency and adaptability in an integrated production strategy, the balance of power has shifted towards TNCs. Given their strategic importance, the perceptions of TNCs about the different choices of location have a critical influence on their investment decisions. Governments can enhance their competitiveness by adopting proactive policies that help create locations in which a cluster of specialized firms can grow. For these poles of growth to emerge, there is a need for pooled talent and an environment that encourages the growth of industries, specialized infrastructure and research centres.

Such proactive policies can be slow to take effect if they replace previous policies of protectionism or a period of inconsistent policy choices and general economic instability. Firms require time to become convinced that the changes are durable. Moreover, given the competing claims for the attention of top management and the inevitable need to alter internal priorities and operational routines, the effects of hysteresis have to be taken into account.

It is in the context of these general strategic changes that the particular circumstances of Brazil are examined in the next chapter. The tests of relative attractiveness at both national and regional levels are critical to support and extend the current upswing of inward investment.

Notes

[1] In some tables, the data are reported on the basis of responses applying to specific product lines, rather than a corporate average. There are important industry differences, and corporate policy in diversified TNCs often reflects those differences in both policy and asset configuration around the world.

[2] For details, see Stopford and Turner, 1985, p. 230.

[3] This section is based on UNCTAD, 1993a.

[4] For detailed examples and analysis, see Stopford, 1992.

[5] European investors may be undergoing a similar process as regards FDI in Asia; see European Commission and UNCTAD, 1996.

[6] Source: private communication.

[7] For evidence and a discussion of how alliances are affecting competitive structures, see Yoshiko and Rangan, 1995.

[8] Source: private communication.

[9] A substantial literature has evolved around these issues. For example, Contractor and Lorange (1988) introduced a model for cooperative ventures, Borys and Jemison (1989) introduced certain propositions with respect to hybrid structures of strategic alliances, and Ohmae (1989) pointed out the necessity for strategic alliances across the regional trading blocs of Europe, United States and Asia. Perlmutter and Heenan (1986) echoed the sentiments of most of today's TNCs that, increasingly, to be globally competitive, these corporations must be globally "cooperative". International business reality now calls for a more realistic discussion of what competition or cooperation means between companies within an industry.

[10] The President of General Electric, quoted in Collins and Doorley, 1991.

[11] For some details of how these networks operate, see Gomes-Casseres, 1996, and Lorenzoni and Baden-Fuller, 1995.

[12] In all such cases, the firms required control worldwide.

[13] For some details, see Stopford, 1992.

[14] For a detailed exploration of the distinctions and the policy challenges, see Stopford, 1997b.

CHAPTER III

THE DETERMINANTS OF FOREIGN DIRECT INVESTMENT AND BRAZIL'S RELATIVE ATTRACTIVENESS

In this chapter, the focus of attention is to link the analysis of firms' strategies discussed in chapter II to the overall patterns discussed in chapter I, so as to explore the particular circumstances and considerations that affect the flow of FDI to Brazil. Part of the discussion is based on the realization that the historically important factors influencing FDI decisions have been significantly altered by the changes in TNC strategy described in chapter II. The dynamic forces at work in a period of transition make it difficult to test theoretical arguments with certainty. Nonetheless, there is sufficient evidence from the survey to suggest that Brazil faces a great opportunity to build on the recent upturn in the trend line and to sustain or even further increase the flow of inward FDI. The survey data from major TNCs that have not yet invested significantly in Brazil are particularly important, for they indicate both the crucial importance of managerial choice and the difficulty in shifting to new priorities.

The managerial themes of choice, the sequencing of investment, and the changing form of global networks should be balanced against the economic reasons why investors choose when and where to invest. Although countries now compete directly with one another for investors' attention, one observer commented only a few years ago that "Brazil has managed its image poorly. We have been unable to show the world that we are a good credit risk" (Kanitz, 1995, p. 30). That was changing by the mid-1990s for portfolio and especially for inward FDI flows, though the financial crisis of 1998 discouraged portfolio flows.

The chapter first reviews the recent history of inward FDI to Brazil. This sets the scene for an exploration of the changing balance of forces affecting FDI decisions. In general terms, the data show that investors regard Brazil to be akin to other large developing markets. However, the development of the Southern Common Market, the MERCOSUR, presents Brazil with a particular opportunity to become the regional hub for some types of investments. A further enhancement and sustainment of Brazil's attractiveness to investors depends critically on the development of a variety of factors consonant with the changing emphasis in TNCs' corporate strategies and with the role of government in influencing the investment climate.

TNCs place particular emphasis on the following factors when considering investment in Brazil:

- **Large deposits of natural resources.** Brazil contains abundant reserves of many minerals that could be exploited, provided the types of provision discussed in chapter I are made available. Note that natural resources do not feature strongly in the data that follow, because the sample included very few natural resource investors.

- **The large size of the domestic market.** Market-seeking investors find Brazil's large domestic market an attraction. However, large size alone is not a sufficient condition for investment. Investors, and especially many of the non-investors, included in the survey, are becoming more selective in their choices of sites and are seeking those that offer freedom to operate internally with the minimum of bureaucratic intervention.

- **A stable regulatory and macroeconomic environment.** All investors, and especially those seeking efficiency gains, are attracted to countries with a stable macroeconomic environment. Further, an increasing number of TNCs are looking for consistency in policy agendas and over time. Such consistency is usually associated with investors' confidence in the transparency of the public process.

- **Growth and productivity prospects.** Both market- and efficiency-seeking investors give preference to regions where growth prospects make it easier to justify investments that have delayed pay-offs in terms of building efficiencies for the world-wide system or in terms of creating new forms of specialization. The expectation of growing productivity is an important variable in the choice.

- **The freedom to operate and control.** Efficiency-seeking investors give preference to countries that permit relative freedom to operate across borders. This preference reflects the need to optimize the system globally, especially when corporate scale and highly specialized investments for supply across borders are crucial. Freedom to operate, both domestically and internationally, is closely associated with the need investors feel to control their own strategies. Control needs are heightened as TNCs develop strategies that employ strategic alliances as a means to accumulate new resources quickly. Countries with legal systems that discourage control from being exercised through contracts may receive less investment than those with more transparent legal systems.

- **A well-developed infrastructure and human capital.** Investors tend to give preference to countries that can supply certain external benefits such as resource-strengthening services, specialized and efficient infrastructure and human capital that accelerate the ability of the local affiliate to absorb new technologies.

- **The availability of local suppliers and a good business climate.** Similarly, they give preference to markets where there is a strong climate of competition and dynamic local suppliers. Government attitudes and general policies towards business, both local and foreign, are regarded by many investors as important.

- **The acceptable risk of entry.** Potential investors in Brazil are likely to invest only when they are convinced that the costs of both economic and "psychic "distance have been reduced to acceptable levels. In this respect, the survey data can be taken to imply that the success of those already operating in the country will provide an important *demonstration effect*. Reinforcing the success of incumbents and helping to publicize that success thus becomes an important aspect of government's role in fostering a welcoming climate for investors.

It must be emphasized that these factors are determined by investors' attitudes and opinions, although these opinions are not always consistent across firms as discussed below. Where possible, attention is drawn to differences in industry effects or in investment motivation that explain such seeming inconsistencies. Moreover, investors are not always consistent in their views. Even though they demand of government the need for stability, consistency and transparency, they may not always take their own medicine. Furthermore, as noted in box II.1, due to changes that have taken place since the interviews (which were held in spring 1996) some of the concerns of foreign investors are no longer relevant. Finally, it should be noted that, in this chapter, the emphasis is on the views of the investors, which may or may not represent clear perceptions of appropriate policy or real conditions. Thus, this chapter makes no statement about appropriate policy. The purpose is to inform policy makers about investors' perspectives and beliefs, for these may drive the decisions more than the "facts" as perceived by others.

A. Recent trends in FDI flows into Brazil

⌈ Brazil was, until 1979, by far the single largest host country among developing countries to inflows of FDI. In addition, its accumulated stock of inward FDI was the largest among developing countries, which was the seventh largest in the world. From that impressive base the country's share in developing countries' inflows declined sharply (figure III.1) during what many regard as the "lost decade" of the 1980s. While some investment continued during the 1980s (figure III.2), much of it is thought to have been investment needed to service the existing stock. Many prospective new investors surveyed were apparently deterred by the high rates of inflation, the debt problem spiralling out of control, political instability and a society that sometimes appeared to be hostile to foreigners.

Figure III.1. Share of Brazil in FDI inflows to developing countries, 1970-1998

(Per cent)

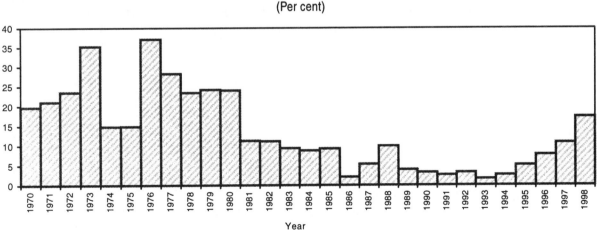

Year

Source: UNCTAD, FDI/TNC database.

Figure III.2. FDI inflows into Brazil, 1970-1998

(Billions of dollars)

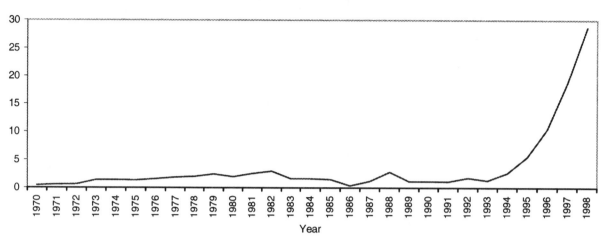

Source: UNCTAD, FDI/TNC database.

In 1990, Brazil attracted less than $1 billion of inward FDI, representing less than half of the flow in 1979 and only one third of that in 1982. Since 1995, however, inflows began to increase sharply, doubling to $9.6 billion in 1996 and reaching almost $29 billion in 1998 (figure III.2). And despite the financial crisis, the FDI inflows surpassed $31 billion in 1999. These figures suggest a strong recovery in confidence among foreign investors, not affected by the financial crisis. Indications are that the strongest growth impulses have come from investors already in Brazil and from first-time investors attracted by the policies of privatization and the opening up of parts of the infrastructure to foreign ownership.[1] Many potential new investors still keep Brazil on their "wait-and-see" list, preferring alternative locations. It is this group of potential investors whose interests are of particular importance in judging how Brazil might recover from the "lost decade" and how the country could fully realize its FDI potential.

The recent acceleration of FDI inflows raises the question of what constitutes an appropriate rate of such inflows for Brazil, and, for that matter, for any other country. The answer has to be linked to the basic choice of policy for the development of the economy and the role accorded to FDI in this respect. Another question is what is a country's potential as regards FDI inflows. Given the liberalization of FDI policies and the globalization of the world economy, relative measures across countries provide an indication (table III.1).

One measure of the attractiveness of a country for FDI as well as that of its unexploited potential is the inward flow or stock relative to the size of its economy. Another is to measure FDI as a proportion of gross domestic fixed capital formation and per head of population (table III.1). Ideally, these measures should be disaggregated by major sector – primary, secondary, tertiary – in order to allow for distortions due to both natural resource investments and differential regulations. In practice, however, such breakdowns are not available consistently across countries. Thus, aggregate measures of all flows should be used for all three indicators:

- In 1980, Brazil attracted FDI inflows as a share of GDP at a ratio above that of developed and developing countries' averages, but below that for Latin America and the Caribbean (table III.1). During the 1980s and into the early 1990s, Brazil underperformed compared to Latin America as a whole, and declined relative to all

Table III.1. Brazil's record in attracting inward FDI: relative measures
(Dollars and per cent)

A. Ratio of inward FDI flows and stock per $1000 of GDP[a] (dollars)

Region/economy	Flows										Stock
	1980	1985	1990	1991	1992	1993	1994	1995	1996	1997	1997
Developed countries	6.0	4.7	10.5	6.6	5.9	7.1	7.2	9.4	9.5	12.4	105
Developing countries	3.4	6.3	9.8	11.5	13.5	18.0	20.6	19.3	22.4	26.9	165
Latin America and the Caribbean	10.1	10.2	9.2	14.5	17.4	14.0	19.3	19.5	25.3	33.9	172
Brazil	8.1	6.5	2.4	2.8	4.6	3.0	4.7	8.0	14.0	23.3	159
Mexico	10.7	10.8	13.8	19.6	24.4	16.7	29.3	33.2	27.4	31.9	125
South, East and South-East Asia	4.5	4.7	12.6	12.5	15.0	24.8	26.0	24.2	25.8	27.8	184
of which :											
South-East Asia	13.1	10.0	35.5	34.2	26.6	30.0	31.4	29.1	31.0	32.9	251
Seven economies[c]	12.0	7.6	21.3	21.3	15.0	18.5	20.1	17.0	19.4	23.2	201
China	0.3	5.7	9.8	9.8	26.7	64.7	62.5	51.4	49.3	48.2	235
Indonesia	2.5	3.5	10.3	10.3	13.9	12.7	12.0	21.9	27.4	21.7	286
Central and Eastern Europe	0.1	0.2	2.8	2.8	10.0	14.8	10.3	20.6	15.2	22.3	83
of which :											
Three countries[d]	0.1	0.2	3.8	17.0	21.1	30.3	22.9	49.5	33.7	36.2	182
Russian Federation	..	..	..	..	7.1	6.5	2.3	5.8	5.6	13.9	32

B. Inward FDI flows as per cent of gross fixed capital formation

Region/economy	Annual average 1985-1989	1990	1991	1992	1993	1994	1995	1996	1997
Developed countries	4.2	5.0	3.2	2.9	3.6	3.7	4.7	4.8	6.5
Developing countries	3.2	3.8	3.9	4.3	6.4	8.0	7.3	8.4	10.3
Latin America and the Caribbean	4.0	4.4	6.7	7.8	6.0	9.1	9.4	12.5	16.1
Brazil	2.0	1.2	1.5	2.4	1.5	2.3	3.8	7.1	11.9
Mexico	8.2	7.2	9.7	11.4	9.0	15.2	20.6	15.5	16.3
South, East and South-East Asia	3.4	4.5	4.3	4.8	7.3	8.5	7.6	8.2	9.1
of which :									
South-East Asia	6.5	10.6	10.0	7.9	9.3	9.5	8.4	8.8	10.1
Seven economies[c]	6.4	6.8	5.6	4.7	5.7	6.2	5.1	5.8	7.2
China	2.4	3.5	3.9	7.6	12.2	17.3	14.7	14.3	14.3
Indonesia	1.6	2.6	3.3	3.6	4.3	3.8	6.7	8.9	7.0
Central and Eastern Europe	0.9	1.7	6.7	8.5	7.7	3.3	9.8	7.0	10.5
of which :									
Three countries[d]	0.5	2.1	8.0	10.0	15.4	11.1	23.6	14.7	15.1
Russian Federation	..	..	..	..	3.4	1.1	2.9	2.8	7.2

C. Inward FDI flows and stock per capita (dollars)

Region/economy	Flows										Stock
	1980	1985	1990	1991	1992	1993	1994	1995	1996	1997	1997
Developed countries	59.0	51.2	206.0	135.8	128.7	155.3	168.7	238.6	240.3	309.3	2 617
Developing countries	2.4	4.2	8.6	10.2	12.9	18.3	23.1	23.8	29.8	37.4	229
Latin America and the Caribbean	20.9	18.4	23.8	37.5	47.9	43.8	67.7	69.7	96.2	140.1	710
Brazil	15.7	10.7	7.6	7.3	11.5	8.4	16.5	34.4	65.2	114.9	785
Mexico	30.9	26.3	40.5	67.3	93.7	76.3	138.0	104.5	99.1	136.1	536
South, East and South-East Asia	1.4	1.8	7.2	7.5	9.6	17.0	20.7	22.3	26.0	28.3	187
of which :											
South-East Asia	6.7	5.6	28.2	30.0	26.6	34.4	41.6	45.0	53.1	55.9	427
Seven economies[c]	16.3	12.4	72.0	69.0	63.0	83.0	101.3	97.1	117.9	135.4	1 172
China	0.1	1.6	3.1	3.8	9.6	23.5	28.6	30.1	33.4	36.4	177
Indonesia	1.2	1.9	6.0	8.0	9.4	10.5	10.8	22.0	30.9	23.0	302
Central and Eastern Europe	0.0	0.0	1.7	7.2	13.1	20.0	17.5	42.3	36.8	55.1	204
of which :											
Three countries[d]	0.2	0.3	8.0	38.6	53.5	79.9	66.0	181.1	134.3	140.9	709
Russian Federation	..	..	..	..	4.7	8.1	4.3	13.6	14.0	42.3	97

Source : UNCTAD, based on data from UNCTAD FDI/TNC database, the IMF and the United Nations Population Division.

[a] GDP data in this table are not fully comparable with those in tables I.6 and I.10.
[b] Based on new figures for stock, revised upwards by the Central Bank of Brazil. In 1996, this stock was $108 billion.
[c] Includes Hong Kong, China; the Republic of Korea; Malaysia; the Philippines; Singapore; Taiwan Province of China and Thailand.
[d] Includes the Czech Republic (data for 1980-1991 refer to the former Czechoslovakia), Hungary and Poland.

other developing countries. From 1994 onwards, Brazil's attractiveness began to recover, but by 1995, was at the same level as in 1980, and was only less than half of the rate for Latin America. In 1997, the last year for which these data are available, the distance narrowed.

- If FDI is taken as a proportion of gross domestic capital formation, the picture of relative performance that emerges is similar to that provided by the earlier measure. Brazil underperformed between the first half of the 1980s and early 1990s and, since then, showed significant improvement, rising to almost 4 per cent by 1995 and 12 per cent in 1997.

- If inward flows per capita are considered, again, a similar trend emerges: a deterioration during the 1980s and the early 1990s, and an improvement from 1994 onwards.

- The stock-data indicator for the most recent year, based on the recent upward revisions of the stock by the Bank of Brazil, provide a picture largely similar to that emerging from the recent flow-data indicators: the gap between Brazil and a number of countries or groups of countries (table III.1) is closing; but still some of these countries perform better than Brazil.

Data for 1997 suggest that, at best, Brazil's ratio of FDI flows to GDP is approaching those for Mexico and South-East Asia but is still far from the Chinese ratio and those of the three largest host countries of Central and Eastern Europe. As regards the FDI/domestic investment ratio, the situation is much the same: Brazil's ratio is approaching the Mexican ratio, is much below the Chinese and the three countries' ratios but higher than the ratio for South-East Asia.[2] Also the ratio of FDI flows per capita shows unexploited potential: it is lower only for countries with very large populations, such as China, or for groups of countries including India (South-East Asia). For some measures, Brazil's ratio was lower than the average ratios for all developing countries including Latin America and the Caribbean. It is likely that these differences in the ratios as compared with the developing and Latin American countries further diminished in 1998 and 1999, or perhaps even disappeared. But this means that Brazil is only catching up with the average for developing countries including in its own region.

Yet, as discussed in chapter I, Brazil stands out among developing countries as regards most, if not all, existing and potential locational advantages. Furthermore, if it maintains its newly regained dynamism and stability, and improves the operating conditions for TNCs, it should be able to perform much better than most, if not all, developing countries and countries in transition in attracting FDI.

Realizing fully this potential will not be easy. The privatization programme, begun in the mid-1990s, may fuel FDI inflows for a number of years, but when all companies to be privatized are sold, this source of FDI will subside (though it does not have to dry up entirely, as discussed in chapter I, because of the possibility of sequential and associated FDI). Existing investors can be an additional source of extra FDI flows in the years to come. But most likely they alone will not be able to make up for the declining privatization-related flows in the future.

Therefore, Brazil – should it wish to attract sustained higher levels of FDI – would need to prepare itself now to be able to attract increasing flows in the future from various additional sources discussed in this volume, and especially from new investors still sceptical about the country's prospects and attractiveness.

An additional consideration regarding FDI trends and prospects concerns the geographical source of investment. For Brazil, the United States has been the predominant foreign investor, accounting for 26 per cent of the total stock in 1995, and 29 per cent of the inward flows in 1997. For United States TNCs, too, Brazil is very important in Latin America and the Caribbean, surpassed only by Mexico in terms of employment in foreign affiliates (clearly influenced by proximity) (table III.2). The responses of managers of United States TNCs to the questionnaire may have been biased in that their favourable views on Brazil's attractiveness could reflect, to a certain extent, the fact that they have a large asset to defend. United States managers also responded with a greater perception of opportunity for the future. The

Table III.2. Employment in United States foreign affiliates in manufacturing, 1992 and 1997[a]

	Number of employees (Thousands)		Per cent	
	1992	1997	1992	1997
Total	3 269	3 880	100.0	100.0
Developed countries	2 114	2 357	64.7	60.7
Brazil	253	238	7.7	6.1
Argentina	33	46	1.0	1.2
Mexico	372	454	11.4	11.7
Venezuela	34	41	1.0	1.1
Malaysia	72	119	2.2	3.1
Singapore	67	79	2.1	2.0

Source: U.S. Department of Commerce, Bureau of Economic Analysis.

[a] United States investment abroad, revised 1992 estimates and preliminary 1997 estimates.

implication is that investors from other countries and regions are generally less sanguine about the past record and future prospects. This possibility of bias is examined carefully in the data presented later in this chapter.

The TNCs interviewed attributed the decline of inward FDI during the 1980s to many factors. The most important were the failure to manage the macroeconomic instruments of control, inconsistency of policy between the various administrations, stagnation in the growth line for productivity – a crucial indicator of economic prospects, watched closely by TNCs – and policies that at times seemed to be hostile to foreigners.

Their fears about macroeconomic situation were heightened between 1988 and 1994 when the inflation rate ranged between 400 and 2,500 per cent annually.[3] The failures of successive plans for reform and shock therapy suggested to many in the international community that the Government had lost its ability to exercise control. That sense of political and institutional failure was surmounting its problems and amplified by the success of its neigbour, Argentina, in creating conditions of economic stability and growth. A further sense of Brazil as an unattractive place to invest was fostered by the persistent stories of kidnapping and assassinations that threatened companies and their executives in a very personal way.

The Plan Real has had a powerful impact on the economy and has shown that macroeconomic order can and has been restored. Growth has been resumed, productivity has begun to rise at rates last experienced in the 1970s, and inflation fell from over 2,000 per cent in 1994 to nil in 1998. Because investors watch these issues closely, a discussion of their views is deferred until later in this chapter, as part of an examination of the perspectives that influence managers' choices of investment locations. In the short-term, investors know that the country's FDI policy has been liberalized to attract FDI to support both short-term stabilization efforts (through adding further investment to help accelerate growth) and long-term economic objectives (such as increasing competitiveness through technology transfer or restructuring). The upturn in inward FDI enjoyed in 1995 continued thereafter at impressive rates of growth, and was not affected much by the financial crisis. Yet, several potential foreign investors – needed if Brazil is to realize its FDI potential, presented above – remain unconvinced that Brazil has a better claim on their investment budgets than other competing territories. Why this should be so is a matter of considerable interest, for the answers will go far in revealing both how managers view investment opportunities in the late 1990s and how difficult it is to change investors' perceptions.

B. Assessing national attractiveness

The main reasons why firms chose to invest rather than to serve foreign markets by other means have been discussed in chapter I. This chapter describes the firm as having competing motivations: natural resource-seeking, market-seeking, efficiency-seeking and strategic asset-seeking. For each motivation, a firm has a complex range of considerations to sort out when it comes to the question where and when it should invest. It has been well established, for example, that firms seeking markets do so in sequences of action, for they cannot expand everywhere simultaneously (Chang, 1995). Thus, in a world of scarce managerial resources, a key question is what determines firms' choices among alternative locations.

Considerable research evidence exists to suggest that three factors in a host country dominate many of the other possible reasons for investment (UNCTC, 1992):

- the size of the internal market (Green and Cunningham, 1975; Dunning, 1980; Ajami and Ricks, 1981);

- the growth of the market, either historically (Kobrin, 1976; Root and Ahmed, 1979)[4] or in prospect (Brash, 1966; Hill and Johns, 1985);

- the stability of the environment for business, a finding derived from research that in the main has correlated instability with a negative impact on investment decisions. Stability refers to the macroeconomic policy regime, together with other social and political indicators of an operating environment. For example, a study of eight Latin American countries found that political events which worsened the environment significantly deterred potential investors (Nigh, 1986).

Evidence from the survey undertaken for this study supports these general findings and adds new data to indicate how the dynamics of global strategies are acting to alter the balance of effects. The overwhelming importance of size and growth was discussed in chapter II. Both, those firms with Brazilian investments and the non-investors agreed that large, growing host markets were important to support a growth-oriented global strategy. This sense of importance applied even to those firms pursuing a strategy of specialization, where the main growth dynamic was tied to a firm's global system rather than to the local environment. "Better to operate in a benign environment than fight for externalities in a hostile local climate", seemed to be the dominant theme. However, as indicated later, there is emerging evidence that, for efficiency-seeking investors, even growth in the host economy is becoming relatively less important than other considerations for the effective implementation of specialized strategies for supply enhancement.

Similar importance was accorded to indicators of stability: general indications of political, economic and social stability ranked highest for almost all investors (figure III.3). There was no significant difference between firms of different national origin, by industry or according to whether they had already invested in Brazil or not. Many firms made statements that are similar to the following quotations: "We would be encouraged by a rational, commercial approach, but discouraged by dogmatic policies or irrationality in the way policies were applied" (an energy company); "Inconsistent policies discourage us" (an electronics company); and, "We work where we believe there will be long-term stability". The importance of the relative calculations TNCs are making was underscored by a consumer-goods company: "Political and economic stability has always been better in Asia than Latin America, but the latter has become more democratic in the past 10 years or so". Similarly, the importance of currency volatility showed up as a powerful negative influence on location choice; as one firm observed, "Adverse changes in regulations, particularly in the fiscal area would discourage us from investing in a country".

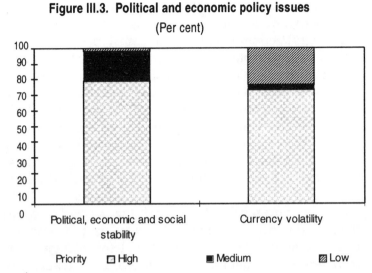

Figure III.3. Political and economic policy issues

(Per cent)

Source: survey results, based on corporate responses of all interviewed TNCs.

A further aspect of stability is the ability of firms to integrate their operations across borders. This is to be expected, and is of growing importance in a world of specialized, networked global strategies, for it has a direct impact on the efficiency of the corporate systems as a whole. Many plants and activities have scale requirements that far exceed the demand functions in country such as Brazil. Without opportunities for integration into the global production system, they would be inefficient and probably would not be built.

Three measures can be used to test the sensitivities of firms to these considerations (figure III.4). The first two concern freedom to transfer both money and technology. One capital goods manufacturer captured the mood of many: "It is important to us that a government views foreign investment favourably and that the policies they introduce are supportive of such investments. For us, it is key that their policies

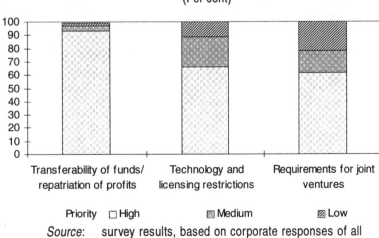

Figure III.4. Ability to integrate in the world economy

(Per cent)

Source: survey results, based on corporate responses of all interviewed TNCs.

include the ability to repatriate profits and dividends freely". A consumer goods firm added, "Restrictive trade policies discourage us from investing in a country". This general sense of requiring freedom as regards the transfers of money and technology contrasted with a strong preference for protective legislation for patents, brands and intellectual property of all sorts. One pharmaceutical firm went so far as to say, "We only invest where we can be sure that our patents are protected", and a capital goods producer stated: "We need to be sure about intellectual property regulations in countries where we invest".[5] (Section I in this chapter interprets these general statements in the context of some of the recent developments.) Investors generally favoured an appropriate combination of these freedoms and protection as part of their desire to be able to exercise control in optimizing their operations. Yet, on other accounts, they favoured "appropriate" incentive and other non-market stimuli to investment and development.

The third sensitivity concerns the freedom to choose the form of ownership, though here the considerations are a little different. It is the freedom to choose whether or not a joint venture can be established that is important. Requirements that insist on joint ventures irrespective of commercial considerations and the resources available from prospective partners are generally seen as negatives in the investment decision. (This issue was examined in some detail in chapter II.) However, it is worth emphasizing that, while there was a preference among both manufacturing and service investors for 100 per cent or strong majority ownership in equity terms, the most important criterion was management control, about which some companies were adamant; they stated that they would not operate without equity control and that requirements by host countries for local partners would preclude any investment. However, most indicated that, while this may have been the case in the past, minority positions were now acceptable providing management control was assured. The same sorts of consideration applied to those who were developing alliances and contract-based forms of control.

The move by TNCs to greater specialization and refocusing of their global strategies has meant that the importance of scale is less a matter of national calculation and increasingly a matter of the optimization of global corporate systems. This may have the effect of weakening some of the historical relationships that determine locational attractiveness. There are hints from the survey data that this is already happening. There is also strong evidence that the new global strategies are placing an altered emphasis on specialized infrastructure, unit labour costs and the importance of tax and incentive structures in influencing choices.

Most strategies of thinking globally but acting locally require high degrees of specialization for some parts of value-creating operations. At the same time they tend to diminish the importance of taxation regimes, for only part of the total value-added is involved in any one location. If one assumes, as the respondents did, that there was freedom of financial transfer and that disputes on transfer pricing were not an issue, then the location decision itself is less swayed by overall levels of corporation tax than would be the case for a company designed for import substitution. The weighting given to these factors (figure III.5) reflects the differing degrees of progress towards a transnational strategy made by the companies interviewed.

The aggregate data in these figures obscure important differences in perspective, depending on the original investment motivation. For example, the commentary from some of the efficiency-seeking investors that have made significant progress towards a full transnational strategy indicate the declining power of incentives to influence decisions: "Financial incentives are irrelevant and companies should not be over-influenced by them" (a consumer electronics company); "If companies want to invest – and the major criteria are reasonable – financial

Figure III.5. Importance of fiscal issues and specialized infrastructure
(Per cent)

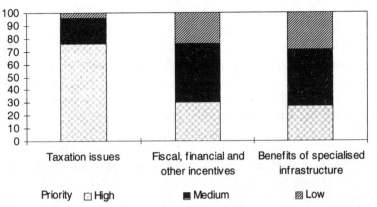

Priority □ High   ■ Medium   ▨ Low

Source: survey results, based on responses of all interviewed TNCs.

incentives will only be the 'gilt on the gingerbread'" (a consumer-electronics company); "Subsidies are broadly the same everywhere, it depends on how they are managed as to whether they are helpful or effective" (a chemicals company). By contrast, incentives were more likely to assume greater importance for market- and scale-seeking investors within the MERCOSUR, as discussed below.

Efficiency-seeking investors also tend to give more attention to ownership restrictions as a discouragement to investment, and to the benefits of specialized infrastructure as an incentive. This is entirely consistent with the argument in chapter II about the growing significance of clusters of resources in new poles of growth. However, as investors did not see Brazil as fostering such clusters, there was little specific discussion of this issue in the context of Brazil.

Further and more detailed evidence about sensitivities to local operating conditions was collected (figure III.6) for all the firms surveyed, with no significant differences emerging among the various categories of firms. The factors involved were generally seen as being less important than those directly affecting the freedom to integrate the corporate network across borders. Though they are seldom sufficient by themselves to make or break an investment decision, taken together they indicate how important it is for host countries to create a consistent set of operating conditions.

The desire for stability is repeated with regard to the conditions for permits to operate. The impact of employment legislation has to be interpreted as the desire for legislation that allows firms freedom to adjust their operations as market imperatives dictate. Just as many TNCs have been favouring the United Kingdom for their European investments because of the greater labour flexibility and

Figure III.6. Sensititity to the operating climate within Brazil
(Per cent)

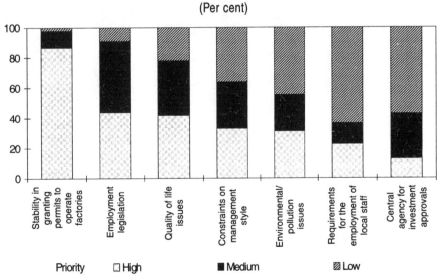

Priority   □ High   ■ Medium   ▨ Low

Source: survey results, based on responses of all interviewed TNCs.

legislation limiting the power of unions, the surveyed firms look for equivalent flexibility where they can find it. Much the same applies to the figures concerning constraints on management style (i.e. the ways in which the local enterprise is directed and managed).

Quality of life issues, while regarded as important for all employees, are directly related to the ability to employ foreign nationals. Especially in conditions of political instability and social tensions, expatriates are also concerned about absolute levels of security; if these are perceived to be too different from those at home, it is difficult to persuade senior home country managers to relocate, even for short periods, with their families. It is precisely because a poor quality of life can impede executives' mobility that firms become concerned.

The same considerations seem to apply even more forcefully with regard to employment legislation. Perhaps surprisingly, investors were little concerned about requirements to employ local staff. One firm explained this was "because we expect to employ locals for the vast majority of the posts. We would object, however, to any controls (such as ethnic quotas) over who we should employ, and we would seriously object to constraints on our ability to employ key expatriates". More generally, the development of local management was recognized as a high priority. In addition, the survey clearly indicated that the question of control is closely associated with the ability to employ foreign nationals in top management positions in foreign affiliates. This is especially important in the context of integrating across countries, as most firms have their own formula for successful integration. To translate this formula into practice, firms want to use the expertise of their expatriate managers, especially in top management positions. Indeed, one chemicals firm went so far as to say, "We absolutely require that we have freedom to move our key executives. This is one of the most important ways in which we manage an increasingly integrated network. Where this freedom is denied we will not invest".

Pollution issues attracted less concern, as many respondents claimed, "We have higher pollution control standards than many host countries and have adopted common procedures world-wide, irrespective of local legislation, so as to allow easy transfer of both personnel and product". Sceptics might challenge this frequently repeated statement, but it represents a serious perception on the part of senior management.

All these general indicators underscore the fact that investment decisions in those companies whose FDI strategies call for a high degree of specialization and cross-border integration are particularly sensitive to the following factors: freedom to operate, efficiency, stability and support. Growth in the host economy is, for such firms, no longer the main determining or differential factor. However, many respondents to the survey warned that even if a country rates highly in all these areas, it may not be successful in attracting FDI if stability is not a key part of the value system, beliefs and abilities of the host Government.

C. Brazil's relative attractiveness

The general conclusion in chapter II is that TNCs have to make clear choices of investment location, and typically need to work out a sequence of development that permits them to learn effectively how to manage increasing complexity. These conclusions are supported by the survey responses. As one executive put it, "We try to fund all good projects wherever in the world they arise. The only serious constraint on our overall FDI strategy is the availability of good management"; but he went on to observe positively, "Brazil is a net exporter of good managers". These relative measures are important indicators of how official policy might influence future increases in FDI inflows. For these purposes, two measures of relative attractiveness are needed. One concerns each TNC's global policy and the other concerns the MERCOSUR. Each of these is discussed in the following section.

The survey asked executives to compare Brazil with other countries in order to test whether there were special considerations that might explain why the flows of FDI had declined so sharply and had recovered so slowly, albeit recently at rates faster than for the MERCOSUR as a whole. In very general terms, the answers indicated two important considerations:

- Investors seek in Brazil the same sorts of conditions that are important to them elsewhere. In many respects, Brazil is rated favourably, especially in terms of its size and potential. There are no special conditions that influence investors' ratings, such as uncertainties in China, or issues of a "pariah" state as was the case for South Africa under apartheid.

- Turning a rating of attractiveness into investment action is quite a different matter. Most of the TNCs not established in Brazil and some of the large established TNCs have reservations about the prospects for continued stability and were deliberately holding back investment there at the time of the interviews.

The more detailed answers to the question (table III.3) show a range of opinions and convey a sense of mutual contradiction. They highlight some of the investors' sensitivities, discussed in chapter II, to problems of past instability (the "psychic" distance problem) and to the need, even in a developing economy, for modern facilities and support. Yet, two-thirds of those surveyed discounted the problems of the "lost decade" and looked for the same features of attractiveness in Brazil as in other countries. Indeed, many in this group of firms regarded Brazil much more as a developed country. They emphasized the inappropriateness of using the same scales of attractiveness as for other developing countries. Such views were held exclusively by United States-based firms, all of which were looking for ways to integrate Brazil more fully into their integrated international production networks of increasingly specialized production.

The general determinants of Brazil's attractiveness were strikingly similar to those applied elsewhere (figure III.7).[6] Reflecting Brazil's turbulent past, the most significant variation is the greater priority given to political, economic and social stability. The slightly higher weight given to "access to natural resources" is a feature of the sample of companies interviewed.

Table III.3. Opinions on Brazil, compared to other developing countries
(Per cent)

Opinions	Per cent of responses
Positive	
"Brazil differs from the normal developing country profile. We treat it as quasi-developed."	27
Neutral	
"We look for the same things there as elsewhere."	41
Negative	
"It is a laggard economy, marginal to our strategy."	14
"It remains unstable and unattractive in general terms."	18
Total	100

Source: survey responses of all TNCs.

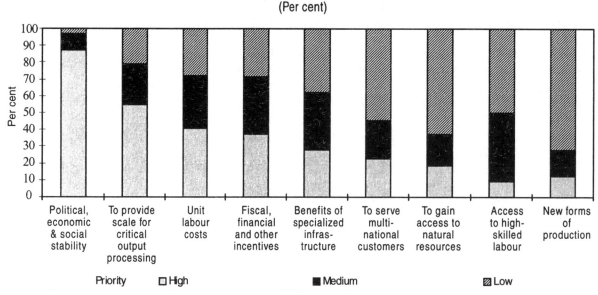

Figure III.7. Key determinants of FDI in Brazil
(Per cent)

Priority   □ High   ■ Medium   ▨ Low

Source: survey results, based on responses of TNCs established in Brazil.

Much of the important data about firms' views on Brazil is found in the commentaries provided by many firms, which gave perspectives that could not readily be captured on numerical scales, often because the nuances were important. Frequently, the sense of choice and relative ranking can only be determined within the context of a firm's particular experience and strategy. For example, one automotive firm said, "Our priorities are time dependent. Brazil is currently third out of four. This is difficult to identify because of our global approach, but Brazil is now part of our [global] projects while, some years ago, it wouldn't have been". Another firm provided considerable detail about the problems of gaining consensus within the firm, a necessary pre-condition for them for sanctioning investments. The head of a major product division said, "Our regional office in Latin America now considers their region to be less risky than China. But they have a vested interest in saying that and are not convincing. We will not invest significantly there for the time being."

To capture the nuances of such commentary, investors in Brazil are divided into two categories: those who are very optimistic about post-reform developments in Brazil, and those who recognize the progress of reforms, but who are concerned about sustainability. A third group comprises those who have not invested in Brazil and share many of the negative perspectives of the second group. There was no pattern discernible by industry, but there were strong regional biases: United States firms were the most positive, and Japanese firms the most negative. The opinions of European firms are almost equally divided between these two camps.

1. Optimistic views

Consider first the optimists. Many commented on the impact of the recent reforms, both on market attractiveness and on their own decisions. A common remark was, "We were winding down our Brazilian operations a few years ago, but that has now been reversed". Others, particularly in consumer goods, were impressed by the developments in society and the effect on the nature of domestic demand. One European consumer firm said, "Brazil is a very modern market. Customer behaviour demands more product investment"; and another added, "The emerging middle classes are important". Another executive claimed, "Brazil is now our number one priority in Latin America". A United States machinery producer stated, "Brazil has been the lead operation in updating our products. It is not a typical developing market". For him, the attractiveness was limited to domestic conditions, for he went on to observe that "A combination of macro policies and an over-valued currency have made Brazil unattractive as an export base". (The issue of currency value and exporting is discussed later in the section on trade behaviour.)

Typical of the optimists was the observation from a consumer goods producer , "We have always slowed down our rate of investment in times of crisis in the past in Brazil, but this experience has not deterred us from continuing to expand there". The value of such, often hard-won, experience cannot be overestimated for it allows the firm to prosper where others can find only problems and losses. Becoming an "insider" can be crucial, especially when the business depends on government purchasing and local technical specifications. How to make it easier for newcomers to consider themselves as valued "insiders" should be on the agenda for government action.

2. Pessimistic views

The pessimists hold quite different views about Brazil, except that everyone included in the survey agreed on Brazil's economic importance. Where many have welcomed the advent of deregulation as a sign of progress towards an open economy, some see only short-term penalties. One European automotive supplier said, "While the economy was closed, there was a high motivation for companies interested in staying in Brazil to establish manufacturing facilities. Now, however, deregulation has slowed this down. Brazil has become more costly and its competitiveness has been diluted." Others held the view that the potential for instability was greater than elsewhere. Common expressions of concern included: "We are attracted by the size of the market and the labour supply, but we worry about political and economic volatility"; "We are not convinced that the reforms will stick"; and "Currency volatility is more of a problem in Brazil than elsewhere".

Pessimists were also concerned that the Government's ability to manage the transition of the economy was very limited. One firm stated that "Energy is becoming a concern as there is a capacity problem associated with growth". Inflexibility was identified as an obstacle to progress in the labour market and in the dealings with the bureaucracy: "Brazil adds unnecessary red tape", said one Japanese firm.

Inconsistency was another problem for some: "Continually changing import taxes causes great problems"; and "The regulations are inconsistent and volatile". Pessimists were also those who trusted Government least. One capital equipment producer said, "We have been burned there before by believing the official policy. We are now much more cautious and, at present, though we like the rhetoric, we feel too much is being left to chance". A European industrial products company elaborated on that theme, suggesting, "Brazil has not got the best record in relation to continuity of policy on FDI. But we regard it is an important market and will therefore live with that situation. Brazil's record is not really acceptable".

The range of responses has an important implication for Brazilian policy makers. They cannot count on the large scale of the internal market as necessarily being a magnet to draw in investment. Among the existing investors, the concerns that have bred pessimism may not be sufficient to make firms leave the country, especially in view of the inertia effects that deter exit.

But concerns can seriously influence the propensity to undertake sequential investment, and they can deter prospective investors. The evidence shown later provides some support for the proposition suggested at the beginning of the chapter, namely that a perception gap exists among those who do not know Brazil.

Determining precise cause-and-effect relationships is not possible. Yet, it is possible to indicate some of the ways by which a climate of opinion is formed to influence managers' perceptions. Far from being driven always by rational considerations and perfect information, managers have human biases and can ignore evidence when it suits them to do so. The very differences in perception of Brazil among the optimists and the pessimists – and their sharply different investment behaviour, even in the same industry – shows how the same information can lead to different outcomes. A full discussion of these considerations, and how they affect the three groups of investors, is deferred until after data and some assessment of the MERCOSUR and the export behaviour of foreign affiliates in Brazil have been added to the discussion.

D. Regional integration: the impact of the MERCOSUR

As indicated in chapter I, the great majority of investors regarded regional developments as being of great importance to their strategies (figure III.8). The data, however, show the importance of experience in conditioning perspective. Those who already had investment experience in Brazil underscored the MERCOSUR's importance. Non-investors included many who considered the MERCOSUR to be of little significance. Perhaps, because many of these firms had little investment in Latin America as a whole, they were implying that their strategic priorities were elsewhere. One Japanese chairperson reported that, for himself and his business, "Brazil is about as far away as possible. I simply do not have time to go there to find out what is really happening. Besides, there are so many other growth opportunities nearer to home which we cannot adequately meet with our present resources that I cannot see either Brazil or Latin America being important to us in the near future." Note that strategic priority has a direct bearing on how executives spend their time and on the information they receive. As has been documented many times (see, e.g. Baden-Fuller and Stopford, 1994), executives can be relatively ignorant about low-priority territories, making it difficult for them to react quickly to opportunities as they arise there.

The interpretation of what investors really mean when they rate the importance of regional developments is by no means straight forward. For some it can mean that, for example, regional integration enlarges markets and encourages new investment. For others, it can serve to reinforce the wisdom of their earlier judgements and makes no difference in terms of actions. For yet others, it can be an important milestone in building a base-level of confidence needed to influence relative

Figure III.8. Importance of the MERCOSUR to regional strategy

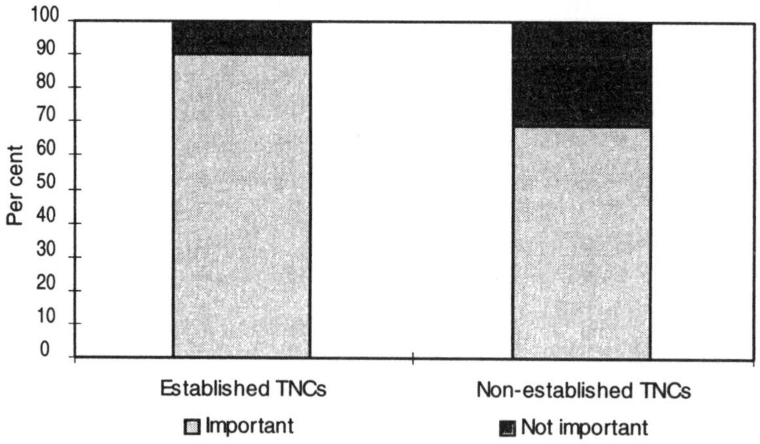

Source: survey results, based on corporate responses of all interviewed TNCs.

rankings among competing regions and move this part of Latin America higher on their global yardstick.

To test some of these general considerations for the region as a whole, the survey included a series of questions about overall confidence and about the respective importance of key provisions in the agreements leading to the creation of the MERCOSUR. Among the investors already in Brazil, the MERCOSUR has reinforced the favourable perceptions of the optimists and has gone some way in reducing the negative impressions of the pessimists. [7] One stated that "It opens the door to a wider range of products". A chemicals company said that it "creates a more important market in terms of size and growth potential". One of the European firms added, "Our investment priorities are changing. We are getting out of mature areas and going into new product areas. The MERCOSUR allows us to think about the region in terms of optimizing our production arrangements". Moreover, most of these firms considered that the emerging commitments were solidly grounded in regional politics and, therefore, they had confidence in acting upon the agreements already in place. These views are strongly consistent with experience in the EU where the deepening of regional integration created new FDI as a means to capture scale benefits and lower costs (see chapter I). They are also consistent with a survey of confederations of industry in Germany, which showed that regional integration schemes had a favourable impact on TNCs' decisions to invest in Latin America (Nunnenkamp and Agarwal, 1993, p. 51).

It is possible to speculate that market-seeking investors may be stimulated to increase their investment in the form of mergers and acquisitions, as has been the case in the EU (Centre for Business Strategy, 1990). The Brazilian merger boom in consumer goods (shown later in Section F) suggests that the European pattern may be repeated, at least in this industry, with Brazilian entities becoming the centre of further, regional expansion. Whether the same will apply to other industries depends critically on the availability of local firms of sufficient quality. Just as BMW waited until Rover had cured itself of long-standing inefficiencies before making a bid, so TNCs may become very selective in choosing their bid targets in Brazil. Where there is a dearth of appropriate local targets, TNCs may be motivated to start more greenfield investments than would be the case in the absence of the MERCOSUR.

Confidence was very important in affecting the timing, if not the form, of future region-oriented investments (table III.4). Non-investors, who generally lack much knowledge of the region, were much less confident than those with more regional experience. To some extent, non-investors' statements may be taken as self-justification for their wait-and-see policies. Yet they were voicing concerns shared by a significant minority of the investors already experienced in the region. They were concerned, as was shown earlier with regard to internal Brazilian conditions, about the possibilities of inconsistency across competing agendas and over time. They did not agree that the MERCOSUR would yield the desired stability. One United States chemicals executive considered that "Brazil hasn't yet fully understood the importance of Brazil as a main base for the MERCOSUR". Like many others, he was worried that Brazil's domestic agenda could

Table III.4. Confidence that the MERCOSUR will deliver on its promise

(Per cent of corporate responses)

Degree of confidence	TNCs established in Brazil	Non-established TNCs
Very confident	17	0
Confident	55	24
Reasonably confident	21	63
Not confident	7	13
Total	100	100

Source: survey results, all TNCs.

take precedence and get in the way of forging durable and irreversible links with its neighbours. Others pointed to the remaining, and sometimes increasing, problems of managing component imports from outside the region.

Sensitivities to the various features of the agreements varied considerably, suggesting which were the main sources of low confidence (figure III.9). Firms assigned the highest importance to the liberalization of intraregional trade and the second highest rating to the external tariff regime. Both of these can lead to a simplification of tariff formalities, thus reducing transaction costs.[8]

The importance of the external tariff regime, however, can cut both ways. High importance was associated with strong negative reactions among those investors seeking freedom to integrate their operations across regional boundaries and to lower global, not only regional, costs. What this means is that, if intraregional efficiencies are being gained by methods that seriously hinder the creation of globally integrated production networks, this would seriously diminish the attractiveness of Brazil to efficiency-seeking investors. By contrast, market-seeking investors, concerned about scale and integration solely within the MERCOSUR, will probably find Brazil more attractive and the cushioning effects of the external protection will be similar to the days of import-substitution policies. They are thus likely to increase their investments, perhaps with Brazil as the hub. In other words, the policies on external trade were likely to divide the opinions and actions of TNCs. The net effect on Brazil will depend on the overall balance of investors' motivations.

Other aspects of the internal workings of the agreements were also important (figure III.9). Half or more of the investors rated various provisions as being of "central importance". Given that intraregional trade is still subject to a variety of government interventions, these ratings are to be expected. Many of the investors regard the impact as negative.

The sensitivities vary across industry, as the impact of intervention is uneven. For example, Argentina and Brazil stipulated that their trade in automobiles and parts should be bilaterally balanced. In the case of FDI, several exemptions from the national treatment for intra-regional investors were introduced in 1994. Most of them applied to Brazil, including industries such as mining, hydro-electric energy, health systems, radio broadcasting and telecommunications, banking, insurance, construction and marine navigation.

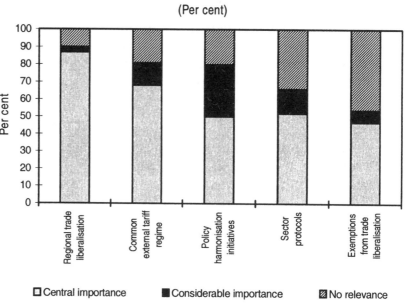

Figure III.9. Importance of the main integration instruments in the MERCOSUR to companies' operation

(Per cent)

Source: survey results, based on responses of TNCs established in Brazil.

Moreover, harmonization of regulations and norms within the member economies is called for to promote mutual trade and investment. There is growing concern about inconsistencies between an increasing number of norms, rules and exemptions related to trade, investment, labour markets, environment protection etc. among the MERCOSUR members. They add to transaction costs and offset the incentives to FDI flows gained from the liberalization of trade. Uncertainties about the application of the source or destination country norms – as is well known from the EU experience – can result in long-drawn legal disputes forcing investors to postpone investment decisions. The gains from liberalization should not be allowed to be sabotaged by domestic rules on product norms.

Insofar as liberalization at the MERCOSUR level will be a slow process, Brazil could take the lead by opening its own markets unilaterally. National policies are crucial for attracting FDI. Unless they are attractive to foreign investors, gains from economic integration under the MERCOSUR may remain at best limited. The Greek experience in the EU suggests that, without a proper policy framework and growth prospects, investors are not impressed by membership in an integration scheme. This applies also to the surveyed TNCs established in Brazil. As one automobile producer put it bluntly, "Brazil must open up its marketplace more. Until we are confident that we can develop specialized production and integrate trade with local production, we will not invest more in Brazil".

By how much the creation of the MERCOSUR has increased investment in Brazil above the level it would have attracted on a stand-alone basis is a matter of some speculation. The survey gives some clues. Most of the investors, especially United States firms, regard Brazil as the essential political leader of the MERCOSUR, as well as the most attractive investment site in the region. Over half of the TNCs established in Brazil regarded their investments there as the centre of an emerging regional hub. Only a few, however, stated categorically that they had added more capacity in Brazil solely because of the regional effect. The other investors believed that regional leadership had yet to be earned in terms of Brazil becoming either the lowest-cost regional site (another aspect of the sensitivities to the currency-adjusted effects of the Plan Real), or the location with the greatest stability or some combination of the two. The non-investors, who were much less confident in the stability and durability of the MERCOSUR, shown earlier (table III.4), were clear that regional developments had yet to make a difference. They were more concerned with Brazil attaining internal stability first. Further scale-based cost-gains reductions were important but would, in the opinion of many, come later.

When asked whether they would invest in any of the MERCOSUR countries without a regional agreement, over half of the investors said they would consider doing so only in Brazil. Another one third of them said they would consider Brazil and Argentina. Automobile producers were especially conscious of the balanced trade agreements for their industry. Some, such as Toyota, had invested in Argentina in light trucks, as a way to access the much larger Brazilian market. Whether Toyota would have done so in the absence of the MERCOSUR cannot be determined.

A general problem involved in trying to disentangle the various causal forces at work is the fact that some firms with export-oriented affiliates in Brazil had expanded capacity to serve many markets, not just those in the MERCOSUR. As discussed in the next section, firms with impressive records of export growth from Brazil reported that they regarded expansion in Brazil as central to their future in the region. The strong impression is that such expansion had more to do with their affiliates' specialization and productivity potential measured against global rather than regional benchmarks.

Clearly, all members will be affected by investors' moves to seek scale benefits from particularly attractive locations. Most probably it is the smaller members (e.g. Uruguay) that will be affected proportionately the most. Whether the effects will be as beneficial, as they have been, for example, for Ireland within the EU, remains difficult to determine. What does seem certain, though, is that such scale-seeking investments will be influenced by Governments' offers of investment incentives of all sorts.

Some speculation is possible about how a further enlargement of the MERCOSUR might affect investors' attitudes and actions. Some of the United States TNCs were enthusiastic about the MERCOSUR in terms, as one machinery manufacturer put it, of "creating a stepping stone, with NAFTA, on the way to an all-American free trade area." If Mexico were to be included in the MERCOSUR, thus creating a more direct link with NAFTA, then the way would be open to a much more far-reaching specialization of investment and the creation of regional core networks. Just as many United States investors have changed the location and specialization of their European investments in recent years, they could do so also for a the MERCOSUR of continental scale. One implication for Brazil of such a speculation is that enlargement could reduce the effect of Brazil as the sole hub. Brazil's ability to attract the majority of new regional investment might be undermined, even though the absolute volume of investment might increase. Most investors, however, were not prepared to engage in such speculation and preferred to work with present arrangements.

E. Export behaviour of foreign affiliates in Brazil

The growing ties between FDI and trade have been discussed in earlier chapters in terms of the general trends towards specialization of production and accompanying changes in corporate strategy and managerial behaviour. The earlier conclusion was that the relationship was complementary, fostered by the liberalization of trade and investment regimes.

The data reported here indicate that, to date, TNCs' trade policies in relation to their Brazilian affiliates are much the same as those for affiliates in other developing countries of similar structure. Performance has been tied closely to the original market-seeking motivations of investors during the 1950s and 1960s. Then, TNCs invested principally for import-substitution to take advantage of the growing and protected domestic market. A few started to export later on to deal with their excess capacity. Some also responded to export incentives and other changes introduced in the trade and foreign exchange regime that helped to offset the inefficiencies of domestic operations (Fritsch and Franco, 1991). In addition, as has frequently been the case of import-substitution in countries with large domestic markets, the early investments were a preamble to exporting, but only by those firms that invested in upgrading their operations and added new skills to make the output internationally competitive (Teitel and Toumi, 1987).

The development of the MERCOSUR is but one of the dynamic forces acting as a double-edged sword on corporate policy and practice. (Table II.6 provides evidence of the rate of change in export behaviour as part of the broader picture of strategic change.) The surveyed firms are clearly developing systems of linked production. These systems have a bearing on the development of exports from their affiliates in Brazil, as the calculation of the appropriate adjustment to regional conditions has shifted to the global level. Just as Brazil is becoming more deeply connected to the world economy, so are Brazilian affiliates of TNCs being managed as more connected parts of increasingly complex networks. And just as some parts of the Brazilian economy are becoming internationally competitive more rapidly than others, TNCs are moving at different speeds and, in some cases, in different directions.

In addition to the differences in trade behaviour caused by different investment motivations (discussed above in the context of the MERCOSUR), there are major differences of behaviour created by the strategic choices discussed in chapter II. Furthermore, the concepts of distance, commitment, consistency of purpose and how favourable or unfavourable earlier experience were, affect sequential FDI decisions.

Both economic and "psychic" distance show up strongly in the contrasting attitudes of United States and Japanese investors (see next section). The comments recorded during the survey show that negative past experiences discourage strong adjustments that might capitalize on the new environment. Such reluctance to invest in extra Brazilian capacity to serve export markets was illustrated by one consumer electronics firm, "We used to export ... to Argentina, but no longer do so because of Brazilian inefficiencies". A comment from another firm was, "We have a history of failure in Brazil. We now only have small plants there that are not export-competitive". Positive past experience has the opposite effect. One automotive firm went so far as to state, "Our production facilities and sales in Brazil are so large, we treat them as extensions of our domestic market". The experience of having successfully weathered the storms of the "lost decade" also acts as a powerful stimulus for further investment and the development of an export orientation capacity from Brazil.

These contrasting perspectives and policies were explored in relation to 28 product lines (table III.5). The enormous variety of product policy, developed from both industry economics and company policy, make company averages meaningless. The figures provide estimates of the dominant tendency in the geographical pattern of exports in the early 1990s. Thus, seven European firms exported worldwide from Brazil, whereas five concentrated their efforts on neighbouring countries in the MERCOSUR, and four exported little or nothing from Brazil.

In the main, United States firms were more optimistic about future export prospects, whereas many Japanese and European firms were, at best, sceptical. These differences should not be taken as representative of all firms from the same home environment,

Table III.5. Direction of exports from Brazilian foreign affiliates[a]
(Number of TNCs)

Home country	Worldwide	North and South America	MERCOSUR	Little or no exporting
Europe	7	1	5	4
Japan	2	1	2	3
United States	5	2	3	3
Total	14	4	10	10

Source: survey results of TNCs established in Brazil.
[a] Emphasis in export policy by product line.

for they are, as suggested below, the product of a complex mixture of forces, past and present. Similarly, it was difficult to detect any strong causality from industry effects. When classified by the industry categories used in earlier chapters, the products showed little difference in general tendencies.

It should be emphasized, however, that large differences in export behaviour existed within the major industries represented in the sample of investors. Such evidence serves to reinforce the analysis in chapter II that strategy is determined at the level of the firm and not predominantly by industry economics. The resulting differences in strategies among firms within an industry are an important consideration for government officials negotiating with exporters.

Those TNCs that had integrated the previously separate parts of their global configuration emphasized that their basic preferences for regional or global networks are prime determinants of their Brazilian exports (table III.6). Indeed, a majority of the investors have policies to use at least some of their foreign affiliates to supply their home markets. The company data are consistent with the earlier discussion about network development with the important addition that many firms are now using their foreign affiliates to prospect for new markets and even to develop new products. "Our foreign affiliates are used mainly to create new markets, but some supply the home market on a pragmatic basis as required" was a common remark.

Table III.6. Number of companies using their foreign affiliates to supply home markets or to create new markets

	To supply home markets		
	Important	Minor effect	None
Europe	3	6	4
Japan	4	2	0
United States	7	1	3
	To create new markets		
	Important	Minor effect	None
Europe	6	1	6
Japan	0	2	4
United States	7	0	4

Source: survey results, based on responses of TNCs established in Brazil.

The survey data did not reveal the extent of exports from Brazilian affiliates to serve the TNCs' home markets. Some impressionistic data, however, strongly suggest that there is some growth of such exports, but also great untapped potential. For example, many Japanese firms have developed extensive Asian networks of production that are increasingly supplying parts of the Japanese market with finished goods. Brazil supplies Japan with natural resources, such as coal and timber pulp, from partially Japanese-owned affiliates, but few finished products. Even though 14 of the 30 established TNCs claimed (table III.5) to have worldwide exports from Brazil, the volumes of exports that go beyond the region are less than they might be.

One important reason why executives reported general constraints on exporting is the short-term impact of volatility on exchange-rate-calculated export-cost competitiveness. Many investors reported that they were having to make adjustments in their international supply systems as the strength of the currency had made some products unprofitable. One consumer products firm reported, "Exports outside the region have stopped because of currency problems", while, on a broader plane, a machinery producer stated, "Currency changes have made it less cost effective to export from Brazil to the rest of the world". This problem might however have been resolved, at least partly, after the devaluation of the real in January 1999.

Others, reflecting the importance of prior strategy choices, reported that they expected their exports to increase regardless of the currency issue. A consumer goods firm stated, "We have changed our policy away from local manufacturing to concentrate production on a regional basis. Thus exports are expected to grow rapidly, for Brazil is a key regional manufacturing centre." Another consumer goods firm had planned to export more than half of its Brazilian output by 1997, while an industrial products company considered that "Brazil is our main developing country exporter".

This latter group of firms is composed primarily of those with a steep and positive learning curve. Just as the effects of learning were shown in chapter II to influence global strategic choices, the same applies at local levels. Many firms reported that they had learned how to work in the Brazilian environment and to overcome obstacles that might deter others. Although the role of instability was a continuing theme as a demotivator for FDI, it is clear that many of the existing investors had learned to cope with the instability that existed in Brazil over the 15-20 years prior to the 1993 Plan Real. To do so, corporate strategies had been the driving force, not factor-cost relativities.

The combination of the local learning curve with the quality of past experience clearly influences export behaviour. It is part of a more general issue of corporate behaviour, namely how managers' perceptions can act to spur or impede change. This theme is developed in the next section as it has a direct bearing on the behaviour of the non-investor group in the survey.

F. Differing perceptions

Given the good news from Brazil that its economy is improving and that policies are in place to resolve known problems, the question naturally arises as to why many large firms, although already highly internationalized, have not yet invested in Brazil. The same question applies, as indicated earlier, to those, labelled as the pessimists, who are hesitating to invest more in Brazil.

1. Contrasting United States and Japanese perspectives

The impact on strategic choice of economic and "psychic" distance was discussed in general terms in chapter II. In the context of Brazil, the influence of these factors is shown clearly by the contrasting opinions of executives in United States and Japanese TNCs. Perhaps reflecting greater geographical proximity, and the historic influence of the United States in the region, United States firms had, broadly considered, far more positive perceptions of Brazil than Japanese ones. Many Unites States managers in the survey felt that Latin America, and Brazil in particular, was nearly as high on their lists of growth priorities as was Asia. In sharp contrast, no Japanese executive listed Latin America or Brazil as an area of high or even medium priority amongst the areas of growth potential for their products.

This difference of opinion cannot be explained by physical distance, given the extensive global coverage of the major Japanese firms. Part of the explanation is, perhaps, illustrated by one electronics firm's response, "Brazil is too far away, too unstable and too tarred with a lousy reputation from past mistakes to warrant much attention". Economic distance, combined with "psychic" distance and opinion based on the poor experience of other firms that they respect can add up to a major impediment to action. Many of the Japanese investors in Brazil are, in varying ways, worried about the record of the recent past and felt that the "poison is still in the system".

Although it is clear that most of the investors in the survey recognize the potential of Brazil, it is also clear that many, though not all, of the Japanese firms have a negative image of the country and share the opinion of one who stated, "It is attractive now, but has not always been so. There is no guarantee it won't become unattractive again either". However, an alternative view is based on the experience of Matsushita, which has an accumulated investment of over 10 billion yen in Brazil and for which Brazil represents its fourth largest market for colour televisions. Yet, even Matsushita is on record as saying that Asian opportunities are taking first priority for the time being.

The sense of a negative bias has, perhaps, been amplified by the fact that Japanese TNCs have suffered losses in Brazil in the past. Because they exchange views among themselves, these experiences have undermined Brazil's credibility with many Japanese companies. The attitudes of Japanese banks have not helped either. The survey recorded many observations of the type, "Our bankers tell us that Brazil remains very risky".

This general lack of interest among Japanese firms also appears in industry data on their medium-term investment plans (table III.7). For example, in the 1995 survey, only 8 out of 37 firms in the electric/electronic parts industry planned to invest in Brazil, and of those, half planned an increase in investments while the other half were holding their investments steady. Only 5 of the 31 chemical firms responding in 1995 had investment plans, and of these, 2 were cutting back on their Brazilian exposure.

Table III.7. Plans for FDI in Brazil by Japanese firms, 1993 and 1995

(Number of firms)

Industry	1993				1995			
	Increase	No change	Decrease	No plans	Increase	No change	Decrease	No plans
Electric/electronic parts	1	2	0	16	4	4	0	29
Electric/electronic assembly	3	3	1	8	8	7	1	9
Auto parts	3	1	0	7	3	2	1	16
Auto assembly	3	1	0	3	3	0	0	4
Chemical (excluding pharmaceuticals)	1	2	1	13	1	2	2	26

Source: Export-Import Bank of Japan.

The recent data show that the main motivation of Japanese TNCs for investment in Brazil is its domestic market. Most were interested in either maintaining existing market share or developing new markets. Lower production costs, opportunities to export to other markets – including other Latin American countries – and tax incentives did not figure prominently in this decision, but there has been increasing interest in parts supply (table III.8).

Table III.8. Motivations of Japanese TNCs for investment in Brazil, 1994-1998

(Per cent of responding companies)

Motivation	Year of survey				
	1994	1995	1996	1997	1998
Preservation/expansion of market share	40	67	64	54	53
Develop new market	40	50	36	54	53
Exports	0	17	18	11	15
Diversification of production facilities	0	0	9	25	15
Access to cheap labour	40	17	18	14	18
Supply parts to assembler (incl. Japanese firms)	0	17	27	21	25
Avoid foreign exchange risk	0	0	0	4	6
Response to trade regulations/tax incentives	0	0	9	0	3
Reverse exports to Japan	20	17	0	0	3
Product development to meet local market needs	0	0	0	4	12

Source: Nishiyama, Kushima and Noda, 1999.

The views of Japanese firms and the associated complaints about Brazil are not new. An earlier study (Hollerman, 1988, p. 133) reported how Japanese executives considered difficulties arising from Brazilian policies and practices both in the public and private sectors. "As a result of their recent experience of rapid economic growth, the Brazilians are forming a new identity that is more nationalistic. This forms a framework for other difficulties that have been encountered by Japanese enterprises in Brazil."[9] The perceived nationalism compounds some other characteristics of Brazil's business environment that trouble Japanese firms. Thus, despite a large population of Japanese origin in Brazil, Japanese TNCs seem to feel a great "psychic" distance from this country. The sharing of experience can become negatively reinforcing as past images become indelible, and overcoming this problem is, therefore, a major promotional challenge.

2. Reinforcing success

Many of the existing investors have, as indicated earlier, been investing to reinforce the strength of the market positions they have established in Brazil over many years. Some of them have been investing to make Brazil an important source of exports. These are the firms that have travelled furthest along the learning curve from the initial conditions of import-substitution and possible inefficiency. They are also the firms with the most positive views about Brazil, today and in prospect. In effect, the path of reinforcing success has had the important effect of reducing the costs of economic and psychic distance as well as conditioning managers' attitudes for future success.

As is shown later, these firms had many critical comments to make about Brazilian policy, and especially the condition of its society and the quality of its infrastructure. These comments were made primarily in the context of providing helpful inputs into the policy dialogue; the aim being to seek improvements in order to be able to grow faster and increase their exports. One materials firm stated, "Plan Real has helped spread earnings a little more evenly in the society, but has increased costs significantly, particularly the costs of labour. However, we are prepared to live with these as Plan Real in the long term will produce stability and low inflation – provided the government sticks to it" – the consistency argument once again.

An example of how the trajectory of reinforcing success can change local conditions is provided by the automobile industry. Only a few years ago, this industry was regarded as inefficient and unduly constrained by regulations. The total stock of FDI in the automotive industry was less than $3 billion in 1995 (Banco Central do Brazil, 1998). However, growth in the sales of new vehicles attracted the attention of many transnational firms. A record number of investments by existing TNC investors and new entrants was announced including several large auto makers such as Daimler-Benz ($1.1 billion), Ford ($1.5 billion), Fiat ($1.4 billion), Renault ($1.0 billion), General Motors ($3.6 billion) and Volkswagen/Audi ($3.3 billion). If every company goes ahead with their planned investments, it is expected that there will be 20 different makes of vehicles in Brazil, more than any in other market including the United States (ECLAC, 1998, p. 157-158).

The automobile industry is a good example of one in which trade liberalization has spurred both efficiency gains and inward FDI. Elsewhere, efficiency gains have often been created by imports and the displacement of local output, which result in a reduction of FDI inflows. What made the difference? One partial answer is that TNCs saw there was sufficient potential for reconstruction and that the policy goal of moving towards export-creating output was achievable. Another partial answer is that the firms, with considerable assets to defend, were spurred into action by a combination of regulatory actions. Even though many complained about inconsistencies in the regulations and the problems of rapid changes in the rules, most saw these as necessary aspects of the transition; change is never entirely smooth nor capable of being freely planned in advance. If the firms had not seen the potential, however, the outcome might have been less positive.

The evidence of recent rapid change in the automobile industry might appear to contradict earlier statements about *hysteresis*. The data, on the contrary, show how even compelling economic arguments to change the behaviour of existing investors can take time to work. Little happened in 1991 when the new policies were announced. Apart from a few minor investments, most of the change occurred rapidly in 1995.[10] What may have become compelling arguments for incumbents can remain inadequate to change the behaviour of potential new entrants, as has been the case for many European firms contemplating Asian investments.

A belief in possibility is an essential component of an investment plan. Thus, attitudes are vitally important, and effort to influence them should be a central part of any investment-promotion project. Clear information to investors as argued in chapter II, is a necessary ingredient to make any policy reform effective. Moreover, to build investors' belief in the credibility of change and in the lasting potential for consequent growth, reforms have to meet the test of consistency.

Part of that consistency involves the building of support systems (such as specialized infrastructure) needed for creating world-class competitiveness. Another part involves the Government's funding of forward-looking change when market incentives remain weak. Some data on TNCs' moves since 1990 to rationalize production and upgrade facilities make the point. A study of 55 TNC affiliates showed that short-term efficiency, cost-reduction and product focus dominated the firms' efforts. The study measured the extent of investment in total quality control techniques, as well as better managerial and administrative procedures. It also found a clear trend towards lower vertical integration, specialization in the product-mix and an abandonment of some high-technology products (Bielschowsky, 1992a). A follow-up study in early 1993 with 104 firms (of which 41 were foreign-owned) gave a fuller picture of the corporate adjustments taking place since the 1980s (Bielschowsky, 1992b). The study showed that managerial attention had been, as might be expected, directed towards cost cutting. Investments in tangible assets had been kept to a minimum, while investments in intangibles, such as training, and research and development were cut back. Data from the Brazilian Foreign Capital Survey confirm that this trend has continued through the 1990s (Banco Central do Brazil, 1998).

The Government can help build a climate in which firms are motivated to look beyond the short term and start out on the now-familiar process of rejuvenation that moves from cost-cutting to investment in new capabilities, to extension of those capabilities to world-market production (Baden-Fuller and Stopford, 1994). The essential ingredients for desirable success is the managerial ability to move beyond cost-cutting of the kind reported above. Such efficiency-enhancing moves are no more than imperative aspects of survival, as cost disciplines are necessary, but not sufficient conditions for international competitiveness.

3. Demonstrate local capability

An important signal to foreign investors that Brazil is already, or can become, a site for world-class operations is provided by the results of local firms. If they can succeed, so the TNC argument goes, foreigners are doubly advantaged: they can harness competitive local resources, and they can transfer their own international systems into a receptive territory.

Indeed, if Brazil can play host to Volkswagen's leading-edge global experiment at Resende, and if an indigeneous firm, such as Embraer, can simultaneously convince the world aviation market that an indigenous Brazilian producer can challenge the leaders, then all investors need to take note of a new sense of serious possibility for next-generation competitiveness.

This sense of possibility is also visible in low-technology markets, especially consumer goods. The restoration of greater fiscal stability has helped greatly to stimulate a consumer boom. Even the very poor have begun to finance consumer durables on credit. The consequence has been to stimulate demand and, therefore, fresh investment in such industries as white goods and consumer electronics, including investment by foreign firms. Brazil's food industry was an early beneficiary of the consumer boom. Sales of packaged foods and beverages rose from $45 billion in 1994 to $59 billion in 1995. As in automobiles, strong market demand pulled in new investment. But unlike automobiles, much of the investment took the form of acquisitions (table III.9) rather than greenfield investment. Brazil possesses many strong local brands. However, many of the local firms do not have the scale and scope to compete on level terms with the giants.

Table III.9. Feeding frenzy: selected recent acquisitions in Brazil's food industry

Year	Target	Buyer	Estimated price (millions of dollars)
1993	CICA[a]	Unilever	284
1993	Confianca[a]	Nestlé	135
1994	Campineira	Danone	35
1994	Perdigao	Brazilian pension funds	157
1994	Adria Prod. Alimenticios[a]	Quaker Oats	100
1995	Arisco	Goldman Sachs	70
1995	Pullman Alimentos[a]	Bunge International	85
1995	Aymore	Danone	..
1995	Laticinios Avaré	Nabisco	..
1996	CCGL	Avipal	178
1996	Lacta	Philip Morris	170
1997	CEVAL - Alimento[a]	Bunge & Born	1 200
1997	Kibon SA	Unilever	930
1997	Molinos de Soya - Sadia	Archer-Daniels-Mid.	165
1997	Agroceres	Monsanto do Brasil	..
1998	Ind. Alim. Carlos de Brito	Bombril-Cirio	..

Source: Banco Pactual, reported in *The Economist*, 9 December 1996 and ECLAC (1998, table II.7).

[a]   100 per cent of capital acquired.

Economic growth during the mid-1990s helped fuel a mergers-and-acquisitions boom (figure III.10). There were about 600 mergers and acquisitions between 1992 and 1997 of which more than half had significant involvement of foreign firms. TNCs acquired, or merged with, over 150 Brazilian firms in the first half of 1998 alone (ECLAC, 1998, p. 167-169). As some of these mergers and acquisitions are likely to have been financed by funds raised locally, the official FDI figures most likely understate the full significance of the assets controlled by foreigners.

In any event, the emerging picture is that economic stability has led to a massive restructuring of some Brazilian industries. The successful domestic firms have acquired an incentive to invest beyond the short term: they can afford to borrow to buy up other local firms which have assets worth developing. A race to accumulate domestic scale has begun, partly to

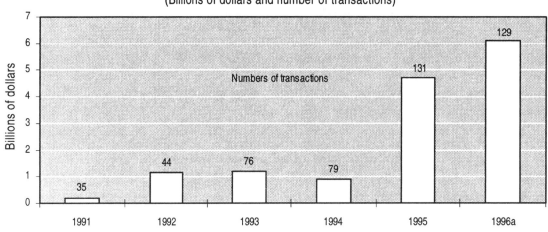

Figure III.10. Mergers and acquisitions in Brazil

(Billions of dollars and number of transactions)

Source: Securities Data Company, reported in *The Economist*, 9 December 1996.

[a] Year up to 25 October.

achieve protection from foreign bidders. Perhaps paradoxically, it is the most efficient and most successful firms that are most vulnerable to being taken over. Because Brazil's overall productivity, as in the automobile industry, remains low by international standards, the opportunity for TNCs to build on previous efficiency-enhancing investments is enormous. The same arguments apply to the growing foreign interest in the privatization of State-owned conglomerates, such as TELEBRAS and ELECTROBRAS (Wheatley, 1996).

Similar developments are beginning to take place in such non-consumer industries as pharmaceuticals. Yet, even in these industries, some senior corporate managers reported in the survey that they remained pessimistic about the chances that these conditions would last.

4. Pessimistic views

Many of the more pessimistic investors in the survey echoed this sense that Brazil had got over the worst of its past performance, but had not yet quite succeeded in building a base for sustainable recovery. Although they believed the reforms were positive, they echoed widespread criticism that reform was proceeding too slowly. They did not share the patience of the optimists, who recognized the length of the legislative agenda, the difficulties in Congress and the extent of what has already been achieved. They were anxious to see their interests recognized and protected before deciding to expand significantly. Echoing the general theme of the need for stability, one firm even offered a benchmark test that needed to be met before it would consider serious expansion again: "For credibility to be restored, there would need to be stability for at least three years, social order (we are concerned for our people), and much less red tape."

Some of the pessimists were fearful that old policies might reappear and constrain their ability to integrate their operations across borders – a repetitive theme. The general fear was expressed by one resources company, "On the whole the Brazilian Government seems to be acting rationally, but there is still some of the old dogma around". A chemicals company was more specific, "Some years ago, Brazil would not allow imports without complementary exports. We would not continue here if that situation reoccurred". Another stated, "The requirement [in our electrical equipment industry] for exports to gain duty drawbacks on imports really hinders us". And an electronics goods producer stated categorically, "Domestic policies still come first and distort trade policy. The result is inconsistency with the international marketplace and a specific deterrent to our further investment."

Others emphasized the deterrents of continued intervention in the structure and conduct of the internal market. One chemicals producer considered that "While there is a more positive attitude to FDI, when shove comes to push, protectionism is still rampant and local investment wins". Another found that "The country's basic instability still remains and state and cartel policies continue to distort the market". Both reported they were holding back on possible investments until they could be confident that open market policies were becoming stable.

The survey data also contained hints that some of the pessimists were, in fact, poised to increase their investments but had not yet sanctioned them. This is one indication of the delayed reaction, or *hysteresis*. There were plans for investment strongly backed by local management, but not yet sanctioned by the main board. For obvious reasons, the survey does not contain details of such circumstances. Yet, the fact that it can happen strongly suggests that, in the short-term, the Government might be well advised to cultivate closer relations with senior executives in the home offices.

5. A perception gap for non-investors

The pessimists' fears and their probable weighting of the evidence so as to exaggerate the negative and downplay the positive is repeated, perhaps to an even greater extent, by the non-investors. For them, the "psychic" distance is likely to be much greater. Their initial perceptions are largely formed by what they read or hear about Brazil. If this is negative, as has been the case for many bankers, they may not bother to investigate further. In the survey, there was much evidence that some do not distinguish between information on Brazil and the rest of Latin America. One consumer-goods executive reported that "Influence on corporate opinion can vary, from the reported level of the crime rate in Rio de Janeiro to issues not connected with Brazil at all, such as the musical 'Evita' or the reported activities of the late President Stroessner of Paraguay." Such lack of discrimination makes the task of overcoming the negative images of Brazil amongst such companies much more difficult.

The survey data contained much negative commentary from the sample of non-investors. Some of this was clearly at odds with actual events, as is only to be expected when the negative image is so strong as to pre-empt any effort to conduct serious research into market potential for the firm's products. One Japanese executive asked rhetorically, "Why should I bother to go as far away as I can from Japan to research a market I know is not going to be of high investment priority in even the medium-term future? No matter what is happening there, I have already too much to deal with in my present markets and in China". Inevitably, some managers will hold such views. They cannot be persuaded to the contrary by rational evidence and argument alone, for they already "know" the answers.

The fact that the survey included some responses of this kind is a good indication that it provides an adequately comprehensive and representative range of what senior executives really feel. Non-investors, to be sure, included some that would probably invest in the near future. Not only were they conscious of the opportunities developing, they were also conscious of the possibility that the "window of opportunity" might close reasonably soon as more new entrants crowded the market. The very best means to encourage more investors to overcome their natural hysteresis is for them to see the powerful combination of a supportive and welcoming Government together with competitors overcoming their inertia and taking advantage of this window of opportunity.

G. Infrastructure

An important set of considerations affecting the climate that conditions investors' attitudes is the state of the country's infrastructure. Brazil's services sector is an important component of the total infrastructure. An executive opinion survey taken in 1998, and data for the same year, indicate that the international community generally regarded Brazil's basic infrastructure as needing rapid improvement – a view largely similar to that held by this group in the mid-1990s (table III.10 and World Economic Forum, 1996). Brazil ranks unfavourably, with few exceptions, not only relative to developed countries and Asian NIEs, but also relative to top performers in Latin America. The assessment of particular service industries reveals the following:

- In the survey, the overall sophistication of financial markets in Brazil is similar to the Latin American and Asian competitors. Nevertheless, some more specific survey results point to major shortcomings. For example, entrepreneurs are concerned about insufficient access to bank credit and exceptionally high capital costs. Furthermore, the stock market and venture capital markets are relatively less efficient than in the Asian NIEs.

- The basic infrastructure in Brazil is somewhat below the average standard in Latin America and considerably below that in the developed countries and Asian NIEs. Serious bottlenecks also appear in transportation (except for air transport).[11]

- The telecommunications infrastructure in Brazil appears to be poor, which seems to represent disadvantage vis-à-vis competitors both outside and within the region. But there are indications that investment in telecommunications is improving. There is evidence, however, that the information and communication technology (ICT) infrastructure is better developed than in other countries in Latin America and Asia and that it is not far below the average of the developed countries.

Opinions about infrastructure were tested in detail by the survey undertaken for this report. There was broad agreement on most items, though the 30 experienced investors differed on some of the details.

More specifically, the survey examined infrastructure in the broadest possible terms and at several levels of aggregation. For purposes of presentation, the discussion on infrastructure is divided into four overlapping categories. The aim here is to show how executives assess the data in terms of decision-making. In many cases, the opinions appear to be rather broad and superficial. Such superficiality implies that actual investment decisions lack rigorous analysis of the detailed issues, but it is another example of how broad attitudes can be formed to affect a firm's internal climate for investment choice.

1. Economic infrastructure

Academic studies into the importance of infrastructure for FDI (Root and Ahmed, 1978, 1979) have concluded that development planning, manifesting itself in the form of an organized economic environment, creates a positive, but not by itself sufficient, climate for attracting FDI. Most firms felt that this was the case, for they could, if necessary, build the requisite infrastructure on their own (e.g. firms exploiting natural resources). But if a country is marginal on other

Table III.10. The state of Brazil's services sector in international perspective, 1999

Industry and indicator	Brazil	Argentina	Chile	Colombia	Mexico	Venezuela	Latin America[a]	Asia[b]	Developed countries[c]
A. Opinion[d]									
Financial services									
1. Legal regulation of financial institutions	5.9	6.2	7.8	5.6	4.2	4.9	5.7	5.2	6.7
2. Financial institution transparency	6.0	5.6	8.0	5.7	5.8	5.9	6.2	4.7	6.0
3. Cost of capital	1.1	2.6	4.9	1.1	1.7	1.7	2.4	4.7	6.6
4. Credit	3.1	3.1	6.8	4.9	1.8	2.7	3.9	4.0	5.9
5. Stock markets	3.9	3.7	6.0	3.1	4.5	3.6	4.2	5.5	6.9
6. Venture capital	3.4	3.0	4.3	2.2	3.3	2.6	3.1	4.4	5.3
7. Access to foreign capital markets	6.9	7.4	7.9	6.0	7.4	7.3	7.2	5.9	8.1
8. Access to local capital markets	8.0	9.0	8.5	7.7	7.8	8.0	8.2	6.2	7.9
9. Availability of finance skills	7.7	7.5	8.3	6.3	5.9	5.9	6.8	5.7	7.1
Average of above	5.1	5.3	7.0	4.7	4.7	4.7	5.3	5.1	6.7
Basic infrastructure									
10. Infrastructure maintenance and development	3.2	3.6	5.1	2.4	3.5	2.4	3.4	5.3	6.5
11. Distribution infrastructure	3.2	4.2	4.7	1.9	4.5	3.4	3.7	5.7	7.4
12. Water transportation	3.1	4.2	5.4	3.0	4.2	4.1	4.2	5.8	7.4
Average of above	3.2	4.0	5.1	2.4	4.1	3.3	3.8	5.6	7.1
ICT infrastructure									
13. New information technology	5.8	6.3	7.6	5.1	5.9	5.2	6.0	6.1	7.0
14. Electronic commerce	5.0	4.3	5.1	3.4	3.9	3.3	4.0	4.7	5.5
15. Year 2000 problem	6.7	5.7	7.5	5.7	6.7	5.1	6.1	6.8	7.3
Average of above	5.8	5.4	6.7	4.7	5.5	4.5	5.4	5.9	6.6
B. Data[e]									
Telecommunications									
16. Investment in telecommunications	0.8	0.7	1.0	1.4	0.6	1.7	1.1	1.1	0.5
17. Telephone lines	121.1	205.3	207.8	159.9	98.1	123.9	159.0	324.2	573.8
18. International telephone costs	2.8	2.8	3.0	2.8	2.4	4.2	3.0	2.1	1.4
19. Connections to internet	1.1	1.7	2.0	0.5	0.9	0.6	1.2	5.7	28.7

Source: IMD, *The World Competitiveness Yearbook, 1999.*

[a] Latin America is the average score of Argentina, Chile, Colombia, Mexico and Venezuela.

[b] Asia is the average score of Malaysia, the Republic of Korea, Taiwan Province of China and Thailand.

[c] Developed countries are the average score of France, Germany, Japan, the United Kingdom and the United States.

[d] The first 15 indicators are from the Executive Opinion Survey. Survey results are scaled from 0 (poor) to 10 (good) and defined as follows:
1. Legal regulation of financial institutions.
2. Financial institutions provide adequate information about their activities.
3. The cost of capital does not hinder competitive business development.
4. Credit flows easily from banks to business.
5. Stock markets (including secondary markets) provide adequate financing to companies.
6. Venture capital is easily available for business development.
7. Access to foreign capital markets is not restricted for domestic companies.
8. Access to local capital markets is not restricted for foreign companies.
9. Skills in finance are available in the local labour market.
10. Infrastructure maintenance and development is adequately planned and financed.
11. Distribution infrastructure is generally efficient.
12. Water transport infrastructure meets business requirements.
13. The implementation of new information technology meets business requirements.
14. Electronic commerce is sufficiently developed for business opportunities.
15. Year 2000 problem is addressed.

[e] The data for telecommunications are defined as follows:
16. As percentage of GDP.
17. Number of main lines in use per 1000 inhabitants.
18. US$ per 3 minute in peak hours to United States (for the United States to Europe).
19. Number of hosts per 1000 inhabitants.

grounds, and has poor infrastructure, then this additional fact can be a deterrent to FDI, as reflected in the poor performance that was commented on earlier in the chapter.[12]

To an important extent, countries are developing efficient and specialized infrastructures as an added inducement to prospective investors – domestic and foreign. The argument is that the effect will reduce total costs, and thus bias investment decisions more directly and effectively than with other forms of incentives. By the mid-1990s, the authorities in Taiwan Province of China, for example, planned to spend some $50-70 billion on infrastructure development over the next seven years in the race for efficiency in infrastructure. Arguably, they perceive the investment to pay off in the form of enhanced competitiveness of local firms. They may in turn attract FDI, depending on regulations and the investment climate.

In terms of Brazil's competitive position in the world FDI market, both actual and potential investors among those surveyed had a number of strongly negative impressions, though there were differences in emphasis (figure III.11). There were no discernible geographic or industry differences in the responses. The inference to be drawn from this is that, where infrastructural issues affect integrated production operations, they have an adverse impact on investment decisions.

Overall, existing investors gave a reasonably good rating to telecommunications and the airways system, but a poor rating to roads, ports and the railways system (figure III.11A). Non-investors shared a similar view, but they perceived the ports as somewhat better (figure III.11B). Responses varied according to the particular concerns of a firm's business. Yet, there were many common perspectives. "The roads are good in the south, but poor in the north"; and, "Our own road system is excellent, but it is isolated from the national system" were typical responses. More specifically:

- From their comments on the roads system, for example, it is clear that existing investors do not view Brazil as an integrated market. This is evidenced by comments about widening gap between the north-east and the rest of Brazil and the state of the roads in the north compared with the south, the latter being seen as distinctly better.

- Brazil's ports were given a poor rating by a substantial majority of existing investors. The three main areas of complaint were costs, congestion and corruption. On costs, most respondents indicated that the charges levied by Brazil's ports were higher than in most parts of the world in which they operated, "Port charges are higher in Santos than in Hamburg", commented one electronics company. A number of companies cited examples of producers in the interior, whose costs are a fraction of the international average before they leave the factory, but are well above it by the time goods have negotiated their way out of a port. Congestion figured high on respondents' list of complaints. Much of the difficulty was ascribed to corruption. "There is considerable corruption in Brazil's ports. This has to be put right quickly, otherwise they will come to a standstill", summed up many of the comments made.

- The question of corruption figured in a number of responses, with many existing investors believing that aspects of Brazilian commercial activity were subject to corrupt influences. This was highlighted particularly by comments on Manaus.

- No existing investor rated Brazil's railway system favourably. "It is so bad, it is

Figure III.11. Perceived quality of Brazil's economic infrastructure
(Per cent)

A. TNCs established in Brazil

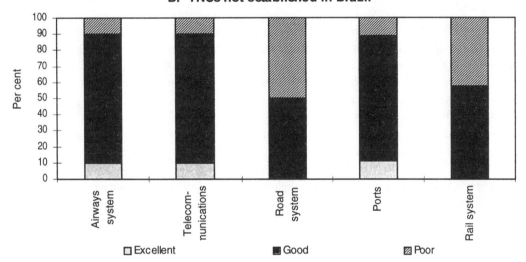

B. TNCs not established in Brazil

☐ Excellent   ■ Good   ▨ Poor

Source: survey results, based on responses of all interviewed TNCs.

almost non-existent", seemed to be the general view. Most respondents were of the view that the only way it could be improved was through private-sector involvement. Many existing and potential investors referred to the high cost of living and to the high cost of utility services, such as telecommunications and energy.

- While the telecommunications sector generally received a good rating, its costs are regarded as too high. "Telecommunications costs were too high. It will take privatization to make them more reasonable, but when that will occur is another matter", was the view of one high-technology company, echoed by many others.

- Energy-supply security and costs were also causing concern to many companies, as reflected in the comment, "Energy is becoming a concern. There is a capacity problem, and this is spiralling up costs." A number of companies were looking into ways of addressing this situation for themselves. One company mentioned that, "We are looking into co-generation with a number of other companies to overcome the possible shortage-of-supply problem". A number of respondents identified the cause of such a possible shortage as the lack of investment in dam construction. This was blamed on both lack of resources and on corruption. One respondent stated, "Until Brazil has got the energy thing right, it won't succeed". Another said, "There is no reason why Brazil should not have an abundance of cheap energy". A number of others indicated that, if utilities were seen as good but expensive, then they were "not good enough".

- This sense of unrealized potential applies especially to Brazil's waterways, which were regarded favourably. However, they were seen as very expensive to use and consequently not enough use was made of them. More competitive prices would increase demand and put pressure on the railway system to become more competitive.

It is clear that most existing investors – as well as potential investors, to the extent that they have looked into the infrastructure situation – did not see the present state of Brazil's infrastructure as being conducive to building future "poles of growth" outside the existing conurbations. While this may not be sufficient to deter all potential investors, if the general perception of it is bad, it will be a deterrent to future major FDI flows into Brazil.

It is also clear that many respondents linked infrastructure improvements to privatization. Note that these opinions did not take into account the range of more general considerations in the debate about the form and function of privatization explored earlier in chapter I. Generally stated, investors were concerned that the pace of privatization was too slow and that little progress has been made in removing the political obstacles. (Since the time of the interviews the privatization programme has been accelerated, attracting , as stated earlier, significant FDI inflows in the second half of the 1990s.) While the Government has been introducing a number of reforms by such means as presidential decrees and ordinary legislation not requiring the two thirds majority needed for constitutional reforms, there is concern about the limit to how much the Government can achieve without changing the constitution. Altering the constitution is seen by all existing investors as "being essential for the long-term success of the economic reforms". A common view was that infrastructure improvements offer an opportunity to attract greater FDI flows into Brazil. As one executive put it, "Given the enfeebled state of public finances, handing over large chunks of the economy to the private sector is the only way to upgrade the economy's infrastructure and raise its productive capacity".

Although it is recognized that progress is being made in privatizing the energy and telecommunications industries, particularly at the State level, there are still many uncertainties. For example, there are regulatory and competition-policy issues not evident in the early stages of the programme. Despite some of the states making use of a law permitting them to grant private concessions for public service projects, there are uncertainties about how the new firms will be regulated at the federal level. It is questionable as to whether foreign investors will be prepared to bear some regulatory uncertainty in return for gaining access to such an enormous market.

2. Social infrastructure

Most respondents offered little more than sweeping generalizations when asked about the social infrastructure. Some of the issues are raised in the next section of this chapter in connection with overall government policy and the dilemmas of striking an appropriate balance among various policies seeking to further development goals. This section is thus restricted to a few of the most commonly stated attitudes. They give a flavour of what investors would ideally like to see without taking into account the costs to the public purse.

The slow pace of change, at both the federal and state levels, was seen by many as the cause of what they regard as Brazil's general underinvestment in all dimensions of social infrastructure. Naturally, many investors want more education, more hospitals and more police. Better targeted spending on training the police to cope with the violence in Brazil's major cities is seen as an urgent priority.

Perhaps the most glaring social problem referred to was the extent of inequalities. Various World Bank data identify Brazil as a very unequal society. The danger of massive social unrest, if this inequality is not addressed as a matter of urgency, was stressed time and time again: "Public security will be affected by the poor standard of education and the inequalities of income distribution. The latter is the most underlying social problem facing the country".

This concern was echoed particularly when regions were discussed: "Development policies have failed to tackle the growing gap between the poor north-east and the rich south." With even less to attract either FDI or domestic investment to the north-east than the south, tax holidays and other fiscal incentives are no longer seen as enough to attract investors, particularly foreign investors, to the north-east. Most respondents were somewhat pessimistic about whether the country's changing economic realities would have any impact in the short term on Brazil's yawning regional and social inequalities. The opposition to the Government's proposals to cut government spending by reforming the social security system and civil service has not helped and is seen to have taken up valuable time. Consequently, these will continue to be of concern to international investors until the social infrastructure is in better balance.

H. Supplier arrangements

It should be remembered that interviews for this survey were largely conducted with senior management at the head offices of the companies selected. When discussing supplier arrangements at that level, therefore, a number of contradictory arguments were put forward. The text below is an accurate report of what was said, although the interpretation is tinged with a degree of scepticism on some issues.

The survey indicates that most companies claim to have clear market-determined policies regarding their use of local suppliers (figure III.12) and that only about one third of them actively encourage their home suppliers to set up alongside their foreign affiliates (figure

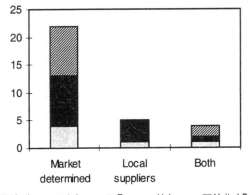

Figure III.12. Policy on use of local suppliers
(Number of companies)

TNCs from: □ Asia   ■ European Union   ▨ United Sates

Source: survey results, based on responses of all TNCs.

III.13). In only one instance was reference made to a general company policy of encouraging suppliers in foreign countries to internationalize alongside the buyer's global network. These general responses need careful interpretation.

One reason for caution is that a policy of supply arrangements being "market-determined" does not mean that supplies are contracted solely on the basis of acceptable quality and services at the lowest price. Many TNCs with market-determined general policies have specific supplier agreements that cross borders and are durable over time in ways that resemble the Japanese *keiretsu* system. These specific practices are seen as essential in the

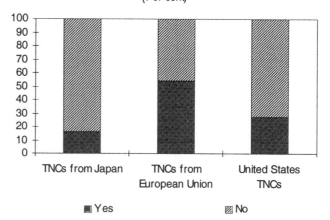

Figure III.13. TNCs encouraging their home suppliers to set up alongside their foreign affiliates
(Per cent)

■ Yes   ▨ No

Source: survey results, based on responses of all interviewed TNCs.

adjustment process undertaken by many major firms to slim down their lists of suppliers. Xerox, for example, has a global supply agreement with EDS for specific services, but it does not have a similar policy for all its suppliers.

The rationale for specific agreements of the Xerox-EDS type is similar to the general rationale for alliances, discussed in chapter II. Increasingly, companies are turning to strategic alliances as a means to expand product lines, to make the company more compatible in existing markets, and to reduce the investment and time it takes to bring good new ideas to the customer. Moreover, suppliers' alliances allow for greater investments to be made by the suppliers in equipment and systems specifically tailored to meet the needs of a major customer. A degree of uncertainty or a short time horizon of contracts often acts to discourage such investments, which is a loss to both parties. Some stability and mutual learning is needed to reap the rewards of greater productivity, and often, greater flexibility, to meet the increasingly demanding needs of global competition.

Such a rationale for specific relationships seems to be so compelling that one might be tempted to conclude that there is now a worldwide trend towards the internationalization of supplier agreements. That conclusion would be premature. Respondents, when pressed on the issue, frequently alluded to the dangers and risks inherent in these agreements. Just as with alliances, there are tensions and different opinions about the need for control, the risks of dependency and related matters. While it seems evident that Volkswagen, in the Resende plant, wishes to explore a new generation of cross-border supplier protocols, others are less confident. Indeed, some respondents went so far as to say they believed the Resende experiment would fail – though perhaps only in terms of not delivering the full set of benefits anticipated by Volkswagen.

When asked whether their local suppliers were foreign affiliates of other TNCs or independent companies, the answer was that, in many cases, they were both. In part, this response reflects the fact that some independent supplier firms – paint makers selling to the automobile industry, for example – have already been pulled through into the international market by buyer demand. It also showed that such "pull-through" demand is continuing.

One reason is that a familiar supplier can reduce the costs of replicating supply-management practices in a new location. In some cases, it is possible to import components from existing suppliers' domestic facilities, but transportation costs, logistic complexity and local production laws can limit this option.

In the case of Brazil, however, high import tariffs have frequently forced companies to buy from local suppliers, rather then permitting firms the freedom to choose which supply arrangement they consider would be most beneficial. In many industries, local firms' lack of both experience and scale have also forced many existing investors to establish links with other foreign suppliers. Many of these foreign suppliers are names familiar from the parents' domestic markets that have set up facilities in Brazil. Thus: "While we use local suppliers to a considerable extent, many of these, however, are local affiliates of transnational companies." Consequently, there has been a substantial reduction in the import of supplies, to the benefit of Brazil's balance of payments. Substantial and continued use of imported supplies has been mainly confined to high-technology industries. As one executive put it, "We import only those items not produced at all in Brazil, such as transmissions, electronics and computers".

A number of companies have created fully integrated supply arrangements of their own. One company observed that, "We build everything we can internally to avoid local inefficiencies". This pattern of supplier arrangements indicates a possible squeeze on Brazilian suppliers (figure III.14). Most respondents viewed them as no more than adequate, with a number giving them "poor" ratings: "Tariffs force us to use expensive and inefficient local suppliers, thus reducing our international competitiveness." Although some improvement is seen, often with technical assistance from TNCs, there are considerable doubts as to whether this will be enough to support the required drive for greater productivity growth and export activity in the economy.

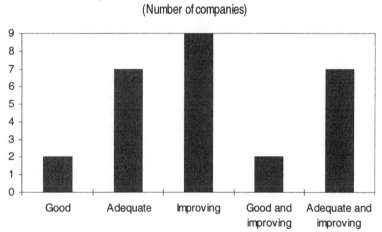

Figure III.14. Quality of suppliers in Brazil
(Number of companies)

Source: survey results, based on responses of all interviewed TNCs.

As was discussed earlier in this volume, SMEs should be accorded specific support, as possible sources of FDI in the future. These supplier pressures add to the earlier arguments. The need for support is due to the disproportionate costs of entry and to the problem of information asymmetry. When existing investors were asked whether they thought that SMEs are able to invest easily in Brazil, the general response was a negative one: "It is not very easy for SMEs to invest in Brazil: not very much encouragement is given to them. That needs changing."

A number of respondents indicated they would be prepared to help foreign SMEs overcome these hurdles in situations where they might become suppliers to their Brazilian operations. In the case of United States-based SMEs, for instance, the American Chamber of Commerce has a scheme for helping small companies wishing to set up in Brazil for the first time. Such informal, market-driven support, however, is not, many felt, sufficient to meet the needs. There was a general view that the "Government needs to support the development and importation of more small businesses through better facilities on financing, information, training and a reduction in bureaucracy".

Precisely the same arguments apply to the development of indigenous, smaller Brazilian companies. As agents of efficiency and flexibility, they also need to become stronger. Linking up with foreign SMEs offers local SMEs the potential to gain scale benefits quickly and gives them access to TNCs' technological developments and managerial and marketing know-how. There is a strong case for government support for forward-looking, local SMEs to enable them to take advantage of such opportunities more readily.[13]

Whether such policies of support would lead to the outward flow of FDI by these firms as they, in turn, come under pressures to internationalize is hard to determine. The data (figure III.14), however, suggest that such an outcome will depend on very considerable improvements being made. These may take some time to accomplish.

I. Government policy and lobbying

The responses of existing investors and non-investors to the question as to whether the policies of the Government of Brazil on FDI are conducive to attracting more investment were broadly similar. This agreement emerged despite the fact that existing investors lived through the turbulence of the 1980s and learned how to deal with local institutions. There was general agreement that the Government's macroeconomic policies, introduced with the adoption of Plan Real, created a much more favourable general environment and that the resulting improvements in the prospects for sustainable growth in domestic demand were attracting increased FDI. There was also general agreement that the favourable climate was fragile, for the track record of the country in terms of consistency of direction and stability of policy had yet to be firmly established. As has been emphasized earlier, it is stability that concerns investors most immediately in any such appraisal of relative attractiveness.

The concerns about consistency and stability were based upon perceptions of slowness in effecting the remaining constitutional changes in the social security, administrative and taxation areas needed to assure continued economic stability. The attitude of many of the respondents can be summed up in the comments of one company representative who said, "The quick implementation of the outstanding constitutional changes would transform our attitude overnight as to the seriousness and longevity of the recent reforms".

All TNCs are keenly concerned about the Government's attitude to investors as agents of development and the extent to which foreign firms are treated equally with local investors. When companies were asked whether the Government's attitude to TNCs was positive, many felt that it had an ambivalent attitude and that in the past they had experienced some element of discrimination against them. A common response was: "The attitude of the Government to TNCs is very important. We would expect to be treated like a Brazilian company and for the Government to be neutral. This has not always been so."

Some investors believed that this discrimination had largely been removed by the mid-1990s. "We hope that the Government will live up to its promise of a better climate for FDI", said one company. Another said, "The recent change in company law removing discrimination between foreign and Brazilian companies is a move in the right direction". Others were not so sure: "We need strong assurances that there is no discrimination in regulation as practiced at operating levels".

Despite this mix of views, most respondents indicated that they had not found any unwillingness on the part of the Government to listen to TNCs, although it has not often acted on what it has been told by them, thus: "The Brazilian Government has always been interested in knowing what TNCs need; in the past, the Government has taken action on the views of economists, but rarely on the views of TNCs."

The Government's attitude to TNCs is, however, an important criterion to most firms that were interviewed, when considering either an expansion of their existing investments or considering investing for the first time. This is seen as particularly important for convincing the internal company's constituency. "We could not convince our divisions that the market opportunity [in Brazil] was sufficient unless we could also show active government support for foreign investment", one high-technology company observed. This comment was echoed by a number of others.

A number of respondents were interested that the Government of Brazil had initiated this study. While some saw it as supporting their view that the Government at least listened to TNCs, others saw it as an indication that, perhaps, the Government was considering more market-driven policies: "Brazil has been fairly one-sided about FDI in the past. This would seem to be changing." Many saw this change of attitude, too, as evidence that Brazil was beginning to wake up to the fact that the competitive stakes for FDI had increased and that companies had changed some of the criteria on which they were investing internationally: "The Brazilian Government seems at last to have recognized that TNCs need a stable political and economic climate for investment."

Most of the existing investors interviewed felt that, if Brazil were to slip backwards or not to press on with further necessary reforms, this would seriously affect their future investment decisions. Similarly, those prospective investors who regard Brazil as an important potential market and who have done some serious market research are wary about their investment intentions, largely because of the country's past record: "Brazil is attractive for us – but it remains a 'jam tomorrow' market". Another company said, "The Brazilian economy will continue to be a bit of roller-coaster, although the dips may not be so great. We are more confident about the long term than three or four years ago." However, they, too, would think about Brazil again if there was any return to the past.

J. Conclusion

It is clear that the reforms of the first half of the 1990s, particularly the introduction of Plan Real, have had a positive impact on the majority of existing investors' views of Brazil. However, as is clear from the specific comments reported above, the actions taken so far are seen very much as a beginning of a long-term process. A representative response was one company's comment that "The Plan Real has had a positive effect on inflation and it has opened up new thinking on global competition. But it still has to be proved for the long term".

It is this concern about the long term that has coloured many of the responses on almost every subject that was covered by the interviews. As was shown in many of the responses, a key consideration here is the perceived need to implement the remainder of the constitutional reforms, particularly in the social security, taxation and administrative areas.[14] While the Government is seen to be achieving partial success in eliminating some of the worst excesses of the present political system through piecemeal legislation, there is concern both about whether the Government's stamina will last, and at the slowness of pace resulting from this course of action.

Overriding the concern about the constitutional reform process is whether it is too closely tied to President Cardoso: "What happens if the President does not succeed in amending the constitution to enable him to stand for re-election?" was a question posed by many respondents. Though this question has been answered by subsequent events (i.e. the constitution was amended and President Cardoso was re-elected), the fact that it was asked so forcefully indicates the seriousness with which TNCs follow internal politics and personalities. It is against this background that most existing investors, while recognizing that substantial economic progress has been made in the two years preceding the interviews, were worried about whether the short-term problems facing Brazil would keep the success aimed by the reform process out of reach.

It was recognized that linking Brazil to its ideal future – defined by most respondents as above average growth, a less intrusive Government and a more just society – would not be easy. Most TNCs welcomed the increased macroeconomic growth and stability, plus greater liberalization and some increases in FDI, and many regarded the problems of maintaining the exchange rate of the Brazilian Real as being a decisive factor. This was evidenced by the Government's difficulty in controlling spending, thus forcing up interest rates to finance its operational deficit.

Most TNCs believed they have a positive role to play in a country's development, and Brazil is no exception. They stated at the time of the interviews that, if Brazil wished to grow faster than was the case, it needed to attract considerably more FDI from both existing investors and new entrants. Referring back to the three categories of investor response, it is likely that those who are most optimistic about the future will continue to develop their interests in Brazil. The pessimistic investors may not feel like withdrawing, but they will wish to hedge their bets and may slow down their investments if they perceive any weakening in present government resolve.

The continued restoration of credibility is, therefore, the essential ingredient that is required, to ensure that any negative attitudes by present investors are overcome and, more importantly, are not mirrored by potential investors. The challenge is to combine progress on the broad macro-agendas with progress on the long list of specific detailed agendas listed at the beginning of this chapter. As one investor remarked, "Brazil is a very competitive FDI market. It doesn't always seem to understand that it has a good story to tell, but it has to tell it consistently".

Notes

1   The data provided by the Banco Central do Brasil can be interpreted in several ways, so the interpretations must be made with some caution.

2   It has, however, to be noted that the latter ratio was reduced during the 1990s because the growth of domestic investment in this group of countries has been rapid.

3   Inflation rates are the GDP inflator.

4   There is some contradictory evidence from Agodo (1978) that investment into African countries was not correlated with growth. However, given the special nature of motivations to invest in Africa under conditions of protection, this evidence can be put to one side in the argument here.

5   A new patent law (no. 9279) entered into force on 14 May 1996.

6   In this figure, the ratings for size and growth are omitted as they were much as expected and in line with the data shown earlier.

7   The recent association of Chile and Mexico to the arrangements came after the interviews were completed.

8   Note that figure III.9 is based exclusively on investors already in Brazil, because the others knew little of the specific provisions.

9   Comment in an interview with Rikuzo Koto, counsellor, Japan-Brazil Businessmen's Economic Committee, Keidanren, in Tokyo, 14 July 1983.

10   The strength of domestic demand and the new automotive regime was important for investment in the automobile industry. Most investments after 1995 took place under the regime that was established by the Government in June 1995. The companies that applied to the regime were given tariff reductions to bring capital goods, intermediate parts and even complete vehicles, subject to certain commitments regarding local content and export performance. The regime was adopted to harmonize the Brazilian regime with that prevailing in Argentina and Uruguay, two other members of the MERCOSUR. In fact a decision taken by the MERCOSUR countries in December 1994 required such harmonization within the customs union established since the Common External Tariff entered into force on 1 January 1995. For those companies that did not invest in Brazil under the regime and felt discriminated against, a tariff-quota regime was established in August 1996 and renewed for another year in 1997. The automotive regime and the requirements attached to it are to expire in December 1999, at the end of the five-year transition period granted under the WTO Agreement on Trade-Related Investment Measures (TRIMs).

11   A survey from the World Economic Forum in 1996 ranks the road and railroad system below the Latin American averge (2.3 vs. 3.1 and 1.6 vs. 1.9 respectively) and well below the Asian NIEs and the developed countries. The survey data on water transportation are the same as those in table III.10.

12   For a review of actions that the Government could consider, see UNCTAD, 1998.

13   As mentioned earlier, a new patent law came into force.

CHAPTER IV

CONCLUSIONS

Although this study was undertaken to support Brazil's objective of increasing the inflow of FDI and dealing with TNCs as part of the wider policy of accelerating the growth of the country's economy, its analysis and conclusions are valid for most countries following similar objectives.

Chapter I examined the changing patterns of worldwide FDI and discussed their implications for Brazil or any other host country. It shows that a truly global world market for FDI has emerged, driven by competition both between firms and between countries. More firms from more countries in virtually all industries are investing abroad; and all countries (and, in many cases, provinces and individual municipalities) are seeking to attract FDI. Chapter II analyzed the forces that are influencing the strategies of TNCs and how these corporations are acting to face intensifying global competition. The most striking observation that comes from examining the recent record of major firms is the sheer power of their innovation processes. It acts to change the sources of competitiveness and so invalidates – or at least seriously modifies – the explanatory power of the models that have routinely been used by economists and government officials in their dealings with the TNCs. Chapter III took a closer look at how major TNCs – both established in Brazil and those not yet present there – evaluate the attractiveness of national markets in general, and how Brazil fits into their overall strategic priorities for building next-generation competitiveness in their global markets. Again, lessons drawn from the Brazilian case may be useful for other countries as well.

The findings from the survey of senior executives' opinions and perspectives provide rich intelligence about priorities, both for understanding opportunities and for removing obstacles to change. It must be recognized, of course, that this type of data is subjective and does not necessarily reflect the facts of operational performance. However, it is a critical determinant of the climate of opinion within a corporation that, in turn, shapes *future* investment choices. These findings leave no room for complacency on the part of any government officials about the inherent attractiveness of a particular country.

While firms compete among themselves, the competition among countries for investment resources and wealth-creating skills has, overall, shifted the relative bargaining power progressively in favour of TNCs. For example, in the 1990s the United Kingdom had to rely on its economic and political record of efficiency building and upgrading capabilities to remain at the forefront of key industries; without such continuing performance, the credibility of the promotional messages being conveyed by the Invest in Britain Bureau would be seriously undermined. Similarly, Brazil can no longer afford to assume that the size and growth of its internal economy by itself will necessarily be a sufficient incentive for investors to accord the country priority for investment, ahead of many other fast-growing open economies, notably in Asia.

The message of contemporary global competition is that countries have to compete aggressively for shares in the wealth-creating resources controlled by TNCs. The changing forms of specialization in which investments are made make it imperative for any Government, wishing to harness resources of TNCs, to take on the role of a trusted partner in progress. TNCs are increasingly seeking partnerships based on such considerations as the ability to provide resources that aid the building of efficiency and productivity in a global framework, yet also permit firms the freedom to adjust to the unforeseen impacts of turbulent market forces.

In summarizing the complexities of the data and the interpretation of their implications for Brazil, this chapter proceeds as follows. First, the important general forces at work are described in the context within which TNCs determine their individual strategies. The salient requirements of a global strategy are stated in terms of central tendencies. In the past firms tended to follow a "recipe" for success and try to match the actions of their key competitors, whereas today they tend to develop unique assets and core competencies that others will find hard to emulate. The resulting variety of corporate behaviour means that a deep understanding of individual firms' strategies will assist in dealing with TNCs. Second, executives' considerations in their search for the most attractive locations in which to invest are described with special reference to Brazil. The chapter concludes with some options for action that could be pursued to attract more TNCs to Brazil as an important investment location.

A. Transformation in the global marketplace

The unprecedented growth of FDI during the past decade has changed, probably irrevocably, the underlying traditional relationships in the world economy. The output of corporate affiliates that are located in one country and owned in another now greatly exceeds the volume of world trade. When trade was predominant, commercial relationships among nations could be controlled at national borders. Now that investors have established salient positions within others' national environments and have to conform to local laws and regulations, the nature of national interdependence has deepened considerably. Just as the growing volumes of exchange transactions and portfolio flows have curbed national macroeconomic discretion, so the growth of FDI and the pervasiveness of TNCs as a contemporary phenomenon has added further pressures on government to abandon policies of "blind" protectionism and, at the same time, to extend their efforts to create an operating environment of openness, transparency and efficiency for domestic and foreign firms alike. The positive powers of the State to encourage the development of new sources of wealth creation are now at a premium.

The most important pattern to have emerged in the growth of FDI is in terms of the development of specialization in the resources being transferred by FDI and their integration into regional or corporate networks. Investment in the manufacturing sector is shifting away from being predominantly a function of transferring full-function affiliates to foreign countries, allowing managers in those countries to operate with considerable degrees of latitude. Today's new investments are often in the form of one or two specialized activities that are part of a corporation's total value chain, and, regardless of where they are being made, they remain integrated in the corporation's value chain. Previously, a foreign affiliate, especially if it was located in countries that emphasized import-substitution as the primary policy goal for FDI, was subject to certain conditions imposed by local authorities. If the country in question was large, the magnet effect of domestic demand gave the local government considerable power to insist certain requirements; today's affiliates are much less susceptible to such pressures. The demands for efficiency-enhancing integration within the parent corporation's global network mean that firms will avoid locating activities in countries in which they fear a possible loss of freedom to operate internationally. National authorities need to be aware that TNCs are increasingly calculating efficiencies and scale effects at the international level, even for their operations in the largest national economies.

Other important features of the changing nature of global competition and of the form and function of FDI include the following:

- The liberalization of the world's trade regime is closely linked to much of the recent growth of FDI in manufacturing. At the same time, the lower costs of information processing have also lowered the coordination costs for the internal operations of the TNCs and made the management of global affiliate networks possible. Thus, many more manufacturing industries are internationalizing. In addition, FDI in services has grown faster than that in manufacturing. Although previously services were more stringently regulated, TNCs in many service industries are now finding that their abilities to internationalize are growing as deregulation for them begins to take hold.

- The recent growth in FDI has been fuelled in part by the rapid increase in the number of new entrants into the international market for investment. They include increasingly SMEs, which are finding that the falling barriers to FDI and trade mean they can, and have to, invest abroad. Many important new investors have emerged from more home counties, including a growing number of developing countries. Given that investors' behaviours and policies are to a certain extent conditioned by their home country conditions where they first gained competitive success, these new entrants can take different, often strikingly different, views of potential for investment locations, as illustrated by the rise of international investment by the Korean *chaebol*. These new investors have not featured in the survey undertaken for this study, nor are they represented strongly in Brazil so far. Their different policies and levels of ability to operate in turbulent environments as compared to leading Western investors is illustrated by Daewoo's exploration of automobile assembly possibilities in Poland. General Motors (GM) had earlier explored the country and had concluded that Fiat had acquired the only desirable asset there. Daewoo saw other possibilities and invested where GM had thought there was little opportunity. It appears that Daewoo's decision spurred GM to take another look and eventually to invest. To capture the potential of such differences requires considerable understanding of the internal workings of individual corporations.

- The survey provided no evidence to support the contention of conventional economic analysis that there is "one best way" to operate in a given industry. The intensification of competition has reinforced trends visible to managers many years ago, namely that firms seek difference and not similarity in their operations as the foundation of competitiveness. Just as Daewoo differs from GM, the survey showed that investors in the same industry can have significantly different global strategies. The survey findings thus add more support to a growing body of evidence that managerial actions to create difference truly matter. Great care is therefore needed in the interpretation of data on trends as regards industry averages. Policy makers need to be sensitive to these differences and to understand the global logic for a firm's strategy in as much detail as they know the local national logic.

- Intensifying competition, combined with technological advances on many fronts, is eroding and blurring the boundaries that used to separate industries. Thus, computing blurs into software; communications and telephone companies compete directly with computer companies; new materials sciences blur the boundaries among metals, ceramics and other inorganic materials; and pharmaceuticals extend into genetics. Where firms compete across traditional boundaries, they have to develop new abilities to manage the resulting complexities and ambiguities.

- An important development as regards the advantages of scale has been the building of corporate scale. The power of TNCs to challenge even deeply entrenched national players rests on their ability to deploy centrally resources that add value to their affiliates around the world. The critical measurement of scale is no longer at the level of the factory or the national unit, but at the level of the corporate system as a whole. For many automobile firms, for example, corporate scale advantages that make a competitive difference are not at the level of the assembly plant (though the cost functions there remain important), but at the level of engineering and design, brand name and loyality, and the logistics systems that provide cost-efficient management for the internal transfer and supply of product to dealers in ever shortening time spans.

  One consequence of the growing salience of corporate scale is that purely national firms are increasingly under threat from international acquisition – as is evident in Brazilian foodstuffs and consumer products industries. In order to survive and prosper in today's market, national firms have to increase their levels of efficiency and, in many industries, expand abroad to gain the advantages of scale and scope. They need to acquire a portfolio of locational assets as a new source of corporate efficiency.

- Competition among TNCs has been likened to a form of strategic arms race, in which the ability to grow both profitably and quickly has become increasingly important. Firms need to explore novel ways in which they can accumulate new resources, build new core capabilities and deploy those capabilities effectively across their increasingly specialized networks. One consequence of this dash for growth has been a dramatic increase in the use of strategic alliances. It is now estimated that over a quarter of all new cross-border business ventures started within the past decade have been in the form of an alliance of one kind or another. Instead of relying on equity ownership for control, TNCs are increasingly exploring the complementary possibility of exercising control through cooperative, trust-based forms of contract. The development of alliances poses considerable challenges to national laws and regulations, particularly as far as competition laws are concerned.

- The need for control has been heightened by the growing complexity and specialization of international corporate networks. Every TNC in the survey emphasized that managerial control was an essential prerequisite for investment. As in the creation of alliances, managerial control is not directly linked to equity participation. Nonetheless, TNCs typically prefer equity control as well as managerial control for those operations they regard as central to their strategies. They are willing to cede equity percentages and even control under two circumstances: for those activities either deemed marginal to their strategies or capable of being outsourced or provided by other quasi-market mechanisms; or else as a temporary price for entry into a country, with the understanding that they have the right, at a later stage, to acquire control. This means that policy makers in host countries need to know, in firm-specific cases, what the management team considers to be of central importance and what is peripheral. Centrally important assets are likely to create much more added value over the asset life than are peripheral assets.

- Just as industry boundaries are blurring, so are the boundaries that define the scope of the firm. The development of alliance networks in many branches of electronic components, for example, means that it is not clear what constitutes the competitive entity, the network, and perhaps even the legal entity. There is growing evidence that it is the corporate network that is increasingly salient for defining the important unit of competitiveness (Gomes-Casseres, 1996). Further, in industries such as electronics, the key question combines the issue of who creates new sources of competitiveness with that of who is best placed to exploit them; some members of a network can learn much faster than others, and the spoils go to the fleetest of foot (Hamel, 1991).

  Similarly, the development of out-sourcing has shifted in emphasis. Instead of the traditional "make-or-buy" decision based on price, many corporations are now choosing their suppliers for long-term relationships and the ability to engage in shared design and development work. Xerox, for instance, has formed a global alliance with EDS for the provision of many internal control and support systems.

- Many of the developments require considerable change in the operations and skill-base of the firm. However, change is often slow to be accomplished, for there can be serious internal resistance: TNCs are not monolithic command structures. This resistance – labelled *hysteresis* in this study – means that the delay function has to be recognized in any negotiations.

- The growth of FDI has been characterized by new calculations of managerial choice, affecting both product ranges and the prioritization of territories. Many TNCs are now finding that their growth is seriously constrained by a shortage of managers capable of handling the growing complexity of the networks needed to achieve scale and to permit sufficient flexibility of adjustment to local conditions. The intensification of competition has forced many firms to slim down their corporate product portfolios to concentrate on a fewer number of businesses in which they can aspire to competitive leadership. The logic of global portfolio choice has implications for local operations, for the ownership of assets can change, or firms can withdraw, for reasons that have little or nothing to do with developments in a particular country.

- Choice also applies to the countries in which TNCs choose to invest. The liberalizing world has opened up so many opportunities that each firm has to work out the limits of manageability of its locational portfolio. There are few TNCs present in all countries. Moreover, the intensification of competition has forced many firms, such make choices akin to those for slimming the product portfolio. Even large firms as Royal/Dutch Shell and General Electric have exited from what they have deemed to be marginal territories in order to focus their energies on more promising areas. The calculation of marginality is not based exclusively on the presumption of needing large market scale. Rather, they are based more on the possibilities of profitable growth. Thus, for a time, Shell quit the large market of Italy when local regulatory conditions made the country unattractive even for one of the world leaders.

- It is important to note that many aspects of choice of territory are affected by concerns of managers to work within boundaries that reduce as much as possible the extra costs of doing business at a distance. In addition to the transaction costs of economic distance, there is much evidence of "psychic" distance: the preference to avoid countries that are culturally different or that suffer from poor reputations. The survey provided evidence that the concerns many investors have about Brazil are simply inaccurate. Yet decisions can be based on inaccurate data. Moreover, those TNCs that have not yet invested in Brazil had held back in part quite explicitly because of their perceptions of "psychic" distance. A later section about possible promotional activities deals with this issue.

The existence of these choices among competing opportunities across the world affects the bargaining power of TNCs in any country. It might be thought that the growth in the number of TNCs would increase competition to the advantage of a particular country, especially in the case of privatizations and the bidding associated with them. The evidence of this survey, however, suggests that, though this may happen, more often the competition is muted and restricted by the range of alternatives each potential bidder faces. Indeed, more often than not, the competition is among national, regional or municipal authorities trying to attract specific projects, and the bargaining that takes place is about the incentives these authorities are willing to offer.

B. National attractiveness

The strategy developments described above directly affect how TNCs assess the attractiveness of any territory for investment. In effect, they make two related calculations:

- One calculation considers the investment as though it were a purely stand-alone venture. In this calculation, the local returns are calculated primarily in terms of the "business-as-at-present" basis, with growth coming purely from the expansion of the market for the known product range. The risk levels are managed in terms of the risk premium added to the required cash flow and the required rate of return on remittable profits.

- The second calculation assesses the likely contribution of the venture to the development of the corporation's international network as a whole. Here, attention is focused on issues of development of new capabilities and the contribution to creating profit streams in other parts of the world.

To the extent that networks are being developed, TNCs are finding that they need to become more risk averse in their calculations of overall attractiveness. Volatility in the affairs of a stand-alone venture is well understood and containable in its impact on the corporation as a whole. In a tightly linked network, however, the risk to the network as a whole from a failure in any one of its parts is great. Thus policy makers in host countries can expect to hear prospective investors asking new questions about risk, performance guarantees, insurance of investment projects and freedom of operation, especially internationally.

The survey responses were concentrated in a number of general areas of relevance to all host countries, not only to Brazil. All TNCs, it would seem, are looking for the same sorts of general features in the environments where they choose to do business. There seemed to be little difference in response due to industry factors or to the conditioning effects of the home environment. Great differences exist, to be sure, in terms of the weighting and the precise sensitivities in the internal decision processes of a firm, but that has more to do with the search, as indicated above, for uniqueness in building sources of future competitive advantages.

Naturally, executives are eloquent in defining their preferred operating environment. In crude terms, they tend to say publicly that nothing short of complete *laissez-faire* policies will meet their needs. That caricature belies a private sophistication and understanding that Governments have a positive role to play in the support of markets and the creation of new assets. Because most respondents to the survey felt that their statements, even behind the cloak of the confidentiality agreement, were on public record, the statements recorded throughout this report emphasize the "ideal" state of affairs, not the pragmatic, workable environment in which stability and transparency are usually more important than an absence of regulation. Consequently, the listing of executive opinion should not be construed as a position of advocacy.

With those caveats in mind, the general requirements applicable to any host country that TNCs identified in connection with developments in Brazil can be grouped under the broad headings listed below:

- *Growth and stability* were the words most frequently spoken first in the review of attractiveness. Firms are looking to grow by being part of growth markets. All the firms surveyed were conscious of the priority attached to growth in Asia. For Japanese firms especially, the growth and proximity of China loomed large, and their policies of building regional core networks of linked supply in Asia means that they give little priority to growth in Latin America. Perhaps surprisingly, many of the United States and European investors looked to Latin America generally, and to Brazil in particular, as a source of much more growth than in developed countries' markets. It was noticeable that those without investments in Brazil gave much less weight to growth prospects in Latin America – some evidence of the importance of perceptions based on "psychic" distance. Perspectives on stability included a broad spectrum of political and economic issues. All items on the list have to do with the TNCs' strong desire to build dynamic, productivity-enhancing efficiencies.

- The second requirement of an attractive location is *freedom to operate*. Investors' concerns about building global efficiency mean that they start from a position of desiring market forces to be the benchmark. They wish to be able to build local systems to capture what they have learned from experience in many markets and to do so without intervention from Government.

- A third requirement in an attractive location is *freedom to operate across borders*. Those with stand-alone units are concerned with the freedom to remit profits. That concern is shared by those with integrated systems, but they have additional requirements. They need to optimize their operating systems across borders. The requirement for freedom to manage is closely tied to the requirements for managerial control mentioned earlier.

- *An efficient economic infrastructure* is generally regarded as an important inducement for investors throughout the world. Given the choice of many alternative locations, investors look for an infrastructure that reduces transaction costs and provides for the rapid movement of goods and services. Inefficient financial markets and distribution network can increase costs to a level that discourages further FDI. The ICT infrastructure has become increasing important in the 1990s as TNCs try to create greater linkages between the parent and its affiliates.

- Investors are increasingly looking for countries to provide a supply of *high-quality human capital* and also a *peaceful, just and safe society*. The former is needed both to ensure that the imported technologies can be fully absorbed and adapted to local requirements and, increasingly, to create new technologies. The latter is needed at the very personal level of ensuring the safety of company personnel, whether expatriate or local.

- Investors look carefully at the degree of *policy and investment support* they receive from central and provincial governments. The sensitivities apply as much to the provision of services and material incentives as to the attitudes of officials. It is, for example, widely repeated in Japanese industry that one reason for the accelerated growth of Japanese FDI in the United Kingdom was the warmth of the relationships formed during the negotiations and the ability of the Government to symbolize its commitment to the welcome by arranging for visits by the Royal Family. For a nation that reveres its own Emperor, this aspect of the welcome was especially significant.

- Investors widely appreciate that all Governments have the important and legitimate role to use their *bargaining power* to advance domestic interests. Though, ideally, many investors publicly proclaim the virtues of market rules, privately they accept the need for Governments to intervene where market failure occurs. In many cases, investors actively require Governments to intervene to create more favourable conditions. They do not always apply to themselves with great rigour the tests of transparency and consistency that they publicly demand of Governments.

Naturally, these are general requirements as seen by TNCs; many of them are probably also shared by domestic firms. But the extent to which a country chooses to meet them is of course a function of its own development strategy and vision (UNCTAD, 1999, ch. XI).

C. Some possible actions

The views presented above are largely the perspectives and opinions of senior executives in major TNCs on what matters to them in host countries, expressed during the interviews undertaken in the Brazilian context in spring 1996. As regards Brazil itself, all the survey respondents were at pains to emphasize that they were freely giving their views and reactions as a means of creating a dialogue in which they could tell government officials how they weighed evidence and made investment decisions. They all concurred with the proposition that it is not legitimate for TNCs to tell any government, at home or abroad, how to conduct its business. Besides, only the elected government of a democracy can determine what domestic costs are acceptable in the search for FDI and growth: there are limits to the benefits provided by incoming foreigners and also, on occasion, great costs. With these disclaimers in mind, the evidence gained from the survey can be used to suggest some options for further work and investigation, not only in Brazil but also in other host countries facing similar challenges.

Above all else, it seems abundantly clear that Brazil is not attracting as much inward FDI as it could even if the increased levels of inflows in 1998-1999 are taken into account (section III.A). The flows recorded in 1996 (when the interviews were undertaken) were, *in real terms*, not much higher than earlier flows, and they were below the proportional rates attracted by other economies with comparable economic parameters and promise. And even though there has been a sharp increase in inward FDI since 1996, there is no question about Brazil's absorptive capacity for much higher inflows (without risking an overheating of the economy). The challenge is not only how to attract greater inflows, but also how to sustain increased inflows over a long period.

Assuming that Brazil, or any country, does want to attract higher FDI inflows, the question becomes: how can that be done? Answering this question goes beyond the scope of this study, but the issues summarized in the paragraphs above suggest some of the possible lines of action that would make present and potential investors more confident of Brazil's future and more likely to upgrade their evaluation of Brazil's attractiveness relative to alternative sites for investment. It is, of course, not certain that such a re-evaluation would lead to more inward investment.

The survey revealed that there are serious misperceptions about Brazil by those who have not yet invested – a problem faced by many host countries. Throughout the study, investors gave evidence of the importance of the experience of learning to live and prosper within the borders of the country. Those who lacked that experience, or who had had particularly bad earlier experiences, held quite pessimistic views about the country and its future prospects. The analysis of opinion showed that TNCs held common views about many aspects of general strategy and locational preference, but that, when it came to Brazil in particular, they fell into three categories, the first two of which applied only to those with extensive Brazilian assets and many years of operating experience:

- The first category consisted of the optimists. Those in this category were predominantly United States-based TNCs that had weathered the storms of the "lost decade" and had begun to prosper once again. Although it was agreed that opinions expressed in the survey would be kept confidential, it was public knowledge – but perhaps not widely appreciated – that Brazil represented the second largest foreign market for Xerox. The extraordinary success of this firm in a country that has experienced such difficulties was an example of the kind of record that undoubtedly made for optimism. While Xerox's corporate opinion of Brazil need not be revealed, it is clear that such successes can form part of the "demonstration effect" to encourage others to follow. Optimists also included some of the European investors.

- The other investors were labelled the pessimists. These included firms that had had poor experiences in the past and felt that conditions had not improved; firms that were finding conditions at the time of the interviews troublesome and were especially exposed to difficulties mentioned above; and firms that had other more pressing strategic priorities. The last group of pessimists included most of the Japanese TNCs, among them many that were not officially part of the survey but about which generalized government-related material was made available to the study team. Japanese firms were, in the main, much more interested in the growth dynamics of Asia, and most found Latin America too far away to be of strategic priority. This collective attitude among manufacturers was reinforced by the recommendations of their bankers who were reported to be providing a stream of negative opinion. The fact that Matsushita's colour television business in Brazil was their number four volume market worldwide did little to counter such pessimism.

- The non-investors were all important TNCs, mainly operating in the same industries as those that had already invested significantly. Their views on Brazil were uniformly much more pessimistic than those of the established investors. In part, their views were based on ignorance and perhaps misapprehension. But, to the extent that views held by executives contribute to investment decisions, they are crucially important for the purposes of this study. Note, however, the composition of the sample of non-investors: it excluded, by design, many prospective investors in services and industries subject to privatization processes. During 1995-1996, these non-investors took more optimistic positions and many, such as Electricité de France, invested large amounts of capital in Brazil for the first time. It is to be hoped that the demonstration effect of these new investors will be backed up by performance and sequential investments and will also act as a further spur to change the opinions of the pessimists.

The objective of increasing the inward flow of FDI cannot easily be met by focusing on the optimists, for they have great knowledge of the country, intimate experience of dealing with key decision-makers and already had plans that gave Brazil priority in the decision queue. While the optimists should not be neglected (and after-investment services are particularly important here), there is considerable potential for increasing FDI by converting the pessimists. In addition, there is an important series of "markets" to be addressed for investments in areas excluded from the survey.

The evidence on the general shifts in composition of FDI flows worldwide reveals several areas of high potential for promoting more investment into host countries, including Brazil, as follows:

- Investors in the services sector are of two kinds: those (e.g. power distribution) that are essentially local and subject to privatization policies; and those (e.g. software and financial services) that are internationalizing rapidly.

- SME investors who are charting new ways to cross borders without the benefit of economies of scale.

- Natural resource investors whose interests cannot be taken for granted simply because a host country, such as Brazil, possesses considerable natural resources.

- Investors from countries that have not featured prominently in the lists of home countries for TNCs. In particular, the Republic of Korea seems to have potential, as do Argentina and Chile. Just as regional trade integration in the EU spurred German firms, for example, to invest in the United Kingdom, the growth of regional trade may be expected to attract investment that is designed to deepen the intertwining effects of trade and FDI.

Each of these categories needs separate treatment, some aspects of which is suggested below. The common ground for all possible actions to encourage more investment is that Brazil needs to address directly the problem of its image gap. As was stated by a Brazilian at the time of the interviews: "Brazil has managed its image poorly" – a situation that probably applies to a number of other host countries as well.

One possible response to the need to generate greater awareness of the "new" Brazil is to make it easier for successful investors to assume the position of trusted and valued "insiders". By this, Brazil could make it possible for foreign firms to play a leading contributing role, for example, in setting technical standards. Brazilian representation at various European Industrial Round Tables might also add impact. Where foreign investors have made particularly noteworthy achievements, as in export development, these could be actively publicized by the Government. There is convincing evidence that promotional efforts can pay off (e.g. Wells and Wint, 1990).

The more general case for a promotional effort appears strong. Perhaps the Government of Brazil should consider establishing an investment promotion agency whose principal task would be to attract FDI to Brazil, particularly that type of investment deemed most important to advance the country's development. (As of November 1999 the World Association of Investment Promotion Agencies had 105 members, from both developed and developing countries). In the case of Brazil, the promotional effort seems best targeted at the categories of investors listed above, rather than being merely broadcast throughout the diplomatic system. The reasons are twofold: the evidence from other countries suggests targeting by category; and the needs of the various groups of firms potentially interested in Brazil are so diverse that they will need separate treatment.

Consider first the findings from other countries. The most successful type of programme mounted by the developed and developing countries studied was one which attracts investors seeking export-oriented facilities – an orientation that, in any event, fits well with Brazilian objectives. The least successful programmes were those aimed at investors to serve the domestic market. For the latter group of firms "it would appear, the domestic market itself is the attraction; to reach that market, investment elsewhere is unlikely to be feasible. Firms that are seeking sites to serve export markets, however, can choose from a wide range of countries. For these firms ... investment promotion and ... pricing via incentives ... [can] have an impact on their investment decisions" (Wells and Wint, 1990, p. 65).

These findings confirm the essence of the survey. Brazil's internal market size is an important magnet for some firms, but not for many others. Some major manufacturers (including, probably, non-investors in the survey) for whom internal size is the dominant motivation for investment have already considered Brazil and made their decisions. No amount of publicity is likely to change their minds, for it is likely to be dismissed by such firms as "rhetoric" and thus lacking credibility. A demonstration that progress is durable and growth rapid in a liberalizing economy will provide more convincing evidence in the future. Publicizing success, such as the return to stability after the financial crisis, may start to rebuild a sense of credibility, provided that the publicity effort is sustained and consistent.

There are, however, important exceptions to this argument, especially for newly internationalizing TNCs and SMEs. They are likely to have an information gap of the kind reported by many Japanese firms – "Brazil is too far away for me to be bothered to go and find out what is happening" – because of several more proximate investment opportunities.

New investors in the services sectors could, as suggested in chapter I, benefit from both better access to information and also from further adjustments in the regulatory framework. The beginning of liberalization of services has already led to a significant increase in FDI. Another step could be the establishment of some form of "services development zone" located in the heart of manufacturing centres. Direct assistance could be provided in the form of help in locating offices, recruitment and the training of staff. Not only might this encourage more service firms to internationalize faster, but also the effect could be particularly advantageous in encouraging more manufacturing investment. Additional service providers would help relieve service and efficiency bottlenecks and simultaneously help to reduce transaction costs.

The information needs and priority types of assistance appropriate for attracting more service firms are likely to be rather similar to the needs of many of the SMEs (UNCTAD, 1998). These are firms that do not have extensive networks of contacts, and that do not posses the resources needed to survive prolonged negotiations or to undertake extensive market research. The successful ones are likely to be those that possess strong entrepreneurial instincts and the commitment to pursue opportunities. Assistance with information is likely to be of less interest than introductions to possible deal makers. These are the firms for which the slogan of "make it easy to feel part of the family" might be appropriate. They do not want prolonged negotiations about permits to enter, nor elaborate consultancy assistance about market averages. The services already provided by SEBRAE (Brazilian Support Service for Small Business) could be boosted, and greater cooperation sought from multilateral agencies such as UNCTAD's programme on entrepreneurship and SMEs. The services have to be provided with some care, for SMEs are generally suspicious of anything that suggests bureaucracy. They look for ways to find out about new markets by "learning by doing"; they are the entrepreneurial engine of future prolonged growth and, therefore, deserve encouragement.

The promotion of more inward investment in natural resources can undoubtedly be assisted in any country, including Brazil, by a removal of restrictions, if any, on foreign control of mining operations. This, combined with important changes in the tax regime, may open the door for much greater inward FDI to provide value-added processing to raw materials. It is noticeable that some large firms had actually stayed in Brazil during the upheavals and restrictions of the recent past. This is consonant with many of the survey responses adopting the view, as expressed by the finance director of the leading minerals TNC, RTZ-CRA : "We always took a long-term view. And we always expected the restrictions to be lifted eventually".[1] Others had a different perspective and so stayed away. Liberalisation, economic stabilization, and new tax incentives could well create a new "gold rush". No particular promotional programme is needed for these industries, now that the crucial reforms are in place and the information about them is readily available.

Yet many firms (especially among non-investors) did not know about these changes in the natural resources sector, which are important signals of the seriousness of the Government's policy intent and could be used to counter some of the criticism mentioned earlier.

Quite different needs apply to potential new investors from countries such as the Republic of Korea or Malaysia (after they fully recover from the financial crisis which resulted in a decrease in outward FDI). For them, provision of information, understanding and creating an attractive climate is essential. The Korean *chaebols* have expanded abroad through outward FDI (that slowed down during the financial crisis) as a result of changes taking place in their home economy and the needs to create new forms of global corporate scale. Their expansion abroad exposed the limits to the information on foreign markets learned by the export sales forces and retained in the head office. One of the authors of this report can attest from personal experience that perspectives are being shaped by personal visits and personal observation. For example, before his visit to the United Kingdom, one company president had an image of the United Kingdom as a country gently subsiding into a form of post-industrial tourist destination. However, a week in London, served to show him a country with a new-found competitiveness and he reversed an earlier decision by locating a leading-edge technology venture in Scotland. His earlier image of the country had dominated his views despite briefings at home by the investment agency, Invest in Britain Bureau (IBB).

It is likely, therefore, that other non-investors might have distorted images of host countries similar to those reported in the survey about Brazil. Promotion in the form of visits and high-level dialogue is likely to be an effective complement to information packages. Like a SME, the *chaebol* is driven by deals, not abstract data. The means to reduce their "psychic" distance from distant host countries, such as Brazil, however, are likely to be quite different from those of Japanese firms, many of which start with negative images and alternative ideas about the signals of opportunity.

In the calculation of targeting promotional efforts of all kinds to boost FDI flows, care needs to be taken to search out the companies that are already, or have the potential to become, competitively strong in their global industries. The message of global competition and the "arms-race" to accumulate resources means that there will be casualties. Even giant trees can fall in a forest. Billion-dollar corporations may lose out in this race, for size accumulated from past success is no guarantee of continuing competitiveness. There is nothing new in this observation, though it seems often forgotten. The example of Chrysler described in chapter II makes the point. In the early 1960s, Chrysler tried to bolster its declining position by using its corporate scale and ability to borrow money to buy significant assemblers in France and the United Kingdom. Yet, its diminishing competitiveness meant that it could not fund its commitments. Host countries, including Brazil, need to be aware of such pitfalls by investing in intelligence about the relative strength of those firms it is actively seeking out for investment.

Finally, it should be well understood that there is a fairly long time lapse before the most important consequences of any promotional programme are realized: the slow adaptation of large systems is a fact of corporate life. To be sure, there may be some quick gains from promotion, but these are likely to pale into insignificance when compared to the longer-term potential. The full returns are likely to be well worth the effort.

Note

1   Quoted in *The Financial Times,* 22 April 1966.

REFERENCES

Agarwal, Jamuna P. (1980). "Determinants of foreign direct investment: a survey", *Weltwirtschaftliches Archiv*, 116, 4, pp. 739-773.

___ (1986). *Home Country Incentives and FDI in ASEAN Countries*, Kiel Working Papers 258 (Kiel: Institute of World Economics).

___ (1994). "The effects of the single market programme on foreign direct investment into developing countries", *Transnational Corporations*, 3, 2, pp. 29-44.

___ (1996). *Does Foreign Direct Investment Contribute to Unemployment in Home Countries – An Empirical Survey*, Kiel Working Papers 765, (Kiel: Institute of World Economics).

___ Ulrich Hiemenz and Peter Nunnenkamp (1995). *European Integration: A Threat to Foreign Investment in Developing Countries*, Kiel Discussion Papers 246 (Kiel: Institute of World Economics).

___ Rolf J. Langhammer, Matthias Lücke and Peter Nunnenkamp (1995a). *Export Expansion and Diversification in Central and Eastern Europe: What Can Be Learnt from East and Southeast Asia?*, Kiel Discussion Papers 261 (Kiel: Institute of World Economics).

Agodo, O. (1978). "The determinants of US private manufacturing investments in Africa", *Journal of International Business Studies*, 9, 3 (Winter), pp. 95-107.

Ajami, R. A. and D. A. Ricks (1981). "Motives for the American firms investing in the United States", *Journal of International Business Studies*, VII, pp. 25-46.

Albert, Michel (1991). *Capitalism contre capitalisme* (Paris: Seuil).

Baden-Fuller, Charles W. F. and John M. Stopford (1994). *Rejuvenating the Mature Business* (Boston, Mass.: Harvard Business School Press).

Banco Central do Brazil (1998). "Census of foreign capitals in Brazil - 1995 base year" (http://www.bcb.gov.br/ingles/censo/980527/hics0500.htm).

___ (2000). "Press Releae – Foreign Sector" January.

Barlow, E. Robert and Ira T. Wender (1955). *Foreign Investment and Taxation* (Englewood Cliffs: Prentice Hall).

Bartlett, Christopher and Sumantra Ghoshal (1989). *Managing Across Borders* (Harvard: Harvard Business School Press).

Bielschowsky, R. (1992a). "Transnational corporations and the manufacturing sector in Brazil", (Santiago de Chile: CEPAL), mimeo..

___ (1992b). "Adjusting for survival: domestic and foreign manufacturing firms in Brazil in the early 1990s", (Santiago de Chile: CEPAL), mimeo..

Blau, P. M. (1964). *Exchange and Power in Social Life* (New York: Wiley).

Borys, B. and D. B. Jemison (1989). "Hybrid arrangements as strategic alliances: theoretical issues in organisational combinations", *Academy of Management Review*, 14, pp. 412-421.

Brash, Donald T. (1966). *American Investment in Australian Industry* (Canberra: Australian University Press).

Bureau of Industry Economics (1995). *Beyond the Firm: An Assessment of Business Linkages and Networks in Australia*, Research Report 67 (Canberra: Australian Government Publishing Service).

Câmara de Comércio e Indústria Brasil-Alemanha (1996). *Arbeitskreis Privatisierung. Aktueller Stand der Privatisierungen in Brasilien*, October (Rio de Janeiro).

Cantwell, J. and E. Tolentino (1990). "Technological accumulation and third world multinationals" (Reading: University of Reading), mimeo..

Centre for Business Strategy (1990). *Continental Mergers are Different: Strategy and Policy for 1992* (London: London Business School).

Chang, Sea Jin (1995). "International expansion strategy of Japanese firms: capability building through sequential entry", *Academy of Management Journal*, 38, 2, pp. 383-407.

Chia Siow Yue (1995). *Foreign Direct Investment and Economic Integration in East Asia*, paper presented at the 8th Workshop on Asian Economic Outlook, Asian Development Bank, Manila, Philippines, 23-24 November.

Chudnovsky, Daniel (1992). *The TNC's Changing Investment*, Technical Report No. 64 (Paris: OECD Development Centre).

___, Bernardo Kosacoff and Andres López (1999). *Las Multinacionales Latinamericanos - Sus Estrategias en un Mundo Globalizado* (Buenos Aires: Fonda de Cultura Economica).

Colebrook, Philip (1972). *Going International. A Handbook of British Direct Investment Overseas* (New York: John Wiley and Sons).

Collins, T. M. and T. L. Doorley III (1991). *Teaming Up for the 90s* (Homewood, Ill: Irwin).

Contractor, Farok J. and Peter Lorange (eds.) (1988). *Co-operative Strategies in International Business* (Lexington, Mass.: Lexington Books).

Deininger, Klaus and Lyn Squire (1996a). "A new data set measuring income inequality", *World Bank Economic Review*, 10 (September), pp. 565-591.

___ (1996b). *New Ways of Looking at Old Issues: Inequality and Growth*, unpublished internal paper (Washington, D.C.: World Bank).

Done, Kevin and Virgina Marsh (1995). "Koreans take the Romanian road", *Financial Times*, 5 May 1995.

Dunning, John H. (1980). "Toward an eclectic theory of international production: some empirical tests", *Journal of International Business Studies*, 11, 1 (Spring/Summer), pp. 9-31.

___ (1993). *Multinational Enterprises and the Global Economy* (Reading, Mass.: Addison-Wesley Publishing Co).

___, R. van Hoesel and R. Narula (1998). "Third world multinationals revisited: new developments and theoretical implications". in J.H. Dunning, ed., *Globalization, Trade and Foreign Direct Investment* (New York: Pergamon).

Dyer, Geoff (1997). "Charge of the heavy brigade", *Financial Times*, 20 August 1997, p. 9.

Economic Commission for Europe (ECE) (various issues). *East-West Investment News* (Geneva: United Nations).

Economic Commission for Latin America and the Caribbean (ECLAC) (1995). *Preliminary Overview of the Economy of Latin America and the Caribbean 1995* (Santiago: United Nations).

___ (1998). *Foreign Investment in Latin American and the Caribbean 1998* (Santiago: United Nations).

The Economist (1996). "Survey: Latin American finance – the rollercoaster region", 9 December 1996.

The Economist Intelligence Unit (EIU) (1996). *Country Report: Brazil.* 1st Quarter (London: Economist Intelligence Unit).

Encarnation, Dennis J. (1992). *Rivals Beyond Trade: America versus Japan in Global Competition* (Ithaca, NY: Cornell University Press).

___ and Louis T. Wells, Jr. (1986). "Evaluating foreign investment", in T. H. Moran et al., eds., *Investing in Development: New Roles for Private Capital?* (Washington, D.C.: Overseas Development Council), pp. 61-86.

Enright, Michael (1993). "Organization and co-ordination in geographically concentrated industries", in Daniel Raff and Naomi Lamoreaux, eds., *Co-ordination and Information: Historical Perspectives on the Organization of Enterprise* (Chicago: Chicago University Press for NBER).

European Commission and United Nations Conference on Trade and Development (UNCTAD) (1996). *Investing in Asia's Dynamism: European Union Direct Investment in Asia* (Luxembourg: Office for Official Publications for European Communities).

Eurostat (1995). *European Union Direct Investment 1984-93*, EU publication (Brussels: Statistical Office of the European Communities).

Fahim-Nader, Mahnaz and William J. Zeile (1995). "Foreign direct investment in the United States", *Survey of Current Business*, 75, 5, pp. 57-81.

French-Davis, R. (1990). "Conversion deuda-capital en Chile", *Cuadernos de Economia*, 82, (Santiago: Universidad Catolica).

Fritsch, W. and G. Franco (1991). *Foreign Direct Investment in Brazil: Its Impact on Industrial Restructuring*, Technical Report No. 52. (Paris: OECD Development Centre).

Funke, Norbert, Peter Nunnenkamp and Rainer Schweickert (1992). *Brazil: Another Lost Decade? Domestic Policies and Attractiveness for Foreign Capital*, Kiel Discussion Papers 188 (Kiel, Institute of World Economics).

GATT (various issues). *International Trade. Trends and Statistics* (Geneva).

Goldhar, J. D. and David Lei (1991). "The shape of twenty-first century global manufacturing", *The Journal of Business Strategy*, 12, 2, pp. 37-41.

Gomes-Casseres, Ben (1996). *The Alliance Revolution* (Harvard: Harvard Business School Press).

Green, R. T. and W. H. Cunningham (1975). "The determinants of U.S. foreign investment: an empirical examination", *Management International Review*, 15, pp. 113-120.

Gundlach, Erich and Peter Nunnenkamp (1996a). *Some Consequences of Globalization for Developing Countries*, Kiel Working Papers 753 (Kiel: Institute of World Economics).

___ (1996b). *Labor Market Implications of Globalization: How the Triad Has Dealt with Competitive Challenges* (Kiel: Institute of World Economics) mimeo..

___ (1996c). *Falling Behind or Catching Up? Developing Countries in the Era of Globalization*, Kiel Discussion Papers 263 (Kiel: Institute of World Economics).

Hamel, Gary (1991). "Learning in international alliances", *Strategic Management Journal*, 12 (special Summer issue), pp. 83-103.

Handelsblatt (1996). *Tokio für mehr Handel zwischen Apec und Mercosur*, August 20, p. 8.

Harbison, John R. and Peter Pekar, Jr. (1993). *A Practical Guide to Alliances* (Los Angeles, CA: Booz-Allen & Hamilton).

Harrison, Bennett (1992). "Industrial districts: old wine in new bottles?", *Regional Studies*, 26, 5, pp. 469-483.

Haspeslagh, Philippe and David B. Jemison (1991). *Managing Acquisitions: Creating Value Through Corporate Renewal* (New York: The Free Press).

Hennart, Jean-François (1982). *A Theory of Multinational Enterprise* (Ann Arbor: University of Michigan Press).

Hiemenz, Ulrich, Peter Nunnenkamp, et al. (1991). *The International Competitiveness of Developing Countries for Risk Capital*, Kieler Studien 242 (Tübingen: Mohr).

Hill, H. and B. Johns (1985). "The role of direct foreign investment in developing East Asian countries", *Weltwirtschaftliches Archiv*, 121, pp. 355-81.

Hilton, Isabel (1996). "Economic reform in Brazil: an interview with Eliana Cardoso", *International Affairs*, 72, 4, pp. 737-750.

Hollerman, Leon (1988). *Japanese Economic Strategy in Brazil: challenge for the United States* (Lexington, Mass.: Lexington Books).

Hu, Yao-Su (1992). "Global or stateless corporations are national firms with international operations", *California Management Review*, 34, 2 (Winter), pp. 107-126.

Hufbauer, Garry C. and Jeffrey J. Schott (1993). *NAFTA - An Assessment* (Washington, D.C.: Institute for International Economics).

Huss, Torben (1994). "Transplants in Mexico's Maquiladoras", *Trade and Investment: Transplants* (Paris: OECD), pp. 99-145.

IMD (1999). *The World Competitiveness Yearbook 1999* (Lausanne: IMD).

Inter-American Development Bank and Institute for Latin American Relations (IADB-IRELA) (1996). *Foreign Direct Investment in Latin America in the 1990s* (Madrid).

International Monetary Fund (IMF). *Balance of Payments Yearbook* (Washington, D.C.: IMF), various issues.

___. *International Financial Statistics* (Washington, D.C.: IMF), various issues.

Jones, L. P., P. Tandon and I. Vogelsang (1990). *Selling Public Enterprises: A Cost-Benefit Methodology* (Cambridge, Mass: MIT Press).

de Jonquieres, G. (1996). "Mercosur trade group under fire", *Financial Times*, 24 October.

Kanitz, S. (1995). *The Emerging Economic Boom* (Rio de Janeiro: Makron Books do Brasil Editora Ltda).

Knickerbocker, Frederick T. (1973). *Oligopolistic Reaction and Multinational Enterprise* (Boston: Harvard University, Graduate School of Business Administration).

Kobrin, Stephen J. (1976). "The environmental determinants of foreign direct investment: an expost empirical analysis", *Journal of International Business Studies*, 6, pp. 29-42.

Kotabe, Masaaki (1996). *MERCOSUR and Beyond: The Imminent Emergence of the South American Markets* (Austin: The University of Texas, Center for International Business Education and Research).

Krugman, Paul (1991). *Geography and Trade* (Cambridge, Mass.: MIT Press).

Kuemmerle, Walter (1997). "Building Effective R&D Capabilities Abroad", *Harvard Business Review*, March-April, pp. 61-70.

Lall, Sanjaya (1983). *The New Multinationals: The Spread of Third World Enterprises* (London: Wiley/IRM).

___ (1997). "East Asia", in J.H. Dunning, ed., *Governments, Globalization and International Business* (Oxford: Oxford University Press).

Lane, Raymond (1996). Chief Operating Officer, Oracle's strategy for the 'networked society', presentation to the Strategic Management Society, Phoenix, Arizona, 10-13 November.

Landström, H. (1992). "The relationship between private investors and small firms: an agency theory approach", *Enterpreneurship and Regional Development*, 4, pp. 199-223.

Levie, Jonathan D. (1994). "Can government nurture young growing firms? Qualitative evidence from a three nation study", in W.D. Bygrave et al., eds., *Frontiers of Entrepreneurship Research 1995* (Wellesley, Mass.: Babson College), pp. 514-527.

Lora, Eduardo and Carmen Pagés (1996). *La legislación laboral en el proceso de reformas estructurales de America Latina y el Caribe*, Inter-American Development Bank, mimeo..

Lorenzoni, Gianni and Charles Baden-Fuller (1995). "Creating a strategic centre to manage a web of partners", *California Management Review*, 37, 3 (Spring), pp. 146-163.

Low, Linda, Eric D. Ramstetter and Henry Wai-Chung Yeung (1996). *Accounting for Outward Direct Investment from Hong Kong and Singapore: Who Controls What?*, NBER Working Paper No. 5858.

Lowe, Jeffrey H. and Sylvia E. Bargas (1996). "Direct investment positions and historical-cost basis", *Survey of Current Business*, 76, 7, pp. 45-60.

Madeuf, Bernadette (1994). "Direct investment/international trade linkages: the issue of transplants", *Trade and Investment: Transplants* (Paris: OECD), pp. 25-79.

Markides, Costas (1996). *Diversification, Refocusing and Economic Performance* (Cambridge, Mass: MIT Press).

Matsushita, Mitsuo (1980). "Administrative guidance and economic regulation in Japan", *The Japanese Business Law Journal*, 1 (December).

Ministry of Foreign Trade and Economic Cooperation (1995/96). *Almanac of China's Foreign Economic Relations and Trade* (Hong Kong: China Resources).

Morris, M. and M. Hergert (1987). "Trends in international collaborative agreements", *The Columbia Journal of World Business*, 22, pp. 15-21.

Nachrichten für den Außenhandel (NFA) (1996). *Mehr Auslandsinvestitionen in Brasilien*, August 27: 2.

Nigh, D. (1986). "Political events and the foreign direct investment decision: an empirical examination", *Management and Decision Economics*, 7, 2 (June), pp. 99-106.

Nishiyama, Yohei, Teruho Kushima and Hidehiko Noda (1999). "EXIM Japan FY 1998 survey: the outlook of Japanese foreign direct investment. The Asian crisis and the prospect of foreign direct investment by Japanese manufactures", Journal of Research Institute for International Investment and Development, 25, (January/February), pp. 4-70.

Nunnenkamp, Peter (1996). *The Changing Pattern of Foreign Direct Investment in Latin America*, Kiel Working Papers 736 (Kiel: Institute of World Economics).

___ and Jamuna P. Agarwal (1993). *Die Bundesrepublik Deutschland und Lateinamerika: Perspektiven für eine intensivere wirtschaftliche Zusammenarbeit im Bereich der Direktinvestitionen*, Forschungsauftrag des Bundesministeriums für Wirtschaft (Kiel: Institute of World Economics).

___ , Erich Gundlach and Jamuna P. Agarwal (1994). *Globalisation of Production and Markets*, Kieler Studien 262 (Tübingen: Mohr).

Odle, Maurice (1993). "Foreign direct investment as part of the privatization process", *Transnational Corporations*, 2, 2, pp. 7-34.

Ohmae, Kenichi (1989). "The global logic of strategic alliances", *Harvard Business Review*, March-April, pp. 143-154.

Oliver, C. (1990). "Determinants of interorganisational relationships: integration and future directions", *The Academy of Management Review*, 15, 2, pp. 241-265.

Oman, Charles (1994). *Globalisation and Regionalisation: The Challenge for Developing Countries* (Paris: OECD Development Centre).

Organisation for Economic Co-operation and Development (OECD) (1993). *Regional Integration and Developing Countries* (Paris: OECD).

___ (1994). *Statistics on International Direct Investment of Dynamic Non-Member Economies in Asia and Latin America*, OECD Working Papers 68, Vol. II. (Paris: OECD).

___ (1995). *International Direct Investment Statistics Yearbook* (Paris: OECD).

___ (1996). *International Direct Investment Statistics Yearbook* (Paris: OECD).

Penn World Table (PWT) (1994). Mark 5.6., (Cambridge, Mass.: National Bureau of Economic Research).

Perlmutter, Howard V. and David A. Heenan (1986). "Co-operate to compete globally", *Harvard Business Review*, March-April, pp. 136-152.

Penrose, Edith T. (1956). "Foreign investment and the growth of the firm", *The Economic Journal*, 66, 262, pp. 220-235.

Porter, Edward (1995). "Privatizations: Brazil's slow sale", *América Economía*, Annual Edition 1995/96, pp. 42-44.

Porter, Michael E. (1990). *The Competitive Advantage of Nations* (New York: The Free Press).

Prahalad, C. K. and Yves Doz (1987). *The Multinational Mission* (New York: The Free Press).

Ramamurti, Ravi (1992). "Why are developing countries privatizing?", *Journal of International Business Studies*, 23, 2, pp. 225-249.

Root, F. R. and A. A. Ahmed (1978). "The influence of policy instruments on manufacturing direct foreign investment in developing countries", *Journal of International Business Studies*, 9 (Winter).

___ (1979). "Empirical determinants of manufacturing direct foreign investment in developing countries", *Economic Development and Cultural Change*, 27, 4 (July).

Rumelt, Richard P. (1991). "How much does industry matter?", *Strategic Management Journal*, 12, pp. 167-185.

Sachs, Jeffrey D. and Andrew Warner (1995). *Economic Convergence and Economic Policies*, NBER Working Papers 5039 (Cambridge, Mass.: National Bureau of Economic Research).

Schemo, Diana J. (1996). "Brazil's moves cheer consumers, but economists see danger", *International Herald Tribune*, 9 September, p. 12.

Simonian, Haig (1996). "Alliances forged in the factory", *The Financial Times*, 4 November.

Stopford, John M. (1992). *Offensive and Defensive Responses by European Multinationals to a World of Trade Blocs*, Technical Report No 64 (Paris: OECD Development Centre).

___ (1995). "Competing globally for resources", *Transnational Corporations*, 4, 2, pp. 34-57.

___ (1997a). "Regional networks and domestic transformation", in R. Kim, ed., *Asia-Pacific Co-operation: Current Issues and Agenda for the Future* (Seoul: Yonsei University), forthcoming.

___ (1997b). "Implications for national governments", in J. Dunning, ed., *Governments, Globalization and National Business* (Oxford: Oxford University Press), pp. 457-480.

___ and Louis Turner (1985). *Britain and the Multinationals* (Geneva: Wiley/IRM).

___ and Susan Strange (1991). *Rival states, rival firms: Competition for world market shares* (Cambridge: Cambridge University Press).

Teitel, S. and F. Toumi (1987). De la substitucion de importaciones a las exportaciones: la experienca de las exportaciones de manufacturas de Argentina y Brasil, *Desarrolo Econonomico*, Buenes Aires, abril-junio, 27, 105, pp. 29-60.

United Nations Centre on Transnational Corporations (UNCTC) (1978). *Transnational Corporations in World Development: A Reexamination* (New York: United Nations), United Nations publication, Sales No. E.78.II.A.5.

___ (1991). *Debt-Equity Conversion: A Guide for Decision-Makers* (New York: United Nations), United Nations publication, Sales No. E.90.II.A.22.

___ (1992). *The Determinants of Foreign Direct Investment. A Survey of the Evidence* (New York.: United Nations), United Nations publication, Sales No. E.92.II.A.2.

___ (1993). *From the Common Market to EC 92. Regional Economic Integration in the European Community and Transnational Corporations* (New York: United Nations), United Nations publication, Sales No. E.93.II.A.2.

United Nations Conference on Trade and Development (UNCTAD) (1989). *Handbook of International Trade and Development Statistics 1988* (New York and Geneva: United Nations), United Nations publication, Sales No. E/F.88.II.D.11.

___ (1993a). *World Investment Report 1993: Transnational Corporations and Integrated International Production* (New York: United Nations), United Nations publication, Sales No. E.93.II.A.14.

___ (1993b). *Small and Medium-sized Transnational Corporations. Role, Impact and Policy Implications* (New York: United Nations), United Nations publication, Sales No. E.93.II.A.15.

___ (1994a). *World Investment Directory, Foreign Direct Investment, Legal Framework and Corporate Data. Vol. IV, Latin America and the Caribbean* (New York: United Nations), United Nations publication, Sales No. E.94.II.A.10.

___ (1994b). *Handbook of International Trade and Development Statistics 1993* (New York and Geneva: United Nations), United Nations publication, Sales No. E/F.94.II.D.24.

___ (1995a). *World Investment Report 1995: Transnational Corporations and Competitiveness* (New York and Geneva: United Nations), United Nations publication, Sales No. E.95.II.A.9.

___ (1995b). *Handbook of International Trade and Development Statistics 1994* (New York and Geneva: United Nations), United Nations publication, Sales No. E/F.95.II.D.15.

___ (1996a). *World Investment Report 1996: Investment, Trade and International Policy Arrangements* (New York and Geneva: United Nations), United Nations publication, Sales No. E.96.II.A.14.

___ (1996b). *Trade and Development Report, 1996* (Geneva: United Nations), United Nations publication, Sales No. E.96.II.D.6.

___ (1997a). *World Investment Report 1997: Transnational Corporations, Market Structure and Competition Policy* (New York and Geneva: United Nations), United Nations publication, Sales No. E.97.II.D.10.

___ (1997b). "Transnational corporations, foreign direct investment and development", Note by the UNCTAD Secretariat (WT/WGTI/W/8/Add.1).

___ (1997c). *Handbook of International Trade and Development Statistics 1995* (New York and Geneva: United Nations), United Nations publication, Sales No. E/F.97.II.D.7.

___ (1997d). *Sharing Asia's Dynamism: Asian Direct Investment in the European Union* (Geneva: United Nations), United Nations publication, Sales No. E.97.II.D.1.

___ (1998). *Handbook on Foreign Investment by Small and Medium-sized Enterprises. Lessons from Asia* (Geneva: United Nations), United Nations publication, Sales No. E.98.II.D.4.

___ (1999). *World Investment Report 1999: Foreign Direct Investment and the Challenge of Development* (New York and Geneva: United Nations), United Nations publication, Sales No. E.99.II.D.3.

___ (forthcoming). *Small and Medium-sized Transnational Corporations and Competitiveness* (Geneva: United Nations), United Nations publication.

U.S. Department of Commerce (USDOC) (1996). "US direct investment abroad: detail for historical-cost position and related capital and income flows, 1995", *Survey of Current Business*, 76, 9 (Washington, D.C.: United States Government Printing Office), pp. 98-128.

___ (1995). "US direct investment abroad: operations of US parent companies and their foreign affiliates", Revised 1992 Estimates (Washington, D.C.: United States Government Printing Office).

___ (1997). "US direct investment Abroad", *1994 Benchmark Survey*, Preliminary Results (Washington, D.C.: United States Government Printing Office).

United Nations Industrial Development Organization (UNIDO) (1996). *Industrial Development Global Report 1996* (Vienna: UNIDO).

Vernon, R. (ed.) (1988). *The Promise of Privatization: A Challenge for U.S. Policy* (New York: Council of Foreign Relations Books).

___ and W. H. Davidson (1979). *The Overseas Spread of Manufacturing for Technology-Intensive Products by US Multinational Enterprises* (Washington, D.C.: National Science Foundation).

World Association of Investment Promotion Agencies (WAIPA) (1997). *WAIPA Directory 1997* (Geneva: United Nations).

Wälde, Thomas W. (1993). "Investment policies and investment promotion in the mineral industries", in Bruce McKern, ed., *Transnational Corporations and the Exploitation of Natural Resources* (London: Routledge), pp. 340-362.

Wells, Louis T., Jr. and Alvin G. Wint (1990). "Marketing a country: promotion as a tool for attracting foreign investment", Foreign Investment Advisory Service, Occasional Paper 1 (Washington, DC: The World Bank).

Wesson, Thomas J. (1993). *An Alternative Motivation for Foreign Direct Investment*, unpublished Ph.D dissertation (Harvard: Harvard University).

Wheatley, Jonathan (1996). "Foreign groups line up for Brazil Telecoms sale", *Financial Times*, 18 September, p. 17.

Williamson, Peter and Q. Hu (1994). *Managing the Global Frontier* (London: Pitman Publishing).

Womak, J., D. Roos and D. Jones (1990). *The Machine that Changed the World* (New York: Macmillan Business).

World Bank (1996). *World Development Report 1996: From Plan to Market* (Washington D.C.: Oxford University Press).

_____ (1999). *Entering the 21st Century World Development Report 1999/2000* (Washington D.C.: Oxford University Press).

World Economic Forum (WEF) (1995). *The World Competitiveness Report* (Geneva: World Economic Forum).

_____ (1996). *The Global Competitiveness Report* (Geneva: World Economic Forum).

_____ (1998). *The World Competitiveness Yearbook* (Geneva: World Economic Forum).

Yoshiko, Michael Y. and U. Srinavasa Rangan (1995). *Strategic Alliances: An Entrepreneurial approach to Globalisation* (Harvard: Harvard Business School Press).

Young, Michael K. (1984). "Judicial review of administrative guidance: governmentally encouraged consensual dispute resolution in Japan", *Columbia Law Review*, 84, 4 (May), pp. 923-983.

ANNEXES

Annex 1. List of interviewed transnational corporations

A. Face-to-face interviewees

EUROPE

Carrefour	**Michel Pinot**, Director General Americas
Fiat	**Roberto D'Agostino**, International Development
	Eugenio Maraghini Garrone, Vice President, International Relations
	Pietro Sighicelli, Vice President, International Development
Hoechst	**John A Graham**, Corporate Center Americas
	Jurgen E Lingnau, Corporate Center Americas
Mercedes-Benz	**Bernhard Mader**, Senior Manager, Corporate Planning Support Group
Nestlé	**Herbert Oberhaensli**, Assistant to Chairperson for Economic Affairs
	Peter E Wagner, Sous-Directeur
Philips Components	**Mr. De Kleuver**, Chairperson & Chief Executive
Pirelli	**Alessandra Meneghini**, Head of Mergers & Acquisitions
Rhone Poulenc	**E. Musa**, Executive Group Vice President (and Chairman, Rhodia)
Robert Bosch	**Rolf Leven**, Robert Bosch Limitada
Royal Dutch Shell	**Mark Moody Stuart**, Managing Director
Saint-Gobain	**Jean-Louis Beffa**, Chairperson and Chief Executive Officer
Siemens	**Anton Thaler**, Executive Director
SmithKline Beecham	**Paul Blackburn**, Director & Vice President International Finance
Volkswagen	**Peter Pohl**, Manager, South American region
Unilever	**Morris Tabaksblat**, Chairperson & Chief Executive Officer

(Sandoz declined to take part due to time being taken up with merger; SmithKline Beecham took their place)

JAPAN

Hitachi	**Yushi Akiyama**, External Affairs Department, International Business Planning and Development Group
	Masayuki Kohama, General Manager, External Affairs
	Ryoko Matsumura, External Affairs Department
	Tetsuo Saito, Manager, External Affairs
Matsushita	**Kazuo Arai**, Corporate Management Division for Latin America
	Shigeru Mizuno, Corporate Management Division for Latin America
	Akira Tsutsumi, Corporate Management Division for Latin America
New Oji Paper	**Yojiro Katoh**, Manager, International Affairs Department
Nippon Steel	Anonymous
Toshiba	**Haruo Kawahara**, General Manager, Corporate Planning
	Yoshihiko Wakumoto, Executive Vice President
Toyota Motor Corporation	**Tetsu Araki**, Manager, Group 2, Latin America & Caribbean Division
	Yoshiharu Gohara, General Manager, Latin America & Caribbean Division
	Toshiaki (Tag) Taguchi, Director, Member of the Board

UNITED STATES

Alcoa	**Richard L. Fischer**, Executive Vice President Chairman's Counsel
Caterpillar	**Robert C. Petterson**, Vice President
Eastman Kodak	**George King**, Vice President/General Manager, Latin American Region
E I Du Pont Nemours & Co	**Michael Emery**, Senior Vice President
General Electric	**Camille Chee-Awai**, Vice President, Latin America Infrastructure Investments, GE Capital **John T. McCarter**, President and Chief Executive Officer, GE do Brasil
General Motors Corporation	**G Mustafa Mohatarem**, Chief Economist **John R. Murtagh**, Area Director
IBM	**Elio Catania**, President, IBM Latin America **Lois Jackson**, Director, External Programs, Office of the President of Latin America
Johnson & Johnson	**Ronald J. Casanova**, Finance Controller **John A Papa**, Assistant Treasurer **Alberto A. Perez,** Controller, Overseas Division
Philip Morris	**Gustavo A. Pineyro**, Director, Planning & Business Development, Latin America Region
RJR Nabisco	**Robert Sharpe**, Senior Vice President/General Counsel
Xerox	**Thomas B. McKean**, Director, Office Document Products, America's Customer Operations **Raymond S. O'Connor**, Director, Marketing & Strategy Integration Planning

B. Telephone interviewees*

EUROPE

BTR plc
Cadbury Schweppes plc
Continental AG
Courtaulds plc
General Electric Company
Lucas Industries plc
Pearson
Redland plc
Rolls-Royce plc
Tare & Lyle plc

JAPAN

Ricoh Corporation
Takada Corporation
A consumer products company

UNITED STATES

CNA Insurance

* *Note*: A further 11 companies were also interviewed on the telephone but expressly requested that their names not be identified in this report.

Annex 2. Research questionnaire

1   What are the main business activities of your company?

2   What are your main product areas in the developed countries where you operate?

3   What are your main product areas in the developing countries where you operate?

4   From how many developed countries do you *export* and of which products? (Please specify)
(Percentages by countries/by product: 50 per cent or more/20-50 per cent/5-20 per cent/
minimal or not at all)

5   Are there any developed countries where you export more than 50 per cent of your output? If
so, where and which products?
(Percentages by countries/by product: 50 per cent or more/20-50 per cent/5-20 per cent/
minimal or not at all)

6   From how many developing countries do you export and of which products? (Please specify)
(Percentages by countries/by product: 50 per cent or more/20-50 per cent/5-20 per cent/
minimal or not at all)

7   Are there any developing countries where you export more than 50 per cent of your output?
If so, where and which products?
(Enter percentages by countries/products where possible)

8   To where and what do you *export* from Brazil? (Please specify)

9   Are your exports from Brazil more than 50 per cent of your output there. If so, in which
product?

10 What dictates your overseas investment strategy today, how has this changed in recent years
and what has dictated any changes, if any?

11 What are the critically important countries for you?

12 In which developed countries do you have an investment presence that is significant to your
business in any of the following: (per cent assets, per cent sales)

    o   manufacturing
    o   sales/service
    o   marketing
    o   full function
    o   other (please specify)

13 In which developing countries do you have an investment presence that is significant to your
business in any of the following:

    o   manufacturing
    o   sales/service
    o   marketing
    o   full function
    o   other (please specify)

14   What is the position with regard to Brazil?

15   Do you have a strong preference for control when considering your FDI strategy?

16   How do you serve the critically important countries in each of your key product areas?

   o   wholly-owned operations
   o   joint ventures
   o   strategic alliances with other TNCs
   o   franchising
   o   other non-equity forms of collaboration with local firms
   o   licensing

17   What is your first priority in each case?

18   How many people do you employ and where?

19   Do you have:
      a)   a general statement about your foreign investment strategy?
      b)   a statement of your foreign investment strategy by countries and/or by product?
      If so, would it be possible to have a copy?

20   Do you produce/publish a consolidated balance sheet for all your global activities?

21   What are the key trends that affect the form of your decisions to invest outside your home country?   (High/medium/low)

   o   new technologies
   o   new or shifting buyer/consumer needs
   o   emergence of new industry segments
   o   shifting input costs or availability
   o   changes in government regulation
   o   privatization
   o   deregulation
   o   competitors' actions
   o   other

22   Have these altered over the last 10 years or so?

23   How do the three key motivations attributed to FDI of

   o   market-seeking
   o   resource-seeking
   o   efficiency-seeking

   apply to your FDI strategy generally and to your investment strategy for Brazil particularly?

24   In your view, is foreign direct investment by transnationals generally becoming more specialized?

25   Over what period has that been happening?

26   Has the pattern of your foreign investment shifted in recent years/during that timespan?

27   If so, in what way?

28   Has it become more specialised by country/function?

29   How do you view Brazil in this context?

30   What are the key determinants of your foreign investment strategy? (High/medium/low)

     o   political, economic and social stability
     o   to provide scale for critical output processing
     o   to serve multinational customers
     o   to add extra volume from host country market
     o   to gain access to natural resources
     o   access to high skill labour
     o   unit labour cost
     o   benefits of specialized infrastructure
     o   fiscal, financial and other incentives by host countries
     o   new forms of production
     o   other

31   Have these altered in the last 10 years or so?

32   Are the determinants of your foreign investment strategy the same for each of your main activities and in what respect?

33   If not, what are the main differences by product area?

34   How do the above determinants apply in relation to your investment strategy in Brazil? (high/medium/low)

     o   political, economic and social stability
     o   to provide scale for critical output processing
     o   to serve multinational customers
     o   to add extra volume from host country market
     o   to gain access to natural resources
     o   access to high skill labour
     o   unit labour cost
     o   benefits of specialised infrastructure
     o   fiscal financial and other incentives by host countries
     o   new forms of production
     o   other

35   What are the factors that make a difference in choosing countries outside your domestic market in which to invest?

     o   attractiveness of the local market:
           -     its size
           -     its growth potential
           -     other
     o   factor availability/costs:
           -     labour
           -     materials supply
           -     energy
           -     working capital/financing
           -     other
     o   currency volatility

36   How do these factors apply to your view of Brazil?

37   Have these altered over the last 10 years or so? If so, how?

38   How do you determine the location and management of the value chain for selling worldwide?

    o   do you still transfer full function facilities?
    o   are you investing by activity now more than before?
    o   if so, what has influenced the change?

39   When looking at location do you consider geographical region (e.g., Latin America) versus individual nation or sub-region within a nation or do you look specifically at countries?

40   Where is the greatest growth in the global economy today for your products?

41   How does that affect your location priorities?

42   Do you do any R&D abroad? If so, where and for what products and technologies?

43   Are you using your foreign affiliates to supply your home market or to create new (third country) markets which you cannot create from your home base?

44   If they are supplying the home market, what is contribution to final product(s) sold in your home market made by foreign affiliates?

45   Does this vary from foreign affiliate to foreign affiliate?

46   How is the contribution to final product from foreign affiliates determined?

47   To what products and to what extent does your Brazilian affiliate make a contribution to your home market?

48   If your foreign affiliates are creating new markets, which ones, where are they creating them and for what product(s)?

49   What percentage of your international trade is in technology payments?

50   What percentage of your technology payments is in the form of transfers among company affiliates?

51   How important are the following issues in your decision to invest in a foreign country for the first time? (High/medium/low)

    o   existence of a central agency to deal with on all matters, including immigration, visas, permits etc.
    o   stability in granting permits to operate factories
    o   requirements for joint ventures
    o   requirements requiting the employment of local staff
    o   restrictions on employing foreign nationals, particularly in management positions
    o   quality of life issues such as housing, education, health
    o   employment legislation
    o   local product content requirements
    o   environmental/pollution issues
    o   taxation issues
    o   technology and licensing restrictions

    o   transferability of funds/repatriation of profits

    o   constraints on style of management (corporate governance)

52   Are there any other issues which you consider when investing in a country for the first time?

53   How does your FDI activity relate to your general international trading strategy as regards:

    o   complementarity
    o   substitutability
    o   integration of the two

54   When deciding to make subsequent investments in a particular country, do the criteria change? If so, how?

55   Does this apply to Brazil? If so, how?

56   In addition to the above factors, what aspects of host government policy, such as trade environment, would encourage/discourage you from investing in a particular country?

57   How do these apply to your investment in Brazil?

58   Do you actively contribute to the debate on the rules governing trading conditions and activities in the countries where you operate?

59   Does this also apply to Brazil?

60   If active, how and why do you make that decision?

61   If passive, why?

62   Do you have clear policies about the extent to which you use local suppliers or is it purely market determined?

63   Do you encourage your home suppliers to set up alongside your foreign affiliates?

64   Would you encourage your existing suppliers outside Brazil to relocate to Brazil to support your operations there?

65   Do you attempt to match your major competitors in every major market around the world?

66   Do you think you will increase the level of your FDI in the foreseeable future?

67   What will drive that increase?

68   Where are the main regions you are likely to invest and in what of percentages? (e.g., 50 per cent European Union, 20 per cent in Asia, 10 per cent in Latin America and then within Latin America)

69   Do you see the form of your foreign investment changing? If so, what and how?

70   What do you see as the drivers of those changes?

Turning now specifically to Latin America and Brazil

71   What are your views on Latin America as a region in which to invest? (Attractive/unattractive)

72   Is it becoming more attractive compared to Europe/Asia/Pacific/other?

73   Are some Latin American countries becoming more attractive than others? If so, which ones?

74   What makes a country attractive to you?

75   How does Brazil fit in with your views on Latin America?

76   With the expected high growth in Asia, do you think that you will invest more there rather than in Latin America and Brazil in particular?

77   Is the MERCOSUR important to your FDI strategy?

78   Which of the main integration instruments in the MERCOSUR are of importance to the company's operation? (Central/considerable/no relevance)

   o   common external tariff regime
   o   regional trade liberalisation
   o   exemptions from trade liberalisation
   o   sector protocols
   o   policy harmonisation initiatives

79   Would you invest in any of the MERCOSUR countries if they were not members of MERCOSUR?

80   Is your policy with regard to the MERCOSUR to replace imports and serve the local and/or regional market or do you see it as a source point for export to other MERCOSUR member countries or to third countries?

81   Would it be more attractive, within the MERCOSUR, to serve the Brazilian market from another member country and, if so, what would be the underlying reasons?

82   Under what conditions could Brazil be considered as a main production base serving the Argentinean and other MERCOSUR markets?

83   What factors would lead you to locate your operations in other MERCOSUR countries and from there export to Brazil?

84   How confident are you about relying on the MERCOSUR commitments?

85   In what areas, if any, is the existence of NAFTA and the recent European Union-MERCOSUR co-operation agreement affecting business opportunities in the MERCOSUR area?

86   How does Brazil fit into your FDI strategy in respect of your main product areas?

87   How long have you been in Brazil?

88   What made you go there in the first place?

89   What is the degree of priority that you give to Brazil compared to the other countries in which you operate?

90   Is your Brazilian affiliate seen as a source of supply of products or components for products for your home market or is it operating in new markets both in Brazil and from Brazil?

91 How are the macro prices implied by Brazil's stabilisation policies and fiscal reforms affecting business practices in your sector(s)?

92 Are there any aspects of your FDI strategy in Brazil with which you are unhappy?

93 If so, what and how would you like to see them improved?

94 How much weight do you attach in your investment decisions about Brazil to the following? (High/medium/low)

   o   overall growth of Brazil's economy
   o   factor availability/cost (materials, energy, labour, working capital and financing)
   o   input costs (local purchases of goods, services, such as telephones)
   o   reliability of the above
   o   regulatory environment
        -    stability in granting permits to operate factories
        -    requirements for joint ventures
        -    requirements for technical transfers
        -    restrictions requiting employment of local staff
        -    labour legislation and practices
        -    restrictions on employing foreign nationals, particularly in management positions
        -    local product content requirements
        -    environmental/pollution issues
        -    taxation policy
        -    technology and licensing restrictions
        -    intellectual property matters
        -    transferability of funds
        -    constraints on style of management (corporate governance)

95 Are you making currency forecasts for the *real* rate against international currencies?

96 Do you perceive there to be any general sense of pressure on Brazil's currency?

97 Do you think that the Brazilian Government's attitudes to TNCs are positive?

98 How important are Government attitudes to TNCs in your criteria when looking at Brazil?

99 Do you think that the Brazilian government's policies on FDI are conducive to attracting more foreign investment into Brazil?

100 If not, what does Brazil need to do to attract more FDI?

101 Are the Brazilian Government's national policy objectives on FDI, such as employment creation, technology transfer, etc., compatible generally with TNC's requirements and with your requirements in particular?

102 If not, in what way do they need to be changed to ensure compatibility of TNC requirements generally and your requirements particularly with national policy objectives?

103 Are there any aspects of Government policy at state level which are important to your FDI involvement in Brazil?

104 If so, are they a positive or negative influence?

105   If a negative influence, how might they be improved?

106   How do you rate the quality of Brazil's infrastructure:
      (Excellent/good/poor)

      o   its ports
      o   its road system
      o   its rail system
      o   its telecommunications
      o   its airways system
      o   its industrial development
      o   other

107   How strong is your local competition and is this a problem for you?
      (high/medium/low relative to your home market competition)

108   What would prevent you from extending your present investment in Brazil?

109   [If you were not already an investor in Brazil, what would be the important determinants
      that would attract you to Brazil?]

110   What is the nature of your outsourcing relationships in Brazil?

111   Is the quality of your suppliers in Brazil adequate/improving?

112   Have you been replacing imports with local suppliers or vice versa?

113   Are those local suppliers affiliates of other foreign companies or Brazilian?

114   What are the products for which you continue to import components?

115   Have you encouraged any of your Brazilian suppliers to support your operations elsewhere?

116   If the answer to question 115 is no, ask: do you intend to do so in the future?

      If no again, ask why. Because it is not the policy of your company to use the same suppliers
      worldwide? or Because Brazilian suppliers would not qualify to undertake such functions
      abroad?

117   If yes, ask why?

118   Are small supply organisations able to invest easily in Brazil or are they subject to an over
      bureaucratic barrier to entry?

119   What do you think would cause a major increase in FDI inflows in to Brazil?

120   Is this any different from what has been happening elsewhere?

121   Why do you think that FDI inflows into Brazil have fluctuated up and down so markedly in
      the last 10 years or so?

122   Is this unique to Brazil?

Selected UNCTAD publications on
transnational corporations and foreign direct investment

A. Individual studies

World Investment Report 1999: Foreign Direct Investment and Challenge of Development. 536 p. Sales No. E.99.II.D.3. $45.

World Investment Report 1999: Foreign Direct Investment and Challenge of Development. An Overview. 75 p. Free-of-charge.

Foreign Direct Invesment in Africa: Performance and Potential. 89 p. UNCTAD/ITE/IIT/Misc. 15.

The Financial Crisis in Asia and Foreign Direct Investment: An Assessment. 101 p. Sales No. GV.E.98.0.29. $20.

World Investment Report 1998: Trends and Determinants. 430 p. Sales No. E.98.II.D.5. $45.

World Investment Report 1998: Trends and Determinants. An Overview. 67 p. Free-of-charge.

Bilateral Investment Treaties in the mid-1990s. 314 p. Sales No. E.98.II.D.8. $46.

Handbook on Foreign Direct Investment by Small and Medium-sized Enterprises: Lessons from Asia. 200 p. Sales No. E.98.II.D.4. $48.

Handbook on Foreign Direct Investment by Small and Medium-sized Enterprises: Lessons from Asia. Executive Summary and Report on the Kunming Conference. 74 p. Free-of-charge.

International Investment Towards the Year 2002. 166 p. Sales No. GV.E.98.0.15. $29. (Joint publication with Invest in France Mission and Arthur Andersen, in collaboration with DATAR.)

World Investment Report 1997: Transnational Corporations, Market Structure and Competition Policy. 420 p. Sales No. E.96.II.D.10. $45.

International Investment: Towards the Year 2001. 81 p. Sales No. GV.E.97.0.5. $35. (Joint publication with Invest in France Mission and Arthur Andersen, in collaboration with DATAR.)

World Investment Directory. Volume VI: West Asia 1996. 192 p. Sales No. E.97.II.A.2. $35.

World Investment Directory. Volume V: Africa 1996. 508 p. Sales No. E.97.II.A.1. $75.

Sharing Asia's Dynamism: Asian Direct Investment in the European Union. 162 p. Sales No. E.97.II.D.1. $26.

Transnational Corporations and World Development. 656 pp. ISBN 0-415-08560-8 (hardback), 0-415-08561-6 (paperback). £65 (hardback), £20.99 (paperback).

Companies without Borders: Transnational Corporations in the 1990s. 224 pp. ISBN 0-415-12526-X. £47.50.

The New Globalism and Developing Countries. 336 pp. ISBN 92-808-0944-X. $25.

Investing in Asia's Dynamism: European Union Direct Investment in Asia. 124 p. ISBN 92-827-7675-1. ECU 14. (Joint publication with the European Commission.)

World Investment Report 1996: Investment, Trade and International Policy Arrangements. 332 p. Sales No. E.96.II.A.14. $45.

World Investment Report 1996: Investment, Trade and International Policy Arrangements. An Overview. 51 p. Free-of-charge.

International Investment Instruments: A Compendium. Sales No. E.96.IIA.12 (the set). $125.

World Investment Report 1995: Transnational Corporations and Competitiveness. 491 p. Sales No. E.95.II.A.9. $45.

World Investment Report 1995: Transnational Corporations and Competitiveness. An Overview. 51 p. Free-of-charge.

Small and Medium-sized Transnational Corporations: Executive Summary and Report on the Osaka Conference. p. 60. UNCTAD/DTCI/6. Free-of-charge.

World Investment Report 1994: Transnational Corporations, Employment and the Workplace. 482 p. Sales No. E.94.II.A.14. $45.

World Investment Report 1994: Transnational Corporations, Employment and the Workplace. An Executive Summary. 34 p. Free-of-charge.

World Investment Directory. Volume IV: Latin America and the Caribbean. 478 p. Sales No. E.94.II.A.10. $65.

Liberalizing International Transactions in Services: A Handbook. 182 p. Sales No. E.94.II.A.11. $45. (Joint publication with the World Bank.)

Accounting, Valuation and Privatization. 190 p. Sales No. E.94.II.A.3. $25.

Environmental Management in Transnational Corporations: Report on the Benchmark Corporate Environment Suvey. 278 p. Sales No. E.94.II.A.2. $29.95.

Management Consulting: A Survey of the Industry and Its Largest Firms. 100 p. Sales No. E.93.II.A.17. $25.

Transnational Corporations: A Selective Bibliography, 1991-1992. 736 p. Sales No. E.93.II.A.16. $75. (English/French.)

Small and Medium-sized Transnational Corporations: Role, Impact and Policy Implications. 242 p. Sales No. E.93.II.A.15. $35.

World Investment Report 1993: Transnational Corporations and Integrated International Production. 290 p. Sales No. E.93.II.A.14. $45.

World Investment Report 1993: Transnational Corporations and Integrated International Production. An Executive Summary. 31 p. ST/CTC/159. Free-of-charge.

Foreign Investment and Trade Linkages in Developing Countries. 108 p. Sales No. E.93.II.A.12. $18.

World Investment Directory 1992. Volume III: Developed Countries. 532 p. Sales No. E.93.II.A.9. $75.

Transnational Corporations from Developing Countries: Impact on Their Home Countries. 116 p. Sales No. E.93.II.A.8. $15.

Debt-Equity Swaps and Development. 150 p. Sales No. E.93.II.A.7. $35.

From the Common Market to EC 92: Regional Economic Integration in the European Community and Transnational Corporations. 134 p. Sales No. E.93.II.A.2. $25.

World Investment Directory 1992. Volume II: Central and Eastern Europe. 432 p. Sales No. E.93.II.A.1. $65. (Joint publication with ECE.) $65.

World Investment Report 1992: Transnational Corporations as Engines of Growth: An Executive Summary. 30 p. Sales No. E.92.II.A.24. Free-of-charge.

World Investment Report 1992: Transnational Corporations as Engines of Growth. 356 p. Sales No. E.92.II.A.19. $45.

World Investment Directory 1992. Volume I: Asia and the Pacific. 356 p. Sales No. E.92.II.A.11. $65.

B. IIA issues paper series

Trends in international investment agreements: an overview. UNCTAD Series on issues in international investment agreements. (forthcoming). Sales No. E.99.II.D.23. $ 12.

Lessons from the MAI. UNCTAD Series on issues in international investment agreements. (forthcoming) 31p. Sales No. E.99.II.D.26. $ 12.

National Treatment. UNCTAD Series on issues in international investment agreements. 104p. Sales No. E.99.II.D.16. $12.

Fair and Equitable Treatment. UNCTAD Series on issues in international investment agreements. 64p. Sales No. E.99.II.D.15. $12.

Investment-Related Trade Measures. UNCTAD Series on issues in international investment agreements. 64p. Sales No. E.99.II.D.12. $12.

Most-Favoured-Nation Treatment. UNCTAD Series on issues in international investment agreements. 72p. Sales No. E.99.II.D.11. $12.

Admission and Establishment. UNCTAD Series on issues in international investment agreements. 72p. Sales No. E.99.II.D.10. $12.

Scope and Definition. UNCTAD Series on issues in international investment agreements. 96p. Sales No. E.99.II.D.9. $12.

Transfer Pricing. UNCTAD Series on issues in international investment agreements. 72p. Sales No. E.99.II.D.8. $12.

Foreign Direct Investment and Development. UNCTAD Series on issues in international investment agreements. 88p. Sales No. E.98.II.D.15. $12.

C. Serial publications

Current Studies, Series A

No. 30. *Incentives and Foreign Direct Investment.* 98 p. Sales No. E.96.II.A.6. $30. (English/French.)

No. 29. *Foreign Direct Investment, Trade, Aid and Migration.* 100 p. Sales No. E.96.II.A.8. $25.

No. 28. *Foreign Direct Investment in Africa.* 119 p. Sales No. E.95.II.A.6. $25

No. 27. *The Tradability of Banking Services: Impact and Implications.* 195 p. Sales No. E.94.II.A.12. $50.

No. 26. *Explaining and Forecasting Regional Flows of Foreign Direct Investment.* 58 p. Sales No. E.94.II.A.5. $25.

No. 25. *International Tradability in Insurance Services.* 54 p. Sales No. E.93.II.A.11. $20.

No. 24. *Intellectual Property Rights and Foreign Direct Investment.* 108 p. Sales No. E.93.II.A.10. $20.

No. 23. *The Transnationalization of Service Industries: An Empirical Analysis of the Determinants of Foreign Direct Investment by Transnational Service Corporations.* 62 p. Sales No. E.93.II.A.3. $15.00.

No. 22. *Transnational Banks and the External Indebtedness of Developing Countries: Impact of Regulatory Changes.* 48 p. Sales No. E.92.II.A.10. $12.

No. 20. *Foreign Direct Investment, Debt and Home Country Policies.* 50 p. Sales No. E.90.II.A.16. $12.

No. 19. *New Issues in the Uruguay Round of Multilateral Trade Negotiations.* 52 p. Sales No. E.90.II.A.15. $12.50.

No. 18. *Foreign Direct Investment and Industrial Restructuring in Mexico.* 114 p. Sales No. E.92.II.A.9. $12.

The United Nations Library on Transnational Corporations. (Published by Routledge on behalf of the United Nations.)

Set A (Boxed set of 4 volumes. ISBN 0-415-08554-3. £350):

Volume One: *The Theory of Transnational Corporations.* 464 p.

Volume Two: *Transnational Corporations: A Historical Perspective.* 464 p.

Volume Three: *Transnational Corporations and Economic Development.* 448 p.

Volume Four: *Transnational Corporations and Business Strategy.* 416 p.

Set B (Boxed set of 4 volumes. ISBN 0-415-08555-1. £350):

Volume Five: *International Financial Management*. 400 p.

Volume Six: *Organization of Transnational Corporations*. 400 p.

Volume Seven: *Governments and Transnational Corporations*. 352 p.

Volume Eight: *Transnational Corporations and International Trade and Payments*. 320 p.

Set C (Boxed set of 4 volumes. ISBN 0-415-08556-X. £350):

Volume Nine: *Transnational Corporations and Regional Economic Integration*. 331 p.

Volume Ten: *Transnational Corporations and the Exploitation of Natural Resources*. 397 p.

Volume Eleven: *Transnational Corporations and Industrialization*. 425 p.

Volume Twelve: *Transnational Corporations in Services*. 437 p.

Set D (Boxed set of 4 volumes. ISBN 0-415-08557-8. £350):

Volume Thirteen: *Cooperative Forms of Transnational Corporation Activity*. 419 p.

Volume Fourteen: *Transnational Corporations: Transfer Pricing and Taxation*. 330 p.

Volume Fifteen: *Transnational Corporations: Market Structure and Industrial Performance*. 383 p.

Volume Sixteen: *Transnational Corporations and Human Resources*. 429 p.

Set E (Boxed set of 4 volumes. ISBN 0-415-08558-6. £350):

Volume Seventeen: *Transnational Corporations and Innovatory Activities*. 447 p.

Volume Eighteen: *Transnational Corporations and Technology Transfer to Developing Countries*. 486 p.

Volume Nineteen: *Transnational Corporations and National Law*. 322 p.

Volume Twenty: *Transnational Corporations: The International Legal Framework*. 545 p.

Transnational Corporations (formerly *The CTC Reporter*).

Published three times a year. Annual subscription price: $35; individual issues $15.

Transnationals, a quarterly newsletter, is available free-of-charge.

United Nations publications may be obtained from bookstores and distributors throughout the world. Please consult your bookstore or write to:

United Nations Publications

Sales Section	OR	Sales Section
Room DC2-0853		United Nations Office at Geneva
United Nations Secretariat		Palais des Nations
New York, N.Y. 10017		CH-1211 Geneva 10
U.S.A.		Switzerland
Tel: (1-212) 963-8302 or (800) 253-9646		Tel: (41-22) 917-1234
Fax: (1-212) 963-3489		Fax: (41-22) 917-0123
E-mail: publications@un.org		E-mail: unpubli@unog.ch

All prices are quoted in United States dollars.

For further information on the work of the Division on Investment, Technology and Enterprise Development, UNCTAD, please address inquiries to:

United Nations Conference on Trade and Development
Division on Investment, Technology and Enterprise Development
Palais des Nations, Room E-9123
CH-1211 Geneva 10
Switzerland
Telephone: (41-22) 907-5707
Telefax: (41-22) 907-0194
E-mail: almario.medarde@unctad.org

QUESTIONNAIRE

FDI Determinants and TNC Strategies:
The Case of Brazil

In order to improve the quality and relevance of the work of the UNCTAD Division on Investment, Technology and Enterprise Development, it would be useful to receive the views of readers on this and other similar publications. It would therefore be greatly appreciated if you could complete the following questionnaire and return to:

Readership Survey
UNCTAD Division on Investment, Technology and Enterprise Development
United Nations Office in Geneva
Palais des Nations
Room E-9123
CH-1211 Geneva 10
Switzerland

1. Name and address of respondent (optional):

    _____

    _____

    _____

    _____

2. Which of the following best describes your area of work?

    Government ☐   Public enterprise ☐

    Private enterprise institution ☐   Academic or research ☐

    International organization ☐   Media ☐

    Not-for-profit organization ☐   Other (specify) _____

3. In which country do you work? _____

4. What is your assessment of the contents of this publication?

    Excellent ☐   Adequate ☐

    Good ☐   Poor ☐

5.	How useful is this publication to your work?

Very useful ☐ Of some use ☐ Irrelevant ☐

6.	Please indicate the three things you liked best about this publication:

_____

_____

_____

7.	Please indicate the three things you liked least about this publication:

_____

_____

_____

8.	If you have read more than the present publication of the UNCTAD Division on Investment, Enterprise Development and Technology, what is your overall assessment of them?

Consistently good ☐ Usually good, but with some exceptions ☐

Generally mediocre ☐ Poor ☐

9.	On the average, how useful are these publications to you in your work?

Very useful ☐ Of some use ☐ Irrelevant ☐

10.	Are you a regular recipient of *Transnational Corporations* (formerly *The CTC Reporter*), the Division's tri-annual refereed journal?

Yes ☐ No ☐

If not, please check here if you would like to receive a sample
copy sent to the name and address you have given above ☐

Printed at United Nations, Geneva
GE.00-50870–May 2000–3,800

UNCTAD/ITE/IIT/14

United Nations publication
Sales No. E.00.II.D.2

ISBN 92-1-112469-7